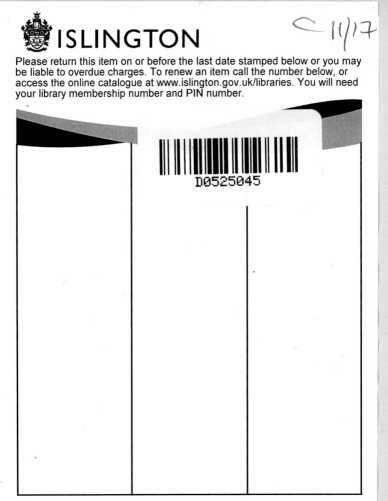

ISLINGTON

⊂ 11/17

Please return this item on or before the last date stamped below or you may be liable to overdue charges. To renew an item call the number below, or access the online catalogue at www.islington.gov.uk/libraries. You will need your library membership number and PIN number.

D0525045

Islington Libraries

020 7527 6900   **www.islington.gov.uk/libraries**

ISLINGTON LIBRARIES

3 0120 02738893 3

Wasting Police Time

The crazy world of the war on crime

PC David Copperfield

MONDAY BOOKS

© DAVID COPPERFIELD 2013

First published in Great Britain in 2006 by Monday Books

Revised and reprinted nine times

Revised editions published in 2007, 2008, 2009 and 2011

This revised edition published in 2013

The right of David Copperfield to be identified as the author of this work has been asserted by him in accordance with the Copyright, Designs and Patents Act 1988

All rights reserved. Apart from any use permitted under UK copyright law no part of this publication may be reproduced, stored in a retrieval system, or transmitted, in any form or by any means, without the prior written permission of the publisher, nor be otherwise circulated in any form of binding or cover other than that in which it is published and without a similar condition being imposed on the subsequent purchaser

A CIP catalogue record for this title is available from the British Library

ISBN: 978-0-9552854-1-7

Typeset by Andrew Searle

Printed and bound by CPI Group (UK) Ltd

www.mondaybooks.com
info@mondaybooks.com
http://mondaybooks.wordpress.com/

To Mrs Copperfield

Acknowledgements

I'd like to thank everyone who helped with the writing of this book and the blog that went before it.

Thanks to Dan Collins at Monday Books, for helping to turn the idle ramblings of a police officer into something that actually made sense.

Thanks to my family for (mostly) keeping quiet about the whole thing.

Thanks to Mike, for his frequent stories from the City of Culture (Liverpool). Thanks to Brian from the Met, for his Frequently Answered Questions. Thanks to Kim and his family, for showing me such hospitality on my most recent visit to the USA.

Thanks to the hundreds of serving and retired police officers from Britain and around the world who have sent messages of support.

And thanks, finally, to my colleagues, who are all funnier and more hard-working than me. If it hadn't been for you I would have left years ago and this book would never have been published.

Any and all mistakes in this book are mine (as long as they're not someone else's).

Foreword

WHAT do you think the police actually *do*?

If you watch a lot of telly, you probably think we spend all day roaring about in our souped-up cars, kicking down doors and shooting people. That is, when we're not unravelling murder mysteries while swanning round in old Jags and listening to classical music.

I'm not sure I thought it was going to be quite that exciting or glamorous when I joined up, but I certainly had visions of nicking lots of criminals and keeping the streets safe.

It turns out, it isn't quite like that.

The signs were there on my first day at training school. I joined the job in my late 20s, a married man with a mortgage to pay and several years working in industry behind me. I finished on the Friday afternoon and turned up at police headquarters on the following Monday morning wearing my old work boots and with the oil and dirt from the factory still ingrained in my hands.

Three days later, we were still talking about prejudice and discrimination; burglars had to wait while we set about changing the racist, homophobic and male-dominated world in which we lived.

Privately, many of us wondered if all this discussion was really necessary. I don't think we were all that interested in skin colour, gender or sexuality. We wanted to get on with what we fondly imagined policing was all about: putting baddies in jail. Whether they were straight black women or gay white men was a matter of supreme indifference to us all. But amid all the diversity training, and rote learning of various statutes, and the occasional bit of marching, something was missing. Nobody seemed very interested in telling us how to investigate crimes, or about the actual criminals themselves. What sort of people were they? How did they break the law? Were there any clues, tell-tale signs, tricks of the trade, which might lead us to them?

Important stuff, you'd think, but we didn't hear a dickie bird about it. Surely it couldn't be that the police weren't actually very interested in catching criminals?

Some of my new colleagues didn't seem too perturbed at this – they were too busy mapping out their career paths to worry much about crime. One lad was so keen to become a traffic officer that he had learned the relevant legislation before the course even started. A few ambitious ones talked about how soon they could be sergeants. Lots of the younger ones wanted to be firearms officers.

Personally, I couldn't remember the legal definition of a car (though I knew one when I saw it), I was still struggling to remember the rank structure above the level of Inspector (it's still something of a mystery) and my wife had already told me I wouldn't be going anywhere near a gun. So I had no particular plans, other than to finish training school and start at the bottom.

Standing on the parade square in my smart new uniform after four months' tuition, I still had no idea what a criminal might look like. I had no idea what I would do if anyone decided to do a runner or start scrapping if I tried to arrest them, or what I was supposed do with them after that. Still, I was absolutely desperate to get out there and put what skills I had into practice.

Although I had yet to speak to a proper police officer, let alone a criminal, I was ready for the streets of Newtown, surely?

Well, yes and no.

Several years on, I'm still a bobby, an ordinary policeman in a nondescript town in England. I'm much like the vast majority of my fellow officers: I don't want to fit innocent people up, I don't want to arrest huge numbers of black people just because of their skin colour and I'm not a violent Nazi.

I love my job, especially the bit where I get to chase after thieves and arrest them. After all, that's why I joined.

The problem is, I hardly ever get to do that. I actually spend most of my life filing, stapling and writing: forms, reports, statements, emails, exhibits… and, now, a book. Oh, the irony.

This is a diary of my working life over the last year or so, together with one or two other bits and pieces that have caught my eye in the recent past. I've changed the names and dates to protect the guilty – that's the name of the game, these days, after all. The place where I work isn't called 'Newtown' and my name isn't PC David Copperfield. But I am a real policeman, and everything you'll read here has happened to me. There's a bit of swearing, some of it from me. It isn't nice, but you couldn't write a truthful account of a copper's life without it.

Some of it (actually, most of it) might not sound all that dramatic. That's kind of the point: being a policeman in modern England is not like appearing in an episode of *The Sweeney*, *Inspector Morse* or even *The* (late, lamented) *Bill*, sadly. It's like standing banging your head against a wall, carrying a couple of hundredweight of paperwork on your shoulders, while the house around you burns to the ground.

This is the first book of its type – written by an ordinary, working copper of the modern era who is telling it like it is. I hope it will give you an idea of the depths of sheer incompetence our police are plumbing, how thousands of officers, both in and out of uniform, are struggling to keep their heads above a sea of paperwork while your money is wasted and the crime books are cooked in ways that would make Gordon Ramsay proud.

PC David Copperfield

YOU'RE ON YOUR OWN, OFFICER

MY MORNING SHIFT begins at 07:00hrs, with a briefing from the sergeant.

This is called a parade, like they used to have in Hill Street Blues, where the old boy would end with a fatherly, 'Be careful out there'.

So what do you imagine our morning parades are like?

Serried ranks of stern-faced constables wearing dark blue capes and carrying truncheons?

Eager hordes of law enforcement freaks champing at the bit to get out there and kick illegal butt?

Two dozen Robocops, checking their CS gas and body armour and practising their take-down techniques?

Er, not *exactly*.

The other day I turned up on my own to the morning parade.

I don't mean I had got the wrong room, or turned up late after everyone had gone.

I mean I was the only uniformed officer on duty that day, in a town of about 60,000 people.

Let me just spell that out again: the population of the town in which I work is about 60,000, and I was the ONLY UNIFORMED OFFICER ON DUTY AT THAT POINT.

True, there were other uniformed officers *inside* the police station; there were even a few officers on duty who were not wearing a uniform. But as for officers, in uniform, on duty and able to deploy to a call from a member of the public, there was only me.

The 'thin blue line' had become a very insignificant dot.

That said, even at full strength, we're hardly going to terrify our local criminals: there should have been three others, not including the sergeant, but one was sick, one was on a course and the other was due at court later that day.

I have always thought the public sector is slightly top heavy on the admin side, so I checked the car park at about 10:00hrs. Sure enough, it was packed.

Our staffing levels are closely controlled and monitored, and we have whole departments within the force geared to ensuring that the

1

right balance of uniformed officers and civilian staff are employed. Staffing is the subject of strategy meetings at the highest level. In fact, the whole issue is so important it cannot be left up to the minds of mere mortals: we have a computer system which plans and manages 'human resources' (people), called HRMS, or Human Resource Management System. I don't think it works very well.

It is a mantra of senior management in the Police Service and at the Home Office that 'ordinary people' overestimate the volume of crime. 'Ordinary people cannot be expected to know the realities of crime and how it can be prevented,' runs the argument. 'Furthermore, they cannot interpret the statistics the way we can. If they could, they would be able to see that crime was actually going down, not up.'

I like to ask ordinary people about how much crime they think there is, and perhaps they do overestimate it.

The thing is, I often ask them to estimate the number of officers on duty, too, and they also overestimate that. Usually by a factor of ten.

OMG! (GEDDIT?)

I HAD BARELY sat down yesterday before I was sent to a criminal damage where a helpful local youth was in the process of altering someone else's property from 'fence' to 'kindling'.

As luck would have it, the offender was identified by two witnesses. He was loitering nearby, drinking cheap lager and fiddling with his fake gold chains. At 16:06hrs, I arrested and cautioned him.

Ignoring the drive out to the address, dealing with the crime had taken me about a minute so far.

Fairly straightforward, yes? A fence has been smashed to pieces, we've got the guilty party and, very shortly, I can be back out on the streets looking for the mugger who just robbed your granny and the burglar who nicked your wedding ring yesterday.

Er, not quite.

Taking the suspect down to the police station and booking him into custody only took half an hour, because there wasn't a queue (if there is a queue, this can treble in length).

Then I returned to the address to speak to a couple of witnesses and take their statements.

One of them was the old man to whom the fence belonged. He was close to tears.

'The thing is, officer,' he said. 'Him and his mates are always hanging around and sitting on our wall. I wouldn't mind, but their language is foul and I don't want my wife to have to listen to that. They leave beer cans and fag packets lying around, and if you ask them to keep the noise down they just swear at you. That lad and his mate were rolling around on our lawn fighting and laughing and squashing all the flowers. When I asked them to stop it they threatened me and he started smashing the fence up. I can't understand it.'

'Yes, it is a tough one, sir,' I said.

'What I want to know is, why aren't they at work or school or something?' he said. 'I probably shouldn't have called you. They'll only come back and next time it'll be worse.'

I reflected on this for a moment. He was probably right. Half a century ago, this sort of mindless, aggressive criminal damage rarely happened, and certainly not in broad daylight in front of witnesses. Can it possibly be that the perpetrators don't fear the forces of law and order any more?

'Well,' I said. 'If they do come back, call us straight away.'

It wasn't much, but it was the best I could do.

I spent a couple of hours on the statements. Total time used up, so far: two hours and 31 minutes.

Back at the nick, I spent another hour waiting for the defence solicitor (of whom, more later) to turn up, and a further hour making disclosure (in which we tell the defence what evidence we have) to said lawyer and interviewing the suspect. He denied everything, so I then wrote a report (called an MG3) to the Crown Prosecution Service (the CPS, which decides on whether suspects will be charged – it has nothing to do with me) and faxed them all the relevant documentation. This preparation, faxing and consulting took a further hour, after which I was allowed to charge the youth with criminal damage to the fence.

Total time so far: five hours and 31 minutes.

Charging, fingerprinting, photographing and DNAing him took a further 45 minutes, so I'd now spent more than six hours on this crime, not counting getting to and from the scene.

The whole enquiry was concluded by about 21:30hrs.

I had something to eat and, at 22:15hrs, I began the file.

A 'file' is a collection of paperwork that consists of all the evidence against the accused, as well as a summary of the case against him.

ACPO (the Association of Chief Police Officers) says it ought to take between four and six hours to complete, which is a rather worrying admission when you think about it. Fortunately for you, the taxpayer (and me), I have the whole process down to about two hours.

I have to record all the evidence, handwritten and much of it duplicated several times, on a series of forms called MG forms (MG standing for 'Manual of Guidance'); standardising the evidence for all our cases is supposed make it easy for the CPS to understand and work through them.

I had to produce a 'Full File' in the anticipation of a Not Guilty plea by the accused. The file preparation consists of the following (NB, all forms are usually handwritten):

1. FCS (File cover sheet containing the offence outline and details of the offender, the offence and the court date).
2. MG1 (Another cover sheet for the CPS, containing offender details).
3. MG3 (The report I prepared for the CPS earlier).
4. MG4 (The charge sheet).
5. MG5 (Details of the case against the offender, running to about three A4 sheets).
6. MG6 (Another summary sheet outlining any details you want to keep from the defence).
7. MG6C (Unused, non-sensitive material eg serial printouts, rough notes, etc).
8. MG6D (Unused, sensitive material eg anything where we might be using police informants, hidden cameras, that kind of thing).
9. MG6E (Anything that may damage the prosecution case).
10. MG11 (Witness statements and IP statements, all of which are handwritten by the officer and are often several pages long; also the officer's arrest statement).
11. MG15 (Summary of what was said on interview).

As well as all that, I also had to prepare the interview tapes for transcribing, and put all of the paperwork generated in the course of the enquiry together in a nice, neat folder.

By now – having arrested the great fence destroyer at 16:06 hrs – it was around midnight. I pinned together a stack of handwritten forms about half an inch thick, handed them to a sergeant for checking and celebrated by going for a quick walk around the town centre before booking off duty.

During the whole shift, I'd spent approximately half an hour outside the police station actually 'policing'.

I appreciate the need for meticulous and accurate evidence-gathering, but here's a question: do you want me to spend an entire shift treating one fence-wrecking moron as though he was the Yorkshire Ripper, or would you rather we could spend a little less time on paperwork and a bit more walking the streets?

I know that's not the sort of question the police normally ask people, but I thought you might like to think about it.

F*CK THE PO-LICE, F*CK THE PO-LICE

I HAVE LATELY (not by choice) been listening to a lot of 'gangsta rap', a genre of music imported from America where it is created by rich black people for consumption by middle-class white youngsters.

Most gangsta rap seems to revolve around killing policemen, being in jail and having sex with 'hose'. It's all a bit of a mystery to me, and the method of its delivery (shouting defiantly, over an insistent drum beat) serves only to make it more indecipherable.

Quite what the idle youths on Newtown's council estates imagine they have in common with the homies of South Central LA I'm not sure – I've been to South Central, and to other ghettoes, and they're quite different from our little town – but it is becoming increasingly common for me to have to conduct stop-searches to the tune of 'Die, motherf+cker, die.'

I suspect that children listen to this music because they like the tunes and find the idea of being rich and famous appealing. It doesn't appeal to us all, though (the music, that is).

The other evening, a lad called Wayne was playing gangsta rap very loudly. Unfortunately, he was in his K-registered Rover 214 outside the corner shop at the time, and not everyone was enjoying it, especially those people living nearby who were trying to get their babies and young children to sleep. Pulling up alongside him, I suggested that the ladies in the area might not appreciate hearing the controversial views of the artist on subjects such as domestic violence, drive-bys and 'bitches'.

I might as well have been talking in Chinese.

'Eh?' said Wayne, the gaggle of teenage morons gathered around his car regarding me with deep suspicion. 'Whayouonabout?'

'I'm not sure everyone wants to hear that music, certainly not that loudly,' I explained.

'Yerwah?' he said, eyes slightly glazed.

'Turn that bloody racket off,' I said. 'Now.'

Grumbling, he turned it down.

'Off!'

He turned it off. 'Why you always be hasslin' de yoot like dis?' he said, though he isn't Jamaican and, in fact, grew up in a rural English village a few miles out of town. 'Man, it's like a f*ckin' police state.'

'More than you know, Wayne,' I replied. I have long-since given up lecturing the young about the errors of their ways, but that never seems to stop them lecturing me about the hardships of living in the 'ghetto', where life is made so hard for them because of the constant interruptions of 'the man'. 'But, be that as it may, if you swear again I'm going to have to lock you up.'

I drove away. I knew he'd turn it on again as soon as I was out of sight, so I did a u-turn 250 yards away.

Sure enough, when I returned, Wayne had the racket up to full blast again.

I warned him under Section 5 of the Public Order Act and sent him on his way.

Sho 'nuff whupped him upside the ass.

VIOLENCE

THE MOST PREDICTABLE thing about being involved in violent incidents is that they are completely unpredictable.

If I respond to a report of thirty youths fighting in the street with baseball bats, I can be fairly certain that on my arrival they will have dispersed and that a subsequent area search will prove negative.

On the other hand, if the local library assistant rings up to report a problem customer returning a book late, I will end up rolling around on the floor with someone somewhere between *Late Medieval History* and *Local Walks*.

I'd like to be able to say that Newtown's A&E unit is just the kind of place where you wouldn't expect there to be much fighting, but the fact that the receptionist has to sit behind a protective glass screen is a bit of a giveaway.

My colleague Paul and I went there the other day to a call of a male shouting and being disruptive. By the time we arrived, he was staging a one-man protest against the NHS by refusing to get off a stretcher and shouting about his treatment.

I began negotiations. 'Do you want to get off that trolley?' I said.

'No, I f*cking don't,' he replied, with some venom. 'I've got a right to be here.'

Paul took a firm grip of his arm and attempted to pull him from the trolley. He resisted, and I began to apply my boot to his hand in a repeated downward motion to persuade him to release hospital property (at least, that's what it says in my statement).

As we dragged him out of the hospital, he maintained his grip on the trolley with one hand and tried to grab my leg with the other. Paul also employed the 'boot method' to subdue the man and eventually we got him handcuffed and in the car, where the fool began to headbutt the window.

I've been to a few fights and met a few violent people, but most of the time the heat has gone out of the situation prior to my arrival and I'm left with a few bruised and battered victims who are really drunk and want someone 'done'.

'His name's John, or something. I think he plays in the same football team as my cousin. If you don't do something, I will. What do you mean, calm down? How can I calm down? I've been hit in the face. Can't you f*cking see? I want him f*cking done!'

Drunk people: that's what the police are really here for, after all.

The trivial nature of most reports of violence has to be seen to be believed. They are a litany of failed relationships, petty neighbour disputes and outbursts of anger, which most people would not bother with but which, in the topsy-turvy world of police bureaucracy and the underclass, create trivial crimes to be detected. You'd like to tell them all just to calm down and take a rational approach, but why bother with that when shouting and screaming has achieved so much already?

They're not always trivial, of course. Sometimes the 30 youths are still going strong when we arrive, which is mildly unsettling. It all kicked off in a big way in town at the weekend. We had a proper punch up, with batons drawn, heads cracked and a few people left nursing bruises and bloody noses on both sides of the argument.

It started with a call to one of our rougher pubs. 'Can patrols attend the King's Head. Reports of 20 people fighting in the car park. No weapons seen.'

I was one of the last there, so didn't see the worst of it. Other patrols had already separated the combatants into 'probably guilty' and 'probably innocent' and the two groups were being held apart by bobbies as they spat and swore at each other (the yobs, not the bobbies).

Several of them were arrested and I was asked to assist a colleague called Karen with one lucky drunk. Karen gave him his one opportunity to come quietly, but naturally he blew it so she and I leapt on him with another couple of officers. I know that sounds like overkill – pictures of five cops sitting on one man always look like police brutality in the papers – but it's actually all about not hurting them. It's very hard to subdue a drunken, violent yobbo without injuring him or you unless you restrain each limb until he calms down.

Eventually, once he was compliant, we turned him onto his front, pulled his hands behind his back and cuffed him in what I can only describe as the 'Home Office-approved manner'. Textbook, it was. He was then thrown in the cage in the back of the van.

By the time he got out at the other end, the injuries he had sustained in the fight and the gravel from the car park had combined to make him look like Freddy Krueger.

'I've been beaten up by these coppers,' he told the desk sergeant.

'Really, sir?' said the sergeant. 'Reason for arrest, please Karen?'

'Hang about,' said the man. 'I've been f*cking beaten up by your coppers, I said. What are you going to do about it?'

The sergeant sighed and put down his pen. 'Let me guess,' he said. 'Did they ask you if you'd get in the van?'

'Yes.'

'And did you refuse?'

'Yes.'

'So they made you get in the van, did they?

'Yes.'

'I see. Karen, reason for arrest please?'

As I say, police attendance at violent incidents like this often results in allegations of brutality. I am usually suspicious of such allegations. It must go on – God knows, a saint would be tempted sometimes – but, hand on heart, I have never overstepped the line myself, or even come close to doing so, and I've never seen it happen.

However, there is a widespread belief amongst the criminal classes that the police *do* beat people up all the time, and that we *like* doing so. I think it has become a sort of self-fulfilling prophecy in their minds. Some thug called Tony is arrested on a night out. He's drunk, he struggles, two officers use a bit of force to cuff him and place him in the van. This, to Tony, is 'police brutality'. (I'd like Tony to go on holiday to Colombia, or even Chicago, and see what happens when he swaggers down the street shouting the odds and attacking the police. That might assist him in developing a bit of perspective.)

The fact is that most police officers hate getting involved in violence. Many are women (and therefore smaller than most of their potential adversaries). Others are terribly unfit: the most exercise the average officer gets is the walk from the car to the police station. Of the rest, most are just ordinary blokes who are mostly interested in getting home on time. They certainly don't want to lose their pension for clocking some halfwit. Would *you*?

That leaves about two psychopathic nutters in the whole of the UK's police strength. If you find out who and where they are, let me know.

No, I hate fighting – especially with people who are bigger and stronger than me. And worst of all is fighting girls. My natural instinct, as an unreformed caveman, is to protect females. Ha, ha. Given a few Vodka Red Bulls and an errant boyfriend, the average Lycra-clad chav-woman will take on a full shift of officers, and possibly win.

Now *that* looks good on CCTV.

A LAND FIT FOR CRIMINALS

I'M SURE LOTS of you, like me, are kept awake at night by the idea that some of our prisons are overcrowded. It's certainly been worrying Lord Chief Justice Phillips of Worth Matravers lately.

Recently, his Lordship suggested that offenders should only be sent to jail 'as a last resort' and that they should really be rehabilitated in the community.

I think they should be rehabilitated chez Phillips, where Lord Phillips can develop a better understanding of what persistent acquisitive criminals are really like while Lady Phillips (nee Christylle Marie-Thérèse Rouffiac) keeps an eye on the family silver.

To understand how bad things really are, I recommend reading *A Land Fit For Criminals* by David Fraser. Fraser is a former probation officer who's had personal experience of dealing with a large number of criminals. His basic thesis is that, in order fully to protect the public, we need to lock up a minimum of 225,000 people (the current maximum is 80,000) and we need a police force of about four times the size that it is now. I disagree with the latter part of that thesis, for reasons I'll explain later, but I agree with the first part.

He firmly believes that prison works, and that all attempts to reform criminals in the community are dangerous experiments which put the public at risk. Not only that, community service doesn't work: people don't turn up and, when they do, they don't really do what they're supposed to do. Jail, on the other hand, is a cast-iron guarantee that the public, and their property, are safe from criminals. While they're inside they can get certificates in all sorts of things from woodwork to 'Enhanced Thinking' (really), but they can't creep into your house and steal your TV.

It's a fact, despite what LCJ Phillips says or thinks, that giving an 18-year-old serious jail time for his third burglary dwelling would ensure the public were protected from literally hundreds of offences.

Fraser reserves special criticism for the probation service, which he says is dedicated to keeping criminals out of jail, and for the civil servants who have consistently viewed jail as counterproductive. He leans rather too much on the fact that most people don't report crime to the police, something that's undoubtedly true but at the same time detracts from the sound arguments in the rest of the book, but it's a recommended read, for all that.

Back to Lord Phillips (Bryanston and Cambridge, Brooks's and The Garrick). I've no idea where the LCJ's houses are (he's probably got several), or what they're like, but I'll hazard a guess. They will be imposing and beautiful pads in low crime areas. They will have walls around them and plenty of open ground that burglars have to cross before they get to the alarmed and well-made windows. He'll probably have a dog or two, and possibly a live-in housekeeper. The local nick will know exactly where he is and they will be on tenterhooks in case they get a call to get out there (if he hasn't got a panic button or some sort of direct comm-link). His neighbours will be charming people with diverse interests, large cars and lots of antique furniture. If he encounters muggers, burglars or general ne'er-do-wells (outside his professional life) it will only be because of extreme carelessness on his part. He certainly won't be glassed in the back garden of the King's Head for brushing the arm of an unemployed yob who has drunk nine pints of Stella.

My question is this: when it comes to deciding how criminals should be dealt with, why should we trust Lord Chief Justice Phillips of Worth Matravers?

JUMPING OFF TALL BUILDINGS

THE STORY OF Barry Chambers reveals, in ways more amusing and unlikely than a mere satirist ever could, the depths of the madness to which Britain is now sinking.

Chambers stole a car in Cheltenham and was chased over to Gloucester by the police until he skidded to a halt by a convenient drainpipe which he promptly shinned up.

He spent the next 20 hours on a rooftop, hurling insults and bricks and slates at the police as they wrung their hands and hopped from foot to foot down below, begging him to come down, *please*, and stop being so silly, we're sure we can sort this out.

Halfway through all this, Barry got hungry and told the police he wanted a Kentucky Fried Chicken lunch. Off hared a bobby (this is the sort of job which would have been given to me if the incident had been on our patch), returning half an hour later with a bargain bucket and a bottle of Pepsi.

'That bottle's too small,' said Barry. 'Get me another, bigger one. And some fags, while you're at it.'

Off hared the bobby again.

Meanwhile, according to press reports, 60 police officers were milling around with dogs and riot shields to stop themselves getting hit with bricks, as 'highly trained negotiators' tried to talk Barry down.

As an aside, I always love hearing the phrase 'highly trained negotiators' – it's a bit like 'bomb disposal expert', which implies that there are loads of 'bomb disposal amateurs' running around the place. (I'm not knocking negotiators, by the way, but there's not a lot of call for it round our way. From time to time, we do get people threatening to kill themselves, but it's always in a very half-hearted fashion, as reflected in the demise of the suicide note which has been replaced by the pre-suicide txt msg: 'Im goin 2 top myslf m8'. Actual suicide is, mercifully, rare, unlike para-suicide which is so common I'm surprised it hasn't got its own form: What's your preferred method of not-committing suicide – pills/drink/slashed wrists/jumping off tall buildings. Delete as appropriate. You may select more than one item from the list.)

Anyway. Where was I? Eventually, after his chicken, a few more insults and a bit of a kip, Barry came down and was led away.

What are we to make of all that? My first thought was, What on *earth* were they doing giving him cigarettes and KFC? Don't they know that's bad for your health? He could sue. The last word on the affair goes to *Sun* letter writer Spencer Arnott, from Holmer Green, Bucks.

'I thought I'd heard and seen it all,' he writes. 'Then Barry Chambers spent all day on a rooftop lobbing bricks at the police while they sent up to him a KFC bucket and some fags. A police marksman should have shot him in the legs.'

Spencer, your application form for the job of 'Highly trained and experienced negotiator' is in the post.

(Update: Barry was later jailed for three years and nine months, which is actually a bit of a result. Or it would be if he was likely to serve more than a few months of it.)

HIDING MY SKILLS UNDER A BUSHEL

TALKING OF NEGOTIATION, I was recently told to check on the welfare of a known manic depressive who had threatened to kill himself.

I knocked on the door.

'Who is it?' he shouted.

'It's the police!' I shouted in return.

'F*ck off, I've got a gun!' he shouted again.

'F*ck off yourself, Sid,' I shouted back. 'You haven't got a gun, you're pissed, and if you don't open this f*cking door right now, I'll break the f*cker down.'

It all ended happily enough, with Sid at the local hospital and me away on time.

Another whose negotiating skills left a lot to be desired was 39-year-old Welshman Dominic Peck. I wasn't involved in this incident, and I'll regret that till the day I die. This may be the funniest story ever.

Peck, a 39-year-old labourer from Barry in Wales, had been a naughty boy and was banned from the area under a restraining order. However, he decided to ignore the order and held a little drinks party for a few friends in a flat in the town.

Eventually, there were just three of them left: Peck, another man and a woman, one Amanda Lacey.

They were settling into a hazy Sunday morning of cider and sherry, as you do, when there was a bang at the door.

'It was the police,' explained Ms Lacey. 'They were shouting, "C'mon Dom, open up we know you're in there". I think they'd come because he'd breached the order.

'Well, he turned to me and winked before shouting back, "F*ck off, I've got a gun and a hostage!" Apparently, he also said he was holding a knife to my throat and had a Glock 9mm pistol and a shotgun, but I can't remember him saying any of that. He certainly never threatened me with any knife. He wasn't like that. He was a big bloke who could look intimidating but he was a friendly giant, really. He was only joking – we were all hammered to be honest.'

They settled back to watching the telly, presumably – and naively – thinking the police would shrug their shoulders and leave.

After half an hour or so, Amanda got up and happened to look out of the window.

'I saw they'd cordoned off the street,' she said. 'There were armed officers in all the neighbours' gardens with their guns pointing at the window. At that point the other guy with us panicked, jumped out the window and did a runner. What we didn't know was that he had the keys on him and the front door was deadlocked – we couldn't get out. For some reason, I never thought much of it.'

She mentioned it to Dom, but he just shrugged and, like anyone would, they went back to the telly and the cider (they got through nine litres of the stuff, Amanda later said, which is impressive on its own).

And the stand-off continued: vanloads of armed police outside, the couple inside blithely channel-hopping and gargling with Strongbow.

At about 6pm, having been drinking all day, a now very much the worse-for-wear Amanda stood up at the window again.

'I looked down,' she said, 'and there were all these little red dots floating around on my chest… it was the laser sights from the police guns. I was really scared and when Dom saw that he really lost his rag. He had a big axe that he'd bought to chop down some trees and he threw it through the window pane. Glass went everywhere.'

Amanda said she could remember the police desperately calling up to her.

'They wanted me to jump to safety. I said, "That's two floors down, you must be joking!"'

Then she had an idea. 'I phoned 999 on my mobile to explain to police that I wasn't being taken hostage, I was just locked in. But before I could say I wasn't in any danger my battery ran out.'

Things reached crisis point just before midnight when a smoke canister came flying in through the window.

'Dom pulled me by the arm into another room but then the door was kicked in and about 10 officers in riot gear with shields came storming in,' said Amanda. 'They pushed me into one room and Dom into the bedroom. I heard a bang and then a lot of screaming. Dom had been shot in the groin by a rubber bullet the size of a baked bean tin.'

Peck got two years in prison, and lost his council flat and one testicle.

But on the upside, what a story to tell his grandchildren (if he ever has any).

Note: For some reason, this story is even funnier if you put on a very strong Welsh accent when reading Amanda Lacey's quotes.

MISSING PEOPLE

CHILDREN SOMETIMES DISAPPEAR, and it must be a terrible ordeal for most parents.

'A 12-year-old girl has been missing for a few days,' said my radio today. 'Please attend the address and see what you can find out.'

Whenever I get a call like that, the dreadful case of Holly Wells and Jessica Chapman flits through my mind.

When I arrived, the television was on. It remained on throughout the duration of my visit, because it was being watched by mum and mum's partner. Over the noise of *Jeremy Kyle*, I tried to get the details of the missing girl: description, last seen by, wearing what etc etc. Then I asked what enquiries mum had made prior to my arrival. The answer, beyond a couple of phone calls to random friends, was none.

I wasn't getting anywhere so, pushing thoughts of Holly and Jessica to the back of my mind, I set off on the hunt. My first call was to the girl's school, 800 yards away... and there she was!

I had a brief talk with her, asked her where she had been, pointed out the dangers of not telling her guardians where she was going and sent her back to class.

I radioed control. 'Panic over,' I said. 'I've found her.'

Then I returned to the house to speak to mum.

'It's OK, she's at school, she's fine,' I said.

The woman stood in the doorway, one eye on the TV. 'That's no good,' she said. 'I want her back here.'

I took a deep breath. 'Well, she's at school. If you're still concerned, how about nipping up there to see her yourself?'

'I haven't got a car.'

'Well, the school is only up the road. You could walk.'

'I'm registered disabled.'

'It's not far,' I said, breathing deeply again.

She turned her baleful gaze on me. 'Look,' she said, as though speaking to an idiot. 'She could be out there being abused right now. I want her back here. It's your responsibility if she gets abused.'

She then shut the door in my face and returned to the television, which I could still hear through the open window.

I stood there, looking at the peeling green paint of the door, and the rotting wood of the frame, and sighed. Then I checked with control, collected the girl and brought her home.

I spoke again to mother. 'Could you please ensure she doesn't run off in the future?'

'No,' she said. 'I can't do nothing about it.'

'Well, can't you lock her in her room or something?'

'No,' she replied. 'There isn't a lock, and I'm not stopping in all night.'

'Where are you going?' I said.

'Out.'

'But I thought you were registered disabled,' I said. 'What will you do if she goes again?'

'I'll call you lot. It's your responsibility to find her.'

NEIGHBOURS

TO A NEIGHBOURS dispute today, one which involved criminal damage, assault and harassment.

How does that distinguish itself from all the other neighbour disputes? Answer: it doesn't. They all involve a combination of the above, plus a belief that the police will sort everything out.

We won't, because we can't.

When I got there, they had all finished swearing at each other but everyone wanted to make complaints about everyone else's foul language.

The male of one of the houses was leaning over his gate as I pulled up. He was out of there and over to the car so quick his nylon tracksuit almost caught fire with the friction. He talked at me as I got out of the vehicle, and continued to do so as I made my way to his garden (I use the word 'garden' in the loosest sense; it was a patch of weed-covered earth with half a car resting in it).

I gathered that the alleged offender was the male of the next door house, whose ratty features I could make out behind the nets in his front window.

'Yeah, like,' gabbled Male One. 'He really sworn at me, like, effing and blinding, and I'm really f*cked off with it, and I want him done for it now.'

I groaned – maybe inwardly, maybe outwardly, I can't remember. 'I'm sorry sir, but we can't arrest for swearing in these circumstances.'

He blinked at me, disbelieving. 'That's not what I've been told.'

'Well sir, I'm sorry but…'

'I don't f*cking believe this,' he said.

'Sir…'

'You're f*cking sh*t, you. You don't know f*ck all. I want that bastard arrested.'

I couldn't help grinning, a tight little grin. 'Look, sir, as I've already explained, I can't arrest him in these circumstances. However, it is an offence to swear at a police officer if you have been warned about your language. I am, as per Section 5 of the Public Order Act, warning you about your language. If you swear again, I'll lock you up.'

He calmed down.

I spoke to both sides and took statements about bad language and other general nastiness. Three hours later, with all the paperwork completed and the incident logged, both parties (independently) said goodbye, and both added, 'I know it's a waste of your time.'

'No problem,' I replied, without a trace of irony. 'That's what we're here for.'

Then I drove back to the police station, feeling like the only adult in a town full of toddlers.

I HATE 'HATE CRIME'

IN THE ABSENCE of organised crime bosses, drug lords and serial killers in the Newtown area this week, I have been left to concentrate on that other menace: hate crime.

Hate crime looms large in the government's priorities.

I don't imagine for a moment that being a victim of such a crime can be a pleasant experience, though I deal with mostly fairly petty examples (if that's not an oxymoron): name-calling, school bullying, offensive text messages, that sort of thing.

I'm not sure, though, that even serious hate crime is any more serious than comparable non-hate crime.

Recently, two men were convicted of the murder of a gay barman, Jody Dobrowski, on Clapham Common in London. They attacked and killed him because he was gay, and they hated gays. They received life sentences, with recommendations that they each serve a minimum of 28 years. Let me say, I abhor their crime. In any civilised, free society, a man's sexuality can't be an excuse for attacking him. I welcome the 28 year sentence, too; that will give them something to think about, and the time in which to do it. I just wish the courts would dish similar terms out to the killers of dads of two who get kicked to death in drunken brawls, or cabbies murdered for their night's takings, or people stabbed for their mobiles.

My current hate crime involves the victim chasing the offender (yes, you read that right; bear with me). The offender managed to evade the clutches of the victim and shout, 'You f*cking Paki!' as he ran off.

'Why were you chasing him?' I asked Jamil, the victim.

'Because he was annoying me, man. Looking at me and stuff.'

'Did he say anything to you before you started chasing him?'

'No.'

'And what would you have done if you'd caught him?'

'I'd have given him a good hiding.'

I sat back, and looked at him. 'So, Jamil, let me get this straight,' I said. 'You were chasing this kid with the intention of beating him up, he called you a Paki and now you want him prosecuting?'

'Yeah, that's right officer.'

Now that all powers of discretion have been taken away and given that this pathetic load of nonsense has been classified as 'racial', I will have to investigate the matter, knowing full well that nobody is ever going to get prosecuted for it.

Sighing, I bent my head to the statement paper and began to write.

We are fortunate in having a Hate Crime Unit in my force – a team of officers whose whole job it is to deal with hate crime. That's the theory, anyway. This unit has its own drawer in the post room, so I know it exists. Moreover, it also sends me emails expressing concern for the victims in cases with which I am dealing. But the Hate Crime Unit 'deals with' hate crime in the bureaucratic sense only: it sends threatening forms advising me of force policy, I tick some boxes and return them. When it comes to *actually* dealing with hate crime – that is to say, arresting, interviewing and charging the offenders – that's *my* job.

The form safely filled in, I received an email thanking me and adding: 'We really need to deal with this as soon as possible.'

This actually means: '*You* need to deal with this as soon as possible.'

By this method, every front line police officer can keep another person in a job who would be otherwise out of work.

I recall being addressed by the new Hate Crime Unit some years ago.

The team visited the uniformed officers and told us how they were going to be able to support us in the front line. Much of this seemed to revolve around sending comforting letters to the homosexual victims of hate crime, but only if they were out.

I found this mildly confusing.

'How are we supposed to know if they're in or out?' I asked. 'And surely it doesn't matter anyway, if you're just sending a letter? If they're out, they'll soon be back, probably by the time the letter gets there.'

'It does matter,' replied the hate crime lady. 'If you were a gay man and you were not out, would you want a letter sent to your house?'

'It wouldn't bother me in the slightest,' I said. 'Anyway, if I'm not out, I must be in. You could come round in person rather than sending me a letter.'

'But you might not want a visit either.'

'Why not?'

'Because you won't be out.'

'Exactly!' I said. 'I'll be in, so you can see me yourself.'

There was a pause at this point. I thought the hate crime lady might be reviewing her options and pondering a change to force policy. She wasn't. After the meeting I was brought fully 'up to speed', as they say in the Hate Crime Unit, with a side of life about which I had previously been entirely ignorant.

THINLY SPREAD

I FIND THE STORY of Nottinghamshire Police most interesting.

At one point last year they had over 30 open murders on their books and had to beg officers from others forces to try to keep up.

One of those killings was that of 16-year-old Colette Aram, who was raped and strangled in the county in 1983. Her killer was never found. An appeal on the BBC's Crimewatch programme in June 2004 resulted in about 300 phone calls. By the spring of 2005, according to media reports, none of those calls had been returned. (If that's right, someone should have been sacked. But then, no-one is ever sacked for incompetence in the police.)

Steve Green, the chief constable, said the problem was that his officers were bogged down with paperwork. Apparently, some of them were also tied up investigating allegations of bears sh*tting in the local woods.

More money and more police officers were what he needed, apparently.

There developed a brief spat of an all-too familiar kind, with Labour replying that Mr Green had enough money, he just wasn't using it right.

The truth is somewhere in between.

The Government is spending lots of money on the police, and there are lots more officers now than there used to be, as the Prime Minister and whoever is Home Secretary this week delight in telling us.

The problem is, hardly any of those new coppers are actually out on the streets policing. Some hardly ever see daylight, but spend their careers behind desks, sending emails, implementing strategies and holding meetings about meeting targets. Those of us who do occasionally leave the nick are back as soon as we've arrested anyone to spend the next six hours filling in forms.

People were very critical of Steve Green, and Nottinghamshire Police generally, when the spotlight fell upon them.

But it's the mandarins of the Home Office and their counterparts in the Nottinghamshire Police Authority who dictate how all the money pouring into the force's coffers is spent. Millions of pounds and thousands of man hours go on coming up with innumerable policy documents, plans to cover every eventuality and a so-called audit trail, so that every last detail of force performance can be monitored by central government. The effect is to ensure that new ideas are implemented on the basis of how well they comply with regulations, rather than how well they deal with criminals and prevent crime.

Every pound spent on paperwork is a pound not spent on front-line policing – something, I think, that people are just starting to wake up to.

Nottinghamshire Police Authority makes some proud boasts on its website, as all these organisations tend to.

We exist to ensure an efficient and effective police service for the County, it says. Among its methods for achieving this, apparently, are 'Consulting with local people about policing' and 'Setting local policing priorities and targets for achievement'.

Who knows? Perhaps Nottinghamshire folk were consulted about Colette Aram's murder, and responded that they'd rather have the police focusing on diversity awareness or best practice delivery of something or other, thanks.

Call me a cynic, but I suspect no-one has ever really asked them what they want.

In fact, just like you, they have no real say in the way their county is policed. They don't elect Steve Green. They don't elect the Police Authority. The Home Office is run by unelected civil servants and presided over by a cabinet minister who spends most of his time in London and represents a far away constituency. What does he know of – or even care about – the minutiae of crime in the towns and villages around Nottingham?

The truth is Nottinghamshire Police, like all forces, is insulated from public opinion.

I'll give you a brief example from my own force. Some time ago, a colleague and I dealt with a complaint about a 'mad dog'. It was actually a rather aggressive little Scotty who could have done some minor damage to your ankles but would have struggled to get much higher. A female had been bitten on the leg and had made a complaint. It wasn't a serious bite, but that wasn't the point; she wanted something done, so we went along. In the course of the interview, she claimed that half a dozen other people nearby had been similarly savaged. No-one else was interested in complaining, though; they were all neighbours who got along together very well and they preferred to deal with the matter by applying their boots to the dog's chops, rather than calling in the force helicopter.

I have no idea what happened to the dog, but the case went to court and everybody except the owner was happy with the result. I've not been back to the address since. Anyway, a couple of weeks ago, I received a note from one of our many bureaucrats about my handling of the crime complaint. It pointed out that the female who had been bitten had mentioned those six other people, some by name and some she didn't know, who had also been bitten by the dog but who did not want to complain.

At this point let me reiterate: everyone was happy, and the police had received no other calls.

However, our bureaucrat stated that, 'in line with Home Office policy', all those six people should be traced and statements obtained from them – even though the matter had already been dealt with by the courts and they did not want to make complaints about the dog.

How ridiculous (though there may have been method in their madness; method associated with a little crime recording scam called 'administrative detections', which I'll tell you about later).

This could easily take a day or more and will be a complete waste of time: time spent with people who don't want to see me, when I might be out dealing with people who do. It is all the more absurd when I tell you that the original incident with the alleged mad dog occurred almost two years ago. What do my local tax payers want me working on? Heroin-addicted burglars or bad-tempered Scotty dogs? Their views ought to count, after all.

Back in Nottinghamshire, Steve Green might be doing the best job he can with the available resources, or he might be a bad manager with no idea of what's going on in his own organisation.

Why not let the people of Nottinghamshire decide?

Update: After advances in DNA technology, 50-year-old Paul Hutchinson was arrested for Collette Aram's murder and convicted in December 2009. He was sentenced to life with a minimum of 25 years (a derisory sentence, when you consider that he had enjoyed 25 years of freedom after committing this terrible crime), but unfortunately died in prison after a year. However, it was a result of sorts.

THE POLICING FOOD CHAIN

IF YOU'VE EVER watched any of those TV *policiers* you'll have a fair idea of the rank structure. It's usually revealed by who shouts at whom. Chief Superintendent Strange shouts at Detective Chief Inspector Morse, who shouts at Detective Sergeant Lewis, and Lewis occasionally grumbles at some muppet in a blue hat (ie me).

But below the surface, there's an entirely different food chain. Where do uniformed bobbies like myself fit in? For non-police readers, here's a rough guide to The Police:

1. Uniformed office-based specialist officers (eg The Hate Crime Unite): The elite, the top of the pile, you can't get any better than this. Experienced officers who have seen a way out and taken it, with impressive results: regular hours, coffee and tea on demand and they get paid more than their shift-working colleagues at the bottom. They remain in-post by performing two invaluable tasks: creating work for other people and moving lots of piles of paper on different days within their offices. They create power-point presentations which are attached to emails and sent to everyone.

2. Civilian support staff: They effectively run the show. Alongside the dispatchers, they decide if crimes have been committed and what forms need to be filled in. They send emails to officers asking for information and create their own

powerful bureaucracies. They certainly don't have to deal with the public.

3. CID (Detective Constables): Far above day-to-day nonsense. Serious crime only, please, don't waste my time. The public love it when detectives turn up because they immediately think that we're taking their problem seriously.

4. Plain-clothes specialist officers (drugs squad, retail crime, vehicle crime etc): Go on 'operations' and wear North Face jackets and jeans. Will attend crime scenes (but not domestics) and make arrests, but only if it falls within their remit.

5. Specialist Uniformed Officers (Dogs, Firearms, Traffic): Arrive as and when required and if the overtime is authorised. Supply statements… sometimes.

6. Dispatchers: Work in nice air-conditioned offices. They become worried if they cannot find a response officer to deal with a problem. Regular meal breaks. They tell officers where to go, what to do and whether a crime has been committed.

7. Community Officers: Usually more experienced and deal with 'community' (ie insoluble) problems. Not tied to the radio, but will occasionally help out. They also attend meetings, a fact which puts them above their response colleagues.

8. PCSOs: 'It's a crime. Not my problem. I'll find a police officer.' Currently seen as the future of policing, unlike response officers who just crash cars and tie up custody with prisoners. Just above the bottom feeders because they only deal with certain things.

9. Front desk enquiry officers: Surprisingly close to the response officers. One up from response, though, in that they only deal with the public through plate glass. The fact they still have to deal with the public keeps them low in the chain, however.

10. Uniformed response officers (Constables, Sergeants and Inspectors): The lowest of the low. Shift-working 'police-oxen' who deal with anything. No regular breaks, no assistance, unable to say, 'Sorry, that's not in my remit.' That's me.

SUGGESTIONS AND OPINIONS

WORKING AT THE bottom of the policing pile, as I do, I am regularly subjected to the latest fads and ideas from both the public and senior police officers. The latter usually arrive by email and are always more numerous, ridiculous and impractical on a Monday morning, when everyone has had a chance to think about stuff over the weekend, discuss things with their wives and come up with an idea to ensure their promotion.

I get lots of suggestions from 'support staff', usually involving me completing an extra form or faxing something to someone else. Some are requests for information: 'Please telephone Mr Jackson and ask him how much the damage to his fence will cost. This is his telephone number.' Apparently, because I am the OIC (Officer In the Case), nobody else can use a telephone.

Another favourite is, 'Please obtain a statement from Mr Herbert. I have established that this is not possible because he is on holiday in Benidorm until next month, but CPS has requested this be done before the trial on Tuesday.' I usually wait until Wednesday before thinking about the problem again, by which time I anticipate it will have been resolved.

Many emails can be deleted, safe in the knowledge that those responsible for sending them will have had an equally silly idea by this time next week which will supersede the earlier one.

But if new ideas from within the force can largely be ignored, ideas from the public are more problematic. In the course of my duties I am subjected to all manner of suggestions, to which I try to appear receptive or, at worst, non-committal.

Some members of the public will even suggest ways of solving crime.

Last week, I went to a robbery victim who had heard one of his assailants call the other 'Pete'.

'What you need to do, officer,' said the unfortunate victim, 'is just find anyone called Pete and see if it was them.'

I thanked him, but had three suspects under arrest by lunchtime using my own old-fashioned methods.

That said, I like listening to ideas from the public because the public makes even me sound like a *Guardian*-reading* criminologist who works part-time in a health food shop which also does a sideline in tatty woolly jumpers and open-toed sandals.

'Death squads for burglars? Well, you might have a point, sir, but it would take a lot of organising.'

'Deporting non-white people apart from the people who run the shop next door? It would probably run into problems, eventually.'

'Bringing back the stocks, madam? Hmm, the human rights people might have something to say about that.'

My own opinions are well-established and are reflected in the work of Sheriff Joe Arpaio, of Maricopa County, Arizona. Sheriff Joe came to my notice because of his somewhat unreconstructed attitudes to punishment. He charged his inmates for their meals, banned smoking and porn magazines in his jail and cut off all TV apart from the Disney Channel. He made them work on chain gangs in temperatures well over 100°F and when they complained it was 'inhumane' he was, not surprisingly, unsympathetic. 'It's 120 degrees in Iraq and our soldiers have to wear full battle gear,' he barked. 'They didn't commit any crimes, so shut your damned mouths! This isn't the Ritz Carlton... if you don't like it here, don't come back!'

With it being a Saturday as I write, I feel a Monday morning suggestion of my own coming on.

* Looking through the manuscript for this book, I notice *Guardian* readers coming in for a fair bit of stick. If you're a *Guardian* reader, don't be distressed; I'm simply using your reading habits as a cipher for woolly-thinking, soft left, do-gooding liberals. I know you're not all like that, I know some of you are even quite sensible.

MORE RABBIT
THAN SAINSBURY'S

HOW ABOUT THIS ONE? A woman called for police assistance because her rabbit had gone missing.

I know, it's scarcely believable. She was standing on her doorstep, wringing her hands, when officers arrived.

'My rabbit has been stolen,' she said. 'I just let him out of the hutch a minute ago for a run round the garden. I know he's been stolen because some kids came round a minute ago and they saw him.'

I am sure it was a very distressing experience for her, but the fact that she couldn't keep her eye on her rabbit and Floppy wanted to explore the great outdoors is hardly a police matter. However, a crime number had to be given, because under government regulations the caller believed a crime had happened and there was no evidence to the contrary. The officer was obliged to investigate and, if a suspect was named, interview him or her under caution. A quick read of a few policemen's logs would soon reveal why the police are so 'overstretched'.

TIEPINS, AND THE LIMITS OF MULTICULTURALISM

I AM ON ANOTHER course at Headquarters.

I'll be back at work soon, but until then criminals will continue to go about their business unmolested and my pencil case will remain unopened.

There's a lot of chat about multiculturalism and diversity here at HQ. I'm not against multiculturalism in theory – I think it would work fine, if everyone was as intelligent, well-mannered and sociable as you are. The problem is, a significant percentage of the British population is stupid, rude and sociopathic, so it doesn't work in practice.

At HQ, of course, they exist in a parallel universe, where things like the truth, facts and the evidence of your own eyes must be denied in favour of the latest politically-correct fad or drive for social engineering.

'Who knows what "Institutional Racism" is?' was one of the questions we had to answer during the course.

This sort of jargonistic talk – along with phrases like 'best practice' or 'multi-agency approach' – have me reaching for my gun (a proper gun, probably an assault rifle).

But bear with me.

Tiepins.

You may wonder what I'm on about. Well, you know what a tiepin is, yes? Many police officers wear them and they come with all sorts of different designs. Some commemorate 9/11, others the fact that the wearer belongs to some minority group or other – they might be homosexual, perhaps, or black, or object particularly strongly to violence against women.

Until recently, I felt that such adornments were unnecessary. They're not part of the uniform and most, if not all, forces dictate that the only other things that may be worn are approved medals (and only then on certain occasions).

However, that's all changed. I've been searching the outer reaches of the Internet and have discovered that North Korea has its own website. Furthermore, it has its own souvenir shop! The irony of clicking the über-capitalist 'Add To Cart' link in a virtual North Korea is delicious (like the food, I'm told). So I've purchased a 'People's Tiepin'.

It's a colourful, enamelled badge emblazoned with the North Korean flag and it looks quite pretty. I shall wear it with pride: at last I have found a cause I can believe in.

Let's look at the evidence: North Korea is anti-American, North Koreans are non-white, North Koreans are suffering and, according to the website, 'In the DPRK there exists a remarkable kind of unity amongst the popular masses that does not exist anywhere else in the world.' (Dermot Hudson, Official Delegate of the KFA in England). So it's fun to live in North Korea as well! Stalinism with a human face! Long Live The Great Leader! (Exclamation marks seem to be a feature of North Korean writing.)

I held out for as long as I could against the special pleading and victim culture of the modern world, preferring a simple life of duty and quiet retirement. But now I have the cause of North Korean Nation to fill my life! Keep an eye out for me; I'll be the one arresting you in a comradely spirit of solidarity.

I'm not the only one moving forward in this way. The Chief Constable of Nottinghamshire, Steve Green (he of the 30 outstanding murders), has got his officers to wear green 'Good Faith' ribbons to show their solidarity with Muslim communities. Apparently, his force area has seen a rise in racism following the terrorist attacks in London last year. While it's nice to be on the same wavelength as the Chief, I can't help thinking that, with such an impressive murder rate, Steve might have other things to worry about. I bet it came after a weekend conversation with the wife, followed up with a Monday morning email. It'll probably all blow over.

Actually, I'm half-tempted by the Muslim green myself. I could also wear an NSPCC badge to stop child abuse, a red ribbon for AIDS, a pink ribbon for breast cancer, a yellow wristband to stop all other types of cancer and black and white wristbands to simultaneously end global poverty and racism. Alternatively, I could cover my uniform in glue and go mental in a haberdashers.

CRIME FIGURES

THE COUNTRY SEEMS to be divided between those who think that things are getting worse, and those who think that things are getting better and that it's all in our heads.

The latter includes most politicians, the liberal left and ACPO. Many of these people earn quite impressive salaries and can afford to live in areas where crime is, for the time being, relatively low. This may explain their optimism.

The former includes: everyone else, many of whom live in areas where crime happens and are people to whom crime happens.

Those who think things are better say, 'Oooh, crime has always happened, it's just that nowadays it's reported more.'

Essentially, this is the ruling elite telling everyone else that there's no need to worry, they'll sort everything out if we just allow them more power and resources.

Mmm, no thanks. Give me a gun and a few acres and I'll take care of myself, if it's all the same to you.

My belief is that greater numbers of police are not the answer to rising crime. I think enough of our money is spent on the police, it just gets wasted. There are enough policemen, it's just that they are all sat behind desks.

Here are some interesting statistics*.

The UK population has risen steadily over the last century or so, from 38 million in 1901 to around 60 million today (note, it hasn't doubled).

In the same period, the total number of police officers employed by the State has risen from around 40,000 to close to 130,000 now (ie it has more than trebled).

What about crime? Well, the number of indictable offences known to the police in 1900 was 2.4 for every 1,000 of the population. In 1997, the figure was 89.1. I'd put my house on the fact that it's gone up since then.

I suppose some cynics might interpret these figures as to show that the police are actually causing crime. I wouldn't go that far. But I do wonder this: where are all these new police officers and what are they doing?

ACPO can probably tell you. Write to them at ACPO, 25, Victoria Street, London SW1H 0EX (or give them a bell – they're on 020 7227 3434). They love to hear from taxpayers.

* All figures from House of Commons Library: Research Paper 99/111 (A Century of Change, Trends in UK Statistics Since 1900).

A DEPRESSING VISIT IN THE SMALL HOURS

I HAD A DEPRESSING visit to make today.

In the small hours, I had to go and see an 18-year-old girl who'd had an argument with her boyfriend. He'd stormed out and she was frightened he was going to come back and attack her.

She lived in a grubby flat, behind a flimsy wooden door with a cheap Yale lock and screw holes where the old one had been before it was kicked off in an earlier row. Inside, the detritus of a disordered life lay everywhere; bedsheets, children's clothes, toys and sweet wrappers strewn throughout the place, a couple of photographs of the kids on the walls and an overflowing bin in the kitchen next to a cat bowl full of Whiskas. In the corner of the living room was a television, with DVD and CD players and a Nintendo Gamecube alongside. A stack of DVDs, CDs and games were shoved behind the telly. The dirty walls were painted pink and the local authority, as part of its environmental drive, had put in double-glazed widows. There were no books and no dining table.

The whole place smelled catty, stale and unaired.

The girl – like so many who spend their lives catering to the whims of the moment – had been out on the town that night. She had left her kids with her boyfriend, and that had been at the bottom of the row. He was not the father of the children, and had taken umbrage when she came home, late and smashed out of her face. He'd restrained himself from delivering the beating he doubtless felt she deserved, but she feared his restraint wouldn't last forever.

'He had a right go at me,' she said, still drunk, and clearing a pile of unwashed children's clothes away so I could sit down. 'I don't want him here any more.'

The children were well-behaved and dressed in dirty pyjamas. It was 3am and they had been up for hours. They were eating crisps and staring at me with dark-rimmed, saucer eyes. A wave of depression came over me, as it always does whenever kids are involved. There was nothing I could do about this young woman's situation because she had not been the victim of a real crime (he hadn't actually beaten her up).

But I started talking to her.

'This isn't great, is it?' I said. 'Your kids up at this time of night, the police here. Never mind this idiot, you need a bloke with a job, someone who can provide for you and the kids. He hasn't got a job, has he?'

'I'm going to college myself soon,' she said. I've heard this a hundred times before.

'He's no good for you, though, is he?'

'I know that,' she said. 'We've broken up twice before. But this time it's for real. He's not coming back in here, no way.'

If I had a pound etc etc.

'Have you ever thought about getting married? Finding someone to take you on, make a commitment to you, that sort of thing?' I said.

She said she was only eighteen and, therefore, too young to marry. I looked at the children; I wanted to point out the obvious, but refrained. Instead, I said, 'Do you get any help looking after the kids?'

'My sister comes round sometimes,' she said, drifting off.

There wasn't much else I could usefully say, or do, so I left, my thoughts turning to the end of my shift and my comfy bed.

The flat wasn't a crack den, the girl wasn't abusing her children, not actively, anyway, and she was not a victim of domestic violence.

Nevertheless, it had been a profoundly miserable experience, and one experienced by every street copper all over the country, all the time: young mums, bringing up children in relative squalor, with no aspirations and no ability to see further than the next few hours. Like so many others, she had been soft-soaped by welfare agencies anxious to preserve the independence of the girl and her ability to make 'informed choices'. The problem is that the choices they make are, almost invariably, the wrong ones, and the result of all this is the systematic neglect of young children and the growth of our underclass.

I got home and Mrs C was asleep. I knew she'd be up soon for work, so I knelt down next to the bed. As she opened her eyes, I gave her a kiss and placed a cup of tea on the bedside table. We had breakfast together downstairs, listening to the radio. She told me she'll be back late tonight because she has to stop at the supermarket; she asked me if she should she buy any of those biscuits I like. I went upstairs, put my shirt in the laundry basket and got into bed.

Mrs C came upstairs, gave me a kiss and said goodbye.

I heard the door lock behind her and I went straight to sleep.

I LOVE MY KIDS...

… IS SOMETHING I GET to hear rather a lot, especially in the Church Road Estate. It usually means one of two things.

'I've got no idea where my kids are.'

Or, 'My kids didn't do whatever it is you say they did.'

Round these parts, love for one's children is articulated at high volume, to save turning off the television, and it's usually peppered with expletives. It's a love that has quite defined limits though: insufficient to warrant the serving of meals at regular times and without chips, for example, but at the same time effusive enough to ensure the provision of great quantities of designer sportswear.

I once spoke to an NYPD officer about the problems associated with youth crime and, in particular, the locating of appropriate adults for interviews. Needless to say, he looked at me with a blank expression. I explained: 'Well, in the UK when we arrest someone under 16 years old, we have to find an adult before you can interview them.'

'What for?'

'So you can get them charged and out of police custody.'

'Why do you care about getting them out of jail?'

'Well, it's not me so much as the custody sergeant.'

'So you ring the mom and tell them their kid's in jail?'

'Yes, but often they don't have a car, so we end up fetching them.'

'So, you guys *actually* drive round to their parents' house, pick up the mom, take her to the police station and drive her home again?'

'Er… yes, pretty much.'

'At least they don't make you give the kid a ride home, eh.'

'Well, of *course* we give the kid a lift home.'

The public's understanding of police procedure in relation to young people is poor. Even if they know the score, because their children have developed quite long criminal histories, they seem to think that the law ought to be suspended with respect to their own offspring; offspring who are, all too often, 'misunderstood'.

I like dealing with parents whose children have been arrested for the first time; it's one of the few opportunities we get to make a difference, and I try to make the experience so terrifying that they never want to come back.

Sadly, the feeling of terror soon fades the next time they're in the shopping centre and temptation is on the display in front of them.

CRIMINAL JUSTICE NONSENSE

TODAY, I SPENT MUCH of the morning sitting in the nick waiting for Dave Dodgy Geezer to arrive so that I could arrest him.

Dave's a Londoner who moved to Newtown after divorcing his wife. He has a rather irritating habit of starting every other sentence with 'When I was dahn London, mate' and ending two thirds of them with 'Know wot I'm sayin', geezer?'

He's in his late 30s and the departure of his missus has led him to attempt to revive his youth. He has blond streaks in his spiky, gelled hair, an orange tan and lots of jewellery. He looks like a juvenile simpleton to me, but some of the young ladies of Newtown seem to find it all rather charming.

I've been trying to arrest Dave for a while now. It all started when his former friend, Joe, popped in to say that Dave had hit him. He was allowed to leave after making the allegation, as there wasn't an officer handy to deal with it. But we jumped at the chance to issue him with a crime number and I had to track him down later to speak to him and get a statement. It only took a week to do that, by which time his very minor injuries had healed. Unfortunately, his ego hadn't and he stuck by his original complaint so Dave still needed to be interviewed.

I telephoned Dave last week. 'Hi Dave,' I said. 'It's PC Copperfield here, from Newtown Police. Look, I'm sorry to bother you but we've had this complaint of assault made against you so you need to come down to the police station to be arrested. You'll be interviewed and released.'

'Yeah, no problem, geezer,' replied Dave. 'Week on Saturday alright for you?'

This fitted in with my schedule, so I pencilled him in. (It might surprise you to know that most of our collars are felt by prior arrangement.)

I never even had to leave the nick.

Unfortunately, he didn't turn up so now I'll have to go looking for him. This is doubly irritating because it's a fairly insignificant offence even if he's really guilty, which I don't believe for a moment he is.

But every cloud has a silver lining, and while I was waiting I caught up on some filing. I also took five minutes to flick through a back issue of *CJS Now*, 'The quarterly magazine for all those working within the Criminal Justice System'.

The cover picture is of a criminal who is not in prison, but is instead serving some kind of community punishment. I don't know about you, but if they're going to insist on these toytown punishments I would prefer to see the offenders in orange overalls. Shackled.

The contents are a sort of liberal *Pravda*: instead of, A further 40,000 capitalist spies have been arrested and imprisoned this month, we are told about the 'Enhanced Community Punishment Order (ECP) – a community sentence in which offenders work unpaid for up to 240 hours on local community projects under close supervision.'

Crikey, talk about the hard coinage of punishment.

I have selected a few of the articles for ridicule (given the content of *CJS Now*, this is a surprisingly easy task).

It all starts with a patronising 'Letter from the Editor', one Helen Stear.

'*CJS Now* aims to demonstrate all the good work going on out there at the frontline', she writes, 'and give you opportunities to share ideas and experiences. Like the… good work going on at Hackney Youth Offending Team in London… I have found myself inspired and encouraged by the people and stories in this edition… I hope you do too.'.

I think Helen needs to get out more – probably on the streets of Hackney after dark.

There's a piece headed 'FRANK is One' which tells us: 'FRANK – the no-nonsense, non-judgmental source of drugs information and advice… celebrated its first birthday in May.'

You might expect the Criminal Justice System to say that drugs are:

    a) illegal;
    b) bad for you;
    c) part of the explosion of acquisitive crime we've
    seen in the last few decades;
    and
    d) damaging society.

But, clearly, the most important thing about drugs advice is that it should be 'non-judgmental'.

Then we read that Christine Knott, 'the first National Offender Manager… will be responsible for reducing the offending of around 320,000 offenders…'

How on earth will she do that? I hear you ask, possibly goggling as you do so.

Ah! She will do it by ensuring 'that offenders… have the maximum opportunity to address their offending behaviour.'

I'm sure we're all for offenders addressing their offending behaviour, but I suspect most people would prefer it if they did so in the comfort of their own small, uncomfortable cell (one run, perhaps, by our friend Sheriff Joe Arpaio). But that is not what *CJS Now* is about.

Positive Activities for Young People (PAYP) is, apparently, a scheme that 'provides a national programme of diversionary and developmental activities for young people who are at risk of social exclusion.'

Well, at least they're at risk of going to prison. And what's this? PAYP has had its first success! 'One young person was found to have very negative views about himself and others... During the self-esteem session, he was challenged by group members about his disruptive behaviour... his mother states he has calmed down.'

Do I need to add anything to that?

The best feature in *CJS Now*, though, is 'Competition Corner'. Perhaps the winner will be the prosecutor who has secured the most jail time, or the police officer who has arrested the most villains, or even the most productive informant? But no. The winner here has to come up with a suggestion '... to improve our service to victims and witnesses.'

Fair enough. These are very important constituents of the criminal justice system and many – most? – of them are currently let down in shameful and ridiculous ways. I wrote off, suggesting putting more offenders behind bars, which I think would strike a chord with your average victim and witness. But the winner, so adjudged by none other than the Attorney General, Lord Goldsmith, was David French from the Criminal Justice Performance Directorate, whatever that rather Stalinist-sounding organisation is. He suggested this: 'Encourage judges and magistrates to recognise and explicitly thank witnesses in court.'

Yep, that should do it, David.

Am I the only person left in this country who believes that the aims of 'Criminal Justice Professionals' should extend as far as, and no further than, putting more guilty people in jail for longer?

RECOGNISING THE UNDERCLASS – A COPPER'S GUIDE

THE SIMPLEST WAY of identifying members of the underclass is to watch the *Trisha* show on ITV in the mornings. I hope I'm not libelling anyone if I say that there can only be two types of people who watch this programme: several million genuine lowlifes and about 30 folks who think it's all rather ironic and amusing. (OK, and a few very bored housewives, students and the odd copper on nights.)

I've lost count of the number of people I've met doing this job who either:

      a) are watching *Trisha* when I go into their house;
      or
      b) have actually been on the show.

Today was a case in point. I arrived at a house on one of our housing estates and was let in by a small child. Inside, several adults were sitting around, smoking and glued to *Trisha*. I sat down, and we all watched it for a while. I don't mean it was on in the background while we all got on with the serious police business of who had been threatening whom. I mean, *Trisha* was the focus of everyone's attention, including mine.

The victims, offenders and witnesses involved in my particular crime all bore a strong resemblance to the participants, hostess aside.

I am sure you have rarely, if ever, been to a police station, either as an offender or the 'IP' (injured party). These people are always there, either under arrest or after being punched by their neighbours (and who can blame the neighbours?).

If I'm not talking to them at home over the sound of *Trisha*, I'm usually meeting them at about 02:30hrs, when they are invariably drunk, fighting and wondering why they are getting arrested.

I quite like interviewing them the next morning, especially the women, when they have sobered up and have suddenly become 'victims' despite the fresh scabs on their knuckles. *Trisha* has so permeated their minds that their every conversation is littered with possible lines from the show.

My favourite exchange was this one.

Female (having been arrested for Section 4 POA): 'I think it was really a cry for help.'

Me: 'Really? I think you just have no idea how to behave.'

More later about the attributes common to the people who regularly visit police stations in this great nation of ours.

GOOD NATURED IRAQIS

TO AN IRAQI VICTIM of crime today, who reported that he had been assaulted by another Iraqi whose name he knew. The unfortunate victim (who had no injuries to speak of) was nice enough and clearly enjoyed the novel experience of speaking to a policeman while not being suspended upside down and used as a human circuit breaker.

In Newtown, we have a large number of recent arrivals from Iraq.

They're an odd bunch but quite good-natured most of the time and they certainly have a lot more get up and go than the average indigenous Englishman of comparable age. They're all working, for a start.

They do share a cavalier disregard for driving documents and an affection for alcohol with our own home-grown people, though.

They used to be quite scared of us (the police) because of their experience at the hands of their own equivalent of the Old Bill; now they treat us with cheerful disregard, quite happily driving around, at speed, without insurance, and with only a passing acquaintance with the rules of the road. Good for them (until they have an accident and kill someone).

I quite like talking to them when I get a chance, and this chap was no exception (I always have a little map on me, and I like them to point out where they're from etc). He didn't speak a lot of English, but he was still able to amuse me with some of his hair-raising experiences at the hands of Saddam's henchmen and the story of how he ended up in Newtown.

The other group I like dealing with is old people. They always have a lot to talk about and are usually quite pleased to see me (a triumph of hope over experience if ever there was one). After lunch I met one, and spent a good hour looking through his old photographs of Newtown to see if I recognised anywhere. To add to the excitement, he was involved in the D-Day invasion, so I spent the rest of the afternoon drinking his tea and listening to his stories about Sherman tanks. It was absolutely brilliant.

I'm sure if this town was made up of only Iraqis and old people we'd all be much happier, and safer.

Talking of tea.

Much is made of the police officer's ability to make decisions. Experienced officers will say that if you go to an interview you will be able decide the issues of guilt and truth and so on in the first few seconds (which probably doesn't fill you full of confidence, but at least our prejudices aren't admissible as evidence).

Well, I'm the same with tea. In fact, the only decision I really trust myself to make is 'Cup of tea… or not?'

In some houses, you don't even want to sit down, let alone drink anything; in others, it's a different story.

I particularly like doing the middle-class domestic. Nice house, clean kitchen, blood on the knives and walls, polite, helpful people and a lovely cup of tea served with a biscuit. Possibly a custard cream. You can't beat it.

Also good for this sort of thing are Asian households. Once again, they're usually lovely people and, whatever the circumstances, they'll always offer you a cup of tea. Best of all (here's a tip if you're in the job and new), if you let them know when you're coming they'll even have something for you to eat. My happiest policing memory to date is sitting down to the best vegetarian curry I've ever tasted whilst dealing with complaints of nuisance phone calls.

I caught up with Dave Dodgy Geezer as well today, so I was an hour late finishing.

He denied assaulting Joe, which didn't surprise me at all. He provided me with an alibi (or at least someone who saw the whole thing and would say Dave wasn't to blame). By the time I get round to speaking to Dave's mate, I'm sure that our alleged victim will have forgotten all about it anyway.

Dave found my interviewing technique a good deal more sympathetic than that which he'd experienced at the hands of the Met while he was 'Dahn London'.

'I got done *right* over by the Old Bill dahn there, geezer,' he explained. 'They took a right liberty, know wot I mean? They had nuffink on me, yeah, they was only on a fishing trip 'cos I knew a few people and they thawt I was dodgy an' all.'

'Well, you are dodgy Dave,' I said.

'Yeah,' he said. 'I know that, but they ditten't, did they?'

TOWARDS A THEORY OF BUREAUCRACY

AS I ARRIVED at work this morning and drove round hunting for a space in the station car park, I was struck by two questions.

Do *all* of these cars belong to people who work in our building? If so, what do they all *do*?

The answer, of course, is that they are *very* busy.

In the civil service, waste is not only tolerated but actually officially encouraged.

All of us have a natural tendency towards bureaucracy. It would have been much easier to chalk up on the cave wall the number of woolly mammoths trapped than actually to go out and trap woolly mammoths. Likewise, nowadays, it is much easier to sit behind a desk and draw graphs about problems than it is actually to get off your backside and sort out the problems.

Of course, in the caveman days people had to kill mammoths to survive. Likewise, in the private sector, unless you make or sell widgets which are good enough that someone wants to buy them, you will, eventually, be unemployed.

No such problems exist in the modern British public sector.

The police are only civil servants in uniform and we are particularly adept at dipping our paws into the rivers of public gold.

We take a massive amount every year from the public purse and virtually everything that isn't spent on pensions gets spent on salaries, though rarely for 'proper' policemen. We have whole departments

devoted to checking and auditing the performance of frontline o\
for every two uniformed cops there's one 'civilian' employee.
been summoned to meetings where there has been standing room
only, yet down the corridor only three front line officers have booked
on duty. We have huge police stations in prime, town centre locations
with only four officers on duty after midnight.

Despite this huge expenditure, and the massive numbers of people
employed by the police, we remain resolutely unaccountable.

Of course, if crime goes down we take the credit, but if it goes up
we blame society or say it's just in your imagination.

What would make a difference?

I would start by getting rid of 25% of civilians and desk jockeys
and using the money saved to bring in more frontline officers. I'd
have them under the command of directly-elected Chief Constables,
responsible to their local electorate. I'd also bring in mandatory jail
sentences for first-time burglars, abandon PACE and remove the
Human Rights Act from UK law.

THREATS TO KILL

THE UNDERCLASS ARE always threatening to kill each other,
whether by phone, text message or in person.

I'm not sure why. I suspect it's a combination of a diet of violent
action films, the fractured nature of their relationships and their
remarkably quick tempers. Or it could just be that they're bored and
have nothing better to do.

At any rate, the threatened party sometimes complains to the
police.

We take statements and interview the suspects, the CPS refuses
to prosecute and then there is a queue of people demanding to know
why their ex-partners and former friends are still walking the streets.

The following week, the cycle begins again.

I can't really blame the CPS.

There are rarely any witnesses to the threats and if the text message
or voicemail hasn't been lost or deleted, it's usually indecipherable.
In fact, if I have to decode one more abusive text or listen to one more
moronic recording, I actually *will* kill someone.

The initial allegation of a threat to kill usually brings a counter-allegation (the immutable First Law of Policing in a consumer-led society), so that then doubles my workload.

Looking on the bright side, a long queue of chavs looking to 'press charges' means I won't have to go outside the police station, where it might be cold and wet, or too hot and sunny, and help people who may actually need my assistance.

Kelly Broxholme nipped in to the station today at about lunchtime, on her way between The Red Lion and Bojangles Wine Bar. Her complaint, that her former friend Sharon had been sending threatening text messages to her, held no surprises for me, though it did make a change. Kelly is known to most officers as 'the offender' – she has a habit of fighting with and threatening people – but for once she was the IP. She was contained, for the most part, in tight hipster jeans and a top which revealed her ample midriff. She's a big girl, taller than me in her heels, and has home-made tattoos of 'Steve 4 ever' on her right forearm and 'R.F.B' on the left. I don't know what 'R.F.B' means and I've never had the courage to ask.

'What do you think of this?' she demanded, waving her mobile phone under my nose.

'Well, it looks very shiny,' I said, 'but, to be honest, I can't tell one from another. Is it, er… 3G?'

'Not the phone,' she said. 'Read the message, will yer?'

'U FUKIN BITCH KELLY U FUKIN GET KILD DED.'

No sooner had I digested this – it sounded like a threat to kill, but a half-decent lawyer could probably come up with an alternative reading – than she whipped it away and, with a blur of thumbs, produced another one, similar in meaning.

When dealing with threats to kill, I first attempt to pour oil on troubled waters by saying that few people who actually are killed receive any warning first, so there's nothing to worry about, is there? That didn't go down well with Kelly.

'Well,' I said. 'What's the root cause of the problem?'

'Yer what?' she asked.

'What's it all about?' I said.

In my experience, it's usually a combination of an excess of aggression and any two of the following:

42

indolence
envy
sexual desire
jealousy
alcohol
drugs
revenge
spite
boredom.

All untempered by any responsibility, intelligence or fear of the law.

'Shaz is just a f*ckin' cow and can't deal with me and Paul being together,' she said.

Ah. Spite and jealousy, then.

I gritted my teeth and carried on to the next stage.

I could have written her statement without even listening to her.

'... I have known Sharon for 18 months since I started going out with PAUL who used to go out with SHARON, but then he and I started seeing each other when SHARON went to Ibiza... In SHAGS nightclub... SHARON said to me "You're f*cking dead, Kelly, I'm going to f*cking kill you, you bitch." I was really scared and really thought SHARON was going to kill me...'

After listening to Kelly for longer than I thought possible, I decided I ought to go and see the offender in the matter, Sharon.

By now, it was nearly 16:00hrs, but Sharon was fortunately still at home (thank God for daytime TV). when I told her the reason I needed to speak to her, she produced her own mobile phone with a flourish and showed me text messages of a similar nature. Of course, these had been sent by Kelly.

Without wishing to downgrade threats to kill – clearly, it can be a very serious offence – this was a load of rubbish that had no chance of coming within a hundred miles of a magistrates' court.

'OK, Sharon,' I said. 'Look, what I'm going to do is make a few more enquiries and then come back to you.'

I'll have to get to the bottom of it, but it will take *forever* and, even after my investigation, after the arrests, statements and interviews have all been completed, and *hours* of police time has been taken up, the CPS won't have the *slightest* interest in this two-bit, six-of-one pile of juvenile tosh, and rightly so.

Now, sorry, did you say your lock-up had been broken into and all your tools stolen? Ah… we haven't got an officer spare just at the moment. Can I come round the week after next?

DRINK DRIVE: EASY PEASY

THERE IS A WAR going on between good and evil but, being a uniformed response officer, I don't have much to do with it.

Instead, I work on the front line of the war of good vs. delinquency, good vs. stupidity, good vs. drunkenness, drunkenness vs. drunkenness and stupidity vs. stupidity.

At the heart of drunkenness, stupidity and delinquency is the drunk driver, one of whom I arrested the other night.

He was a young man who was driving home from the town centre rather erratically – under-steering on the corners and not keeping in a straight line. Oh, and he had forgotten to turn his lights on. But he had got his wipers going. And it wasn't raining. Given that he had committed a moving traffic offence, I was well within my rights to stop him, which I did.

'Would you mind getting out of the car, sir?' I said.

'Naaaah… no problem,' he said. He staggered the short distance and sat in the back of my car.

'I've just stopped you because it's night time and your lights are off.'

'F*CK… oooh… shorry… shwearing… sh*t… I'll turn them off…'

'No, they're already off. They should be on. Do you understand?'

'Sh*t, sorry, yeah.'

'Have you had a drink tonight?'

'Coupleapints, thassall.'

I've long since given up persuading people to blow into the machine if they don't want to: I no longer shout, encourage, threaten, give them ten attempts, explain the procedure again and so on. I simply say, 'The Road Traffic Act means you have to give me a specimen of breath… will you provide me with a specimen? Blah… blah… have you smoked… etc. OK, you've failed to provide a specimen. I'll give you two more goes and if you still won't provide I'll arrest you and take you to the station.'

Anyway, my low-key approach worked and on the second attempt he blew positive. So together we went to the station and, because it was busy, spent the next three hours going through the station breath test procedure and talking about house prices and mutual friends from the Church Road Estate.

Pete (we were on first name terms by this time) failed the station test and was charged the following morning. He will be in court some time next week.

Drunk drivers have few champions in this country and we get loads of calls saying that a particular person regularly leaves the King's Head and drives home whilst drunk. I know it's illegal and I know we should be putting a stop to it, but for some reason I cannot share many of my colleagues' enthusiasm for catching them. The penalty for drunk driving (loss of livelihood, in many cases, and the financial and other penalties that imposes on innocent family members) seems quite severe, especially when you compare it with the penalties many of our proper criminals get.

QUICK! WE NEED A NEW FORM FOR THIS

I READ THE OTHER day about a new police car being ripped apart by fire-fighters so that paramedics could remove a man who was complaining of back pain.

Police officers had been called to a minor collision on the A17 at Clenchwarton, Norfolk, and had put the driver of the crashed vehicle in their car.

But when he subsequently said his back was hurting, there was a dilemma. He said he couldn't get out, so the paramedics who were also there said the roof would need to come off the police car so that they could lift him out, put him on a spinal board and get him into the ambulance.

The Fire Brigade duly obliged. The £25,000 car was scrapped.

If you think this sounds ridiculous, you're right. The emergency services would disagree with you, though. A Norfolk Fire Service spokesman said, 'The well-being of the injured person must always come first in an accident.'

Matthew Ware, of the East Anglian Ambulance Trust, said: 'We considered it unsafe to get him out of the vehicle. The fact that it was a police car and not damaged was taken into consideration, and there were lengthy discussions, but eventually we decided to cut open the roof.'

I'm sure that the discussions wouldn't have been quite so lengthy if the man with the bad back had been sitting in his own car.

'Look mate, we're worried about your back, so we're going to cut the roof off.'

'F*ck off, I'll take my chances.'

BAD NEWS ABOUT POLICE CORRUPTION

THERE ISN'T ANY, really.

OK, there's the odd bad apple but they really are the exception, despite all the nonsense people talk.

The other day, I arrested a guy for possession of a small quantity of Class A drugs.

He hinted that, if I just forgot about this unfortunate episode, he'd see me right. 'Come on mate,' he said. 'Only me and you will know. It happens all the time.'

Well, actually, no it doesn't. Why would I want to take a backhander from someone? I might be tempted if someone offered me a hundred grand in used twenties – I'm only human, after all. But the pension is more money than I'm ever going to get from the kind of people I deal with.

'No thanks,' I said. 'You're coming down the nick with me.'

'You bastard,' he said. 'You'll just keep the f*cking gear for yourself.'

'I won't,' I said. 'I don't take drugs, I'm a *policeman*. And anyway, it's evidence.'

I especially like the way the money is counted out in custody.

Last night, we had a guy in for drunk and disorderly. He was violent and abusive and was searched on the floor, cuffed, with two bobbies on top of him.

The custody sergeant knelt down next to the prisoner, counted out all his money (£2.21), put it in a bag, sealed it, and wrote the seal number down, all inches away from his face and all on camera.

I spent most of the rest of the night filling in some forms whilst eating a sandwich very slowly. The two other officers in the station had their feet up and were drinking tea, an all too brief respite from the war on crime (or is it paperwork this week?). The Sergeant burst in, clutching a printout. 'Have you heard about this?' he asked.

'Yes, we're just about to go,' replied one officer, still watching the television. I think it was Ant and Dec.

'Well, what are you waiting for? It says he's going to commit suicide.'

'Yes, I've read it. We were going to break the door down.'

'You can't do that,' said the Sergeant. 'It says he'll set himself on fire if the police turn up.'

Still watching television, draining the last of his tea, the officer said, 'Don't worry, Sarge. I was going to break the door down with a fire extinguisher.'

I was still chuckling 10 minutes after they'd gone. The man didn't commit suicide, of course. They very rarely do.

I finished the shift with a cuppa myself, and happened upon a copy of our local paper. *New Law Aims To Get Rid Of Graffiti* read the headline on one story.

What a brilliant wheeze, I thought. And why stop there? Why not introduce a law that will stop *all* crime?

Is it just me? Does no-one else realise how stupid people in government are?

PRIVATE POLICING

FED-UP WITH THEIR local police force and soaring crime in their area, neighbours in the London borough of Westminster have clubbed together to pay for the services of a security guard.

About 25 households each pay £1,000 a year for a chap called Yauheni, who works for a private security firm, to patrol the streets in their area and note down any suspicious incidents. He observes people and generally keeps a look out.

Yauheni is from Belarus, but many of the firm's other guards have served in the Israeli Defence Force (IDF).

Officially, I think it's a really bad idea to put people like that out on the streets, with no diversity training.

Unofficially, I think it's a great idea. I know I would feel safer if I knew former IDF soldiers were patrolling the streets where I live. But if I ever suggested it to those in charge here in Newtown, I doubt I would get very far.

'Sir... I've had this idea about going out on foot in one particular area. Let's call it... I dunno... a "beat"? And, well, what we'd do is just sort of walk around, "patrol" you might say, and just keep people on their toes? People will be really happy to see us and we might scare off offenders.'

'Hmmm. It's all very well in theory, Copperfield, but it simply isn't an appropriate use of resources. We're currently flying over the area in the helicopter once a week and are targeting specific areas every third Thursday. Besides, how many detections do you think you'll get if you just walk everywhere? No, we need people in cars to respond to calls within the approved time. Got any new strategies, lad?'

'Sir?'

'*Strategies*, Copperfield. You know, strategies for safer communities, strategies for drug free communities, strategies for policing in diverse environments, that sort of thing.'

'No, sir, I just thought I could have a walk round.'

'No, no, Copperfield, we need *strategies*. Look, why don't you go and see the youth development officer about developing a strategy for this "patrolling"? Then we'll see if we can get some Home Office funding for a pilot scheme. Now run along, there's a good chap.'

The whole Yauheni scheme was orchestrated by one Harriet Sergeant. Like many people, Harriet is of the misguided opinion that the police don't actually do much.

How she can say this? She clearly has no idea about policing in a diverse community and still holds to the old-fashioned idea that police officers should be out there, on foot, getting to know residents and local villains. Nonsense on stilts! As everyone knows, the best thing to do is wait until we get a call and then drive really fast to it. Sometimes we don't even kill anyone on the way and get there when the offender is only a few hundred metres away. We can then dust for DNA, or something.

MAJOR CRIME SCENE

I THINK I MUST have been on television yesterday. I was on 'scene preservation' duty outside a house where a major incident had taken place. Curious, really; I do nothing for ages and then suddenly I'm involved in a major incident. The police organise packed lunches on these occasions, which you can eat when relieved. I couldn't believe the size of mine: it seemed to be full of packets of crisps, biscuits and chocolate bars. I don't normally eat that much, and Mrs C was quite upset when I returned home with her sandwiches uneaten, saying, 'I don't fancy a big dinner tonight.'

I'd like to be able to give you a full report about the forensic techniques used, the organisation behind a major crime scene, an analysis of the chain of command and so on, but unfortunately I can't. I found it most enjoyable though, the weather was quite good and you develop an agreeable sense of self-importance when people keep coming come up and asking you what's going on.

'I'm sorry sir,' you say. 'All I can tell you is that an incident has taken place and an investigation is currently underway.'

Or words to that effect.

The reason you say that is because you don't actually know what's going on either.

The two officers on scene preservation (me and a colleague) were chatting away. 'What do you think's going on?' I asked him.

'Probably murder-related. What do you think?'

'I think Osama Bin Laden's inside.'

'Could be, I haven't seen him lately.'

Fortunately, the neighbours were in and they kept us updated and well-supplied with tea.

The first time they came round, one of them said, 'We've been watching Teletext.'

'Oh good,' I said. 'What's going on?'

Eventually, we found out what it was all about.

I can't tell you, though. All I can say is that an incident has taken place and an investigation is currently underway.

BLACK POLICE NONSENSE

DAVE DODGY GEEZER was due to answer his bail today. The last time we met, he gave me an alibi which I had to check out, so I released him without charge on the expectation that he would turn up today. While waiting for him I was flicking through the paper, when an item caught my eye.

It was about North Wales Deputy Chief Constable Clive Wolfendale's surreal address to the inaugural meeting of the North Wales Black Police Association, in front of black officers and the media. Because – obviously – black people can only communicate through the medium of rap, DCC Wolfendale decided to deliver his message in that style.

I've reproduced the whole thing. If you can get to the end of it without weeping, do let me know.

'I'm just a white boy called the Deputy CC.
They said I'd never make it as a bitchin' MC.
You got it all wrong, 'cos now here I am
Giving it for real in the North Wales BPA jam.
They call me Roxy, or Ms Dynamo on stage.
Unlike my brother here, I never look my age.
I'm goin' to spill it all about the boys in blue,
Show you what it's like within the not-so-solid crew.
So listen! Watcha doin' here today,
Checkin' what the Heddlu Gogledd Cymru gotta say?
Put away your cameras and your note pads for a spell.
I got a story that I really need to tell.
Bein' in the dibble is no cakewalk when you're black.
If you don't get fitted, then you'll prob'ly get the sack.
You're better chillin', lie down and just be passive.
No place for us just yet in the Colwyn Bay Massive.

The Beeb Man stuffed us with the Secret Policeman.
It's no good moanin' 'cos he found the Ku Klux Klan.
Job ain't what it used to be; it's full of blacks and gays.
It was just us white homies in the really good ole days.
So what we bothrin' with this stinkin' institution?
No love, no heart, no sense, no proper constitution.
No-one loves the coppers 'cos we're rotten to the core.
Cross between the devil and a governmental whore.
What is the purpose of a black association?
It's just another stupid race relations job creation.
We got our meetings and our various sub-committees
Packed with some do-gooders and a lot more Walter Mittys.
Forget all of that bullsh*t an' I'll tell u why we're here:
Things are sometimes better than they usually appear.
The New World Order means the streets are gettin' hot.
Trust in one another is really all we got.
The BPA is sayin' that we're all in the same boat.
Black or white in blue, we're all wearin' the same coat.
If this don't happen then the lot of us are screwed,
Caught up in the mis'ry of the international feud.
So Roger, Nick and Larbi will you give us one more chance?
Danny and Silvana, I'd really like to dance.
To Essi and to Imdad I want to give a hand.
Let's hear it for Ms Dynamo and all her backin' band.
There's no time for jam tomorrow, we need the jam today.
That's why we launchin' our association in this way.
Thank you all for coming and remember what we say:
Support your local sheriff and the North Wales BPA.'

I could write a whole book about this alone, but let's confine ourselves to the obvious.

Firstly, the adaptation of the quote from Lenin at the end, 'There's no time for jam tomorrow', suggests that DCC Wolfendale is a reasonably intelligent and educated man, or at least has the Oxford Dictionary of Famous Quotations on his desk.

Secondly, that removes out-and-out stupidity as an excuse for this nonsense and means, therefore, that he is an absolute idiot.

Thirdly, he's also a really, really bad rapper.

And, finally, this is tremendously patronising to the black police officers he was addressing.

Does this idiot really think all black people like rap? Does he think a simple explanation of the ethos behind the NWBPA would have gone over their heads? In my dream scenario, one of them stands up and says, 'Er... actually I'm into Mozart.'

By the way, The Geezer turned up but I hadn't had time to do the relevant enquiries so I re-bailed him. The whole thing's still going nowhere, but I have to go through the motions.

GAY POLICE NONSENSE

HOT ON THE HEELS of the boy Wolfendale's bizarre performance came this, in the *Daily Telegraph*.

'A police force became embroiled in a row over sex discrimination yesterday', it said, 'after it issued a new dress code banning male officers from wearing earrings on duty.

Paul Kernaghan, the chief constable of Hampshire Police, said he was anxious to smarten up the appearance of uniformed officers and it was thought that the public did not want to see male officers wearing earrings. Female officers, however, can continue to wear earrings, as long as they are of the stud variety.

The edict has angered some officers, who feel the ruling is discriminatory. Gay officers said the policy sent out an anti-homosexual message. Wearing a ring in the right ear has become a symbol of homosexuality among gay men. The force has been warned that the policy could face a legal challenge and the Police Federation has said it plans to take up the issue.

A group of gay officers, who declined to be identified, has asked Lee Hunt, a local Conservative councillor, himself a former policeman, to speak for them. Mr Hunt, who represents Southsea on Portsmouth city council, said: "The police force is supposed to be developing more of a live and let live approach, but this sends out the wrong message."'

Is it me? I thought. Is anyone else out there thinking what I am? Am I the only sane person still here?

'Have you seen this, Steve?' I asked one of my colleagues, passing him the newspaper.

He read it with interest and then passed it back with a shake of his head. Apparently it isn't just me. Does your average taxpayer in the town in which I live and work know that some gay men wear earrings in the right ear? Does he or she care? I suspect the whole thing is a joke.

'Tell you what, Dave,' said Steve. 'Most straight blokes like wearing un-ironed shirts and a week's-worth of stubble. We ought to propose that as a way forward, and see where it gets us.'

Things I've never, ever had a victim say to me, No131: 'I'm really sorry, but can I have a gay policeman, please?'

FOILED AGAIN

THIS MORNING I GOT on with some routine enquiries. In a reflection of the trivia that takes up most of my time, Kelly Broxholme's text messages were top of the list. As luck would have it, the missing link (in more ways than one), Paul, was at work. He told me that he knew all about it but it was more than his life was worth to get on the wrong side of Kelly. He therefore declined to make a statement, something that leaves me with one less pointless task to complete and puts the whole job one step nearer the bin.

On the way back to the station, I was diverted to an address near the railway station. The call had originally been classified as 'harassment' by a call centre worker who was convinced that Mr Pilovski was quite sane.

On my arrival I decided, even with my limited understanding of matters psychological, that Mr Pilovski was completely mad. He had called us because he was convinced his neighbours were spying on him via his electricity ring main. In order to try and stop this, he had put tin foil around the plugs and encased his television in the same way.

As I say, I was convinced he was nuts (or had 'mental health issues', as we must nowadays say, in our mealy-mouthed way) and would end up burning the house down very soon.

In fact, I told him so. 'I'm no electrician, but I think you'll *probably* burn this house down soon,' I said.

He thought it was a risk worth taking, what with MI5, MI6 and the CIA also out to get him.

Then he said, 'You don't believe me do you?'

I suggested that the West's security forces had bigger fish to fry, what with the war on terror and all that.

I sat and watched as he foiled up his old radio and, as I did so, I asked myself what on earth I was doing there. Here I was, a vital foot soldier in the alleged war on crime, watching a loony turn his house silver. I think it's called Care in the Community. Mind you, he was harmless and pleasant in a slightly off-kilter sort of way and it was a perfectly enjoyable half hour.

Generally, policing is not frightening. Or exciting. You meet a lot of odd people though, and that's what keeps me going.

FEAR AND LOATHING IN THE TOWN CENTRE

I HATE BEING IN the town centre at chucking-out time of a weekend.

Any sane man in his 30s would hate it, but it's even worse if you're a policeman because we can't just run away from all the thugs like you can.

For some reason, people can't go out for a quiet drink with the wife, maybe have a curry late on and then get a cab back home. Instead, they chuck gallons of fizzy lager and alcopops down their necks, vomit and urinate everywhere and then refuse to disperse without having a good fight first (and that's just the women).

My preferred solution would be to drive a water cannon up the High Street at 02:30hrs and wash all the gobby scumbags away.

Sadly, that's not allowed.

Last night was fairly typical. Two groups of young men had been ejected from a nightclub. As soon as they hit the street they squared up to each other again. A crowd gathered around them, some fearful and hysterical, others gleefully egging them on. I walked over to try to calm things down. It was scary, as it always is, and the symptoms of my fear were the familiar ones: my throat went dry as I tried to make myself heard and my leg started to quiver as what little authority I have started to ebb away.

Just as the warring parties looked like ignoring my instructions, and fighting was about to break out under my very nose, the cavalry arrived in the form of my colleagues and order was once more restored to the streets of Newtown.

In England, if you want to commit a crime, my advice is, do it on a Saturday night. All the police are busy trying to stop people from fighting in town centres across the land. This hasn't escaped the notice of our legislators, who continually put forward new rules and suggestions and strategies about 'binge-drinking' and the consequent disorder. As usual, the solution is simple, but requires political courage:

1. Offence committed on a Saturday night.
2. Arrest.
3. Charge.
4. NO BAIL.
5. Go before the court on Monday.
6. Sentence: one week on the chain gang.
7. Release.

I LIKE TO BE IN AMERICA

OUR POLITICIANS ARE always looking across the Atlantic for solutions to our problems with law and order. At least, that's the impression they'd like you to have.

What they're really looking for are Tony Blair's famous 'eye-catching initiatives': meaningless soundbites, which they can trot out to make themselves sound tough before forgetting them the next week (marching yobs to cashpoints, anyone?). As for actually implementing some of the things which have led to the dramatic falls in crime experienced in many major US cities, that's quite another matter. The reality of US law-enforcement – long, hard prison sentences, locally accountable chiefs implementing zero tolerance policies, and patrol officers with discretion – is too much for most Chief Constables, what with their Masters' Degrees in sociology, and the result is that the best ideas are quietly ignored as being too 'confrontational'.

Today, I'm reading William Bratton's book *Turnaround*, which is all about how he became NYPD commissioner, reduced the crime rate and earned the thanks of the city. So I thought I'd put down some of the main things that Bratton (now chief of the LAPD) and the NYPD got right.

1. Focus on the local commanders. Precinct commanders in the NYPD have to reduce crime. If they don't, they're history. The focus for this is COMPSTAT, a real-time information system which points out, on a map, when and where the crime is happening. At a COMPSTAT meeting you'd better know your crime stats and have some good ideas for getting them down, or else.

This contrasts with the UK, where the copper's main objective is to stay out of trouble. Our police service is just a vast bureaucracy created with the sole aim of covering backs, having everything in writing, avoiding complaints and blaming other people. Officers join the bureaucracy as soon as possible to avoid the twin dangers of making mistakes and getting complained about.

2. Police Control Behaviour. In the UK we think we can stop domestic violence by having an office-bound unit; we think we can stop crime generally by having huge call centres and 'crime audit' departments. (That's those of us who don't think that it's all society's fault, and the police can't or shouldn't actually do anything.)

Bratton knew that the police could get bad people to behave better – by keeping on top of them; furthermore, he knew that law-abiding people feel better when they see police officers walking about and dealing firmly with minor offences.

3. Good Ideas. Bratton wanted people to come up with ideas, or tactics. He understood that low-level tactics help fight crime, and these tactics need to change, sometimes over time, sometimes very quickly. People have to exchange information quickly and be flexible to deal with new crime patterns. He

devolved decision making to the precinct level, and then held local commanders responsible for the results. He had his officers deal with petty offences robustly.

In the UK, it's not a real idea unless it involves a £20 million computer system or another set of forms to fill in.

Notice I've made no mention of numbers, which a lot of police officers go on about a lot of the time. That's because – although the NYPD is certainly well-staffed – I think the problem in the UK is how we deploy and use our police, not their numbers. Numbers is just an excuse. I would be delighted if this book made a small contribution to the furthering of that understanding.

POLICE POWERS

IT IS AN ARTICLE of faith amongst police officers that, in order to deal with crime, we need 'more powers.'

I disagree; in fact, I file it alongside the 'more police' argument. Peter Hitchens' very readable polemic, *A Brief History Of Crime*, describes how the police have changed from being ordinary 'citizens in uniform' to being a breed apart with all sorts of powers to search houses and keep people in custody for days at a time without much more than a shred of evidence. These increased powers have not meant that the police have been any more effective in dealing with crime, argues Hitchens; quite the opposite, in fact.

Unusually for a bobby, I agree with this theory.

Now our powers are on the increase again, as we prosecute the war on terror and fight so-called 'organised crime'.

But while these are serious issues, most people are more worried about 'disorganised crime'. They want a bus that is on time and free of yobs and graffiti; the thought that it might be bombed is a distant one.

Naturally, I don't have much to do with either terrorism or organised crime. My calls, like tonight's, tend to be more prosaic.

'I think my son is being abused by his dad,' the woman said. The boy lived with her ex in another part of town.

This sort of call illustrates perfectly the dilemma facing the libertarian policeman (there are some).

On the one hand, the mother was drunk when she made the call and it was 2am. She might be trying to stir things up.

On the other hand, she might be right; the boy could be suffering terrible abuse.

No choice, really: I did my duty and checked the child out, waking him up and upsetting the whole house in the small hours. He was fine, physically, though obviously quite bewildered and very tired.

As I said goodnight, I reflected on this: who was inflicting the real abuse?

I've been to council estates where there are demonstrations against paedophiles. You stand there, making sure things don't get too out of hand, thinking, 'You're the same parents who sentence your kids to a life of crap jobs, no personal stability, no family life, no support in their learning, no boundaries and no rules.'

The irony almost makes me smile, but it's too sad for that.

CRACK DEALERS ARRESTED

PHEW! HAD A REALLY big day today. You'll probably have read about it in the papers.

I was chasing this car and it crashed into a wall. The people inside got out and I handcuffed them all single-handedly. When I looked inside the car I found 4kg of crack cocaine and £10,000 in cash.

That took care of most of my day.

The rest of it was more mundane. I spent some time studying the posters on one of our walls – they say things like, 'Stop Racism' and 'Handed in a Form 12A/12/36-4 recently? You MUST also copy out a form H1/56/G3-5. Your job may depend upon it.'

After that, I decided to sort out my locker. I knew my file was getting full but I couldn't believe it when I took it out and it all came undone, spilling MG series forms across the desk and floor. It took ages to tidy up.

Then I made some tea.

Note: I made the crack arrest story up. The rest of it is true, though.

THE PEOPLE ARE REVOLTING

EVERY SO OFTEN you get to do something really good and today was one of those days. I don't mean I did something really good for society, like arresting loads of criminals, I mean I did something I really enjoyed (I enjoy arresting criminals, too, don't get me wrong, but it's hard on the wrist, with all the paperwork).

I was at a protest. I won't bore you with the details about what they were against (or maybe for, I really can't recall) but the sun shone and our happy band almost outnumbered the protesters.

After an initial briefing, we all made our way in convoy to the site of the 'demo'. We than drove about two miles away and waited… all day.

Marvellous.

Absolutely nothing happened and I only got out of the car a couple of times, to stretch my legs and go for a little wander.

'This is the life, Adey,' I said, to my colleague, Adrian, when I got back. 'Sunshine, fresh air, birds tweeting, no scumbags.'

He didn't reply, so I looked back into the car. He'd dozed off.

Around about 13:00hrs, we delved into the enormous police-issue packed lunches we'd been sent off with. Two of these took up the whole of the back seat, so much so that our coats and hats had had to go on the floor. We sat, listening to the odd message on our radios, contemplating the scenery and munching contentedly on our sandwiches.

'Tell you what, Dave,' said Adey, eventually. 'These are great lunches, aren't they? Better than my missus makes, that's for sure.' He rooted around in his box and came up with a Mars bar and a mini-packet of custard creams. 'Mind you,' he said. 'Look at these. The Government keeps banging on about healthy eating, and here they are sending us out to ram ourselves full of chocolate and biscuits. What happened to joined-up thinking?'

I chuckled and ploughed on, anxious not to waste anything. I ate the lot before 14:00hrs and was very nearly sick.

Mrs C was once again disappointed that I did not eat my dinner.

PLUS ÇA CHANGE, PLUS C'EST LA MEME CHOSE

IF YOU HAD BOUGHT an earlier edition of this book, then round about here you would have been reading a (probably) rather confusing explanation of a thing called 'administrative detections'. This was a complicated bureaucratic scam by which we 'solved' trivial crimes. We're talking crimes so trivial – a bit of name-calling in the playground, a cup of water thrown over someone, a two-fingered salute – that people didn't actually want to go to court about them, they just wanted to get the matter off their chests. For many modern Britons, the police now provide that outlet, where once a long walk or an adult conversation might have done the trick.

The system of administrative detections has recently been done away with, perhaps after this book found its way to the Home Office, but it's worth explaining what it was for three reasons – first, because other parts of the book refer to the system; second, to show how things have changed; and third, because these things are cyclical and by the time you actually read this administrative detections will probably be back in vogue.

Let's say there's been a bit of mobile phone text abuse going on between a couple of schoolkids – Wayne and his half-brother's ex-girlfriend's new partner's ex, Tracey. Wayne has snt a nsty txt to Tracey so her mum has phoned the police about it; under our system of 'Ethical Crime Recording' (see below), it's therefore officially a crime and we need to sort it out.

We used to 'solve' these sorts of 'crimes' like this:

First, we'd visit Tracey, the IP. She doesn't want Wayne prosecuting – it'll cause all sorts of grief back at school and by next week they'll be best mates anyway. But if we leave it at that we've got a big, fat, unsolved crime sitting there in the middle of our figures, and that's no good for anyone (certainly not for promotion-hungry police chiefs and politicians hoping to get re-elected).

So we'd reassure her that we only wanted to clear it up for the figures, we wouldn't take Wayne to court or even caution him, and could she just make a statement? Usually, she'd agree.

Then we'd visit Wayne, the offender. We'd reassure him, too, that the matter would never go to court, and on that basis he'd agree to be interviewed. During the interview, he'd admit that, yes, he had sent a mildly abusive message to Tracey.

Then, by a process of office-based smoke, mirrors and Biros, we would fill out a few forms, staple the whole lot together and send it off to be 'audited' by the 'crime audit' department.

No-one would ever go to court – indeed, no-one would ever even be cautioned – but… hey presto! The offence would be filed as 'detected'.

Statistically, it would then show up in our figures as a detected crime, balancing out all those tricky undetected burglary dwellings, muggings and genuine assaults.

Even better, during the interview we'd get Wayne to reveal that he had himself received offensive texts from Tracey. So we'd nip back round to her place and go through the whole process again, only this time she would be the offender and he would be the complainant. That makes two detected crimes!

If we could get them to agree to a ripped shirt or a damaged satchel in a bit of playground argy-bargy at the same time, that – a criminal damage – would be three!

Given that the modern British police service is judged almost entirely by Soviet-style figures – Crime down by two per cent! Detections up by seven per cent! – administrative detections were a work of no little genius. They allowed us to report to the Home Office that we were solving lots of things – and, in a manner of speaking, it was even true!

We just crossed our fingers and hoped that nobody noticed that many the crimes we were 'solving' were fairly trivial.

Of course, there was a downside, apart from the fact that it was all a bit of a fiddle on the taxpayer.

It took as much time and work – and sometimes even more – to 'solve' a playground hair-pulling in this way as it does to get a burglar to court. We'd have to visit people, take statements, speak to classmates, interview the offender (having waited for appropriate adults and possibly solicitors and even translators to attend the police station), fill in forms, get the adults to sign other forms, complete a crime report and update the victim before it was all done and dusted. It could take a day or more to sort out.

This meant we were so tied up in investigating spats between Newtown's children for the sake of administrative detections that we couldn't do much about real crime.

I mentioned this paperwork contrivance in passing in the first edition, and we were immediately bombarded with requests for interviews from the media.

Surely, they all said, you must be making this up?

The whole issue of the mad bureaucracy which is strangling our police was even raised in the House of Commons, in a question to our esteemed ex-Police Minister, Mr Tony McNumpty MP.

In response, Mr McNumpty said this: 'Of course, we need the balance between paperwork and bureaucracy, and proper policing. Along with ACPO and the Police Federation, we are trying to ensure that that balance is maintained and to enhance the modernisation that has already taken place. However, the Hon. Gentleman is living in cloud-cuckoo-land if he thinks that that is all that happens in policing – and I would not believe PC David Copperfield either, because that is more of a fiction than Dickens.'

Read into that what you will, but perhaps Mr McNumpty and his colleagues were alarmed by the publicity. A few months later they announced – quietly – that administrative detections were being dropped.

That presents issues of its own, of course.

Firstly, what shall I put in this book in the place where administrative detections were discussed? But, perhaps more importantly, what will be the effect on the average bobby and on crime-fighting generally?

It's early days, but it's looking like it will still involve lots of ballpoint pens and plenty of frustrated victims.

People haven't stopped reporting trivial crimes, you see. And under another key concept in our vast criminal justice bureaucracy – that of 'Ethical Crime Recording' – we are duty-bound to investigate all allegations and treat them equally.

Often, as I've said, the caller doesn't actually want us to do anything about the offence, other than 'have a word with' whoever they think is responsible.

Sadly, for statistical purposes, we don't regard 'having a word with someone' as a successful outcome to a criminal investigation, irrespective of what the victim and his family want. (That said, victims *can* be intimidated into dropping cases and sometimes it's right that people are prosecuted independently of the victim's wishes.)

So we now have to solve these crimes properly – by 'sanctioned detections' (where the offender is brought to court or given a police caution).

In the case of Wayne and Tracey above, we'd now have to arrest Wayne, drag him down to the police station and go through the whole rigmarole in order to 'get the detection'. All for Home Office figures.

We can only speculate as to the effect this (often) gross over-reaction has on the ongoing relationship between the texter and the textee (not to mention the texter's relationship with us, the police).

As for the paperwork, well, it takes just as long. The bureaucracy of the administrative detection has been replaced with the bureaucracy of the unwanted sanctioned detection.

Tony McNumpty and his friends at the Home Office missed a golden opportunity to do something about our form-filling, everything-in-triplicate, fax-it-over-to-me system.

When they did away with administrative detections, they ought to have said this: 'We know that most bobbies are half-sensible people. Moreover, we recognise that they are the people 'on the ground' dealing with crime and criminals. We accept that they are quite able to distinguish between a nasty domestic assault and a bit of handbags between two kids. We'll give them the discretion to write off the minor stuff, and just have a word with the parties. That will free them up more to work on the nasty stuff.'

Of course, the history of modern British policing is littered with missed opportunities, wrong-headed initiatives and politically correct rubbish, so they didn't.

McNumpty may or may not go down in history as a giant of law and order. I know what Sir Robert Peel would have made of the whole thing, though. It's all there in the last of his nine principles: 'The test of police efficiency is the absence of crime and disorder, not the visible evidence of police action in dealing with it.'

Using young people as statistics-fodder, and often giving them criminal records, just so that we can mislead the public about how effective we are is plain wrong. Individual police officers are the ones speaking to the victims and their families, and for that reason they should have at least some discretion about the best way to proceed with an investigation.

KNOW THINE ENEMY

AS A (SMALL 'C') CONSERVATIVE of the lock 'em up and throw away the key school, I am frequently ridiculed (at least, I think that's why they ridicule me).

I know it's not fashionable, but personally I love putting away Burberry-clad ne'er-do-wells. I think it's because I know they are unlikely ever to reform, at least before they hit 30, and that the only respite their neighbours will get from them is if they go to jail.

Such attitudes are (in my experience, at least) rare in our Criminal Justice System, where alternatives to imprisonment are continually being sought and used (tagging, Community Rehabilitation Orders, Community Punishment Orders, that sort of thing). Such alternatives are often called 'progressive' by their proponents, and 'a waste of time' by me (because they are a waste of time; they don't work and the criminals love them). But who on earth comes up with them? And why?

The answer to the first question is, civil servants with degrees in criminology.

The answer to the second question is Rousseau.

A working knowledge of philosophy is not a requirement of police work (at least, not until you become a senior officer), but it's worth knowing about Rousseau if you want to understand why so many criminals are not behind bars.

Jean-Jacques Rousseau was a Swiss philosopher who, in 1754, wrote his *Discourse Upon The Origin and Foundation of the Inequality among Men*. In this work, he says that man should ideally live 'in a state of nature', probably in a forest somewhere, with no clothes on. In such style, 'his wants are completely satisfied.' I'm not sure mine would be, and my wants aren't all that great. But that's by the by.

This wasn't a particularly new idea in itself, being simply a continuation of Primitivism, which had been around for ages. Primitivism was a fairly harmless concept – essentially, it said the outdoors was great and primitive cultures really had got it sorted (think Anita Roddick). But what Rousseau did was to turn primitivism into a political idea: that man's default setting was 'good', and that he became 'bad' when society put pressure on the individual, corrupting him and turning him to criminality. He particularly disliked private property, because he thought it was divisive and led to wars and inequality, and he was one of the seeds from which communism and socialism eventually sprouted. All this is the basis for the 'progressive' notion that, as a society, we should seek to 'treat' criminals rather than lock them up. It is also the basis for 'progressive' education, where children are seen as innocents who must not be disciplined and taught but instead helped to 'discover' knowledge.

It all echoes down through the ages to today's yob: 'It ain't my fault,' he'd say, if he had enough brains. 'Society made me do it.'

And if it really is the fault of society, then surely punishing the individual is immoral?

Rousseau's mistake, of course, was to confuse what he thought human nature was like with what it's actually like. Some people – eg Ken Clarke – are still making that mistake, and little old ladies dare not leave their homes after dark as a result.

HOT BURGLARIES

LAST NIGHT I WENT to an address where I found a very shaken man and woman who had been woken up by the sound of two youths rifling through the drawers in their living room. We raced round as soon as he called us and had a good look round the area and even thought about getting the helicopter out; in the end we decided against it.

The man had gone downstairs and confronted the pair. Thankfully, they had fled instead of taking him on. I say 'thankfully', because I'd hate to have been arresting the chap for assault.

'Unbelievable,' he said to me, as his wife sobbed on the sofa next to him. 'People actually think they can come into your house and take your stuff.'

We've become blasé about burglary but, if you think about it, it is unbelievable. The prevalence of burglars might be connected to the pitiably short sentences, let-offs and general dressing downs handed out to the perpetrators, but then I'm no criminologist.

'They must have got in through the kitchen window,' he said. 'It's not like we've even got much to steal. I mean, do we look rich to you?'

They didn't. He worked as a machinist at a local factory and she was a part-time care assistant.

It was late in the evening and our forensic people had long since gone off duty, so I did what I could to preserve any physical evidence and took a statement about what had happened. I was there for a few hours before I finally left.

In the last year or so, the papers have been full of tales of 'hot' burglaries like this one. A hot burglary is one which takes place when the owner is inside the house. The most famous case of recent times was that of the City financier John Monckton, who was stabbed and killed at his Chelsea home by two lowlife thugs who wanted to steal his property (Rousseau would have been proud).

The widow, herself grievously injured, and the fatherless children of Mr Monckton will doubtless be relieved to know that, according to the Home Office, the burglary rate in England is declining significantly. They will also be pleased with official reassurances that the risk of being confronted in one's own home by a burglar is 'astonishingly rare'.

Not as astonishingly rare as it is in most of the USA, though, where the right to defend your family has not been taken away from you by a State which refuses to do the job properly itself. A huge number – some experts say 50% or more – of all burglaries in England and Wales are 'hot' and while, thankfully, few end in such tragedy, the Monckton case wasn't unique by any means.

In the United States, by contrast, only 13% of burglaries occur when occupants are inside the property.

What accounts for this difference?

Well, the fact that the occupants might be armed and the American burglar knows he might get killed may have something to do with it. This shifts the odds dramatically in the US homeowner's favour and changes the calculation that the burglar has to make: Is it worth dying for the jewellery that might be upstairs? In England, burglars don't have to make that calculation.

Most burglars I meet are actually perfectly rational people who do what they do so they can buy heroin or meet some other desire: they are aware of things like fingerprints and DNA and they know what to say in police interviews. They choose homes with single-glazed rear windows, and try to be quiet when they break in. They keep an eye out for the police and an ear for neighbours. They prefer to go in when a property's empty, but needs must when the devil drives. One thing's for sure: most of them would not burgle a property if they knew the man inside owned a 12 bore, was prepared to use it and would have the law on his side if he did.

When victims take steps to protect themselves, they can have a dramatic effect on crime and I think it's time the British were allowed to do so.

Until then, you'll have to rely on the doctrine of 'reasonable force'. This essentially means that, if you find a man in your house, you are allowed to use reasonable force to eject him. If he has a gun, the courts might agree that you using your own firearm was reasonable, but they'd probably want him to have opened fire first. If he has a stick, you can probably use a stick. If he's unarmed, it's you and him, mano a mano – I wouldn't advise picking up so much as a peashooter.

If the average homeowner actually has to defend himself, it's usually pitch black, he's terrified and the other guy is far more experienced and prepared. But legislators and judges consider abstract concepts like 'reasonable force' in committee rooms and courts where the only real danger is running out of biscuits. I'm sure it's also just a coincidence that they don't live on – in fact, they rarely even visit – the housing estates and rows of old terraces where our burglars are most active; when was the last time you opened the paper to find that half a dozen members of the High Court and a slack handful of MPs have been attacked in their homes in the night?

After the Monckton case, there was talk of making changes to the idea of reasonable force. I wait in vain hope.

The law-abiding English are at their best when they are burgled: the stiff upper lip, the offer of tea, the uncomfortable draught caused by the smashed window in the kitchen ('Don't worry officer, we've not touched anything.'). They display a resignation which I find rather frustrating.

I recently visited a burglary victim called Janet, a hard-working widow in her 50s, who cleaned offices for a living. Her DVD player and £30 in cash had been taken by someone who had kicked her door in while she was at work.

'I suppose it's just kids looking for drug money to feed their habits, officer,' she said.

'Possibly it is, madam,' I said. 'But you shouldn't have to put up with it, should you?'

'Well, it's the family breakdown and that, isn't it?' she said. 'I feel sorry for these kids, in a way.'

I very much doubt this would have been her response 30 years ago: it never ceases to amaze me how quickly, in just a generation or two, the British people have had the fight knocked out of them when it comes to crime and punishment.

'How do you feel now?' I said. 'Are you sleeping OK?'

'Well, I'm a bit nervous,' she said. 'But I've got the dog.'

I looked at the dog, dozing next to her. He was a fat little Jack Russell with milky eyes and rotten teeth who'd looked me up and down when I walked in and then hopped onto the sofa for a kip. He twitched and growled in his sleep, hind legs moving slightly.

'Looks like he's caught them,' I said.

She laughed, and I left.

NOMINALS

A HUGE NUMBER OF the burglaries on our patch – almost certainly including the two we just covered – are committed by 'nominals'.

Nominals is police-speak for repeat offenders, or recidivists.

On the walls of our parade room are photographs of around 15 key criminals. I say 'key criminals', but I'm not talking about Mafia Dons, Triad leaders or international gun runners, I'm talking about hopeless local scrotes who spend as much time with us as they do with anyone else apart from their dealers.

The pictures were taken when they were arrested and brought into custody. They're all male, in their late teens or early 20s, and all are dressed in paper suits that prisoners are forced to wear because their clothing has been seized for forensic investigation. They all, without exception, take heroin and/or crack cocaine, and their faces speak eloquently of years of drug abuse (it starts when they're about 11 around here). Written next to each photograph are details of the subject's known addresses, associates and vehicles, with directions to record and report any sightings.

They all have criminal records stretching back several years.

Essentially, the same faces are up there, year after year. The odd mug shot might disappear from the wall for a few months while the mug in question is in prison. Occasionally, one of them will overdose, or move away, or go to prison for a really long time. But the gap never lasts long; another almost identical male eventually fills the empty rectangular area of white-washed wall.

We spend our careers staring at these pictures. That may explain why police officers don't make particularly enthusiastic penal reformers. In our experience, the only time these people aren't doing any harm is when they're in prison. When they're on the out, they're stealing, mugging, assaulting or defrauding. QED: prison is the only answer for the serious, hardcore criminals who are responsible for the vast majority of acquisitive crime committed in Newtown. Obviously, there's a place for other sentences with first-time offenders. But the really prolific types won't be put off by being ordered to weed gardens, or meet their victims and apologise, or pay pathetic fines off at 50p per week.

Prisons aren't perfect. Proper drug treatment programs are vital, as is keeping jails drug-free. Such programs only really work with prisoners whose sentences last longer than a year, which suggests to me that a minimum year in jail is a sensible starting point. Some education would be useful – they should be taught to read and write and maybe even the basics of a trade.

As regards Newtown, what would happen if all of these 15 individuals were incarcerated for ten years for their next offence? Well, the crime rate would halve overnight. Old ladies wouldn't be robbed in their homes, charity boxes wouldn't be swiped from chippies and bungling cash card frauds wouldn't be attempted. Eventually, more criminals would take their place, of course. But when that happened, we'd simply lock the new customers up, too, if only the courts would let us.

That's the thing about prison. Dramatic effects can be seen almost immediately: crime drops in the area around where the offender lives and the longer the prison sentence, the longer the drop in crime. The quality of life improves in those areas in many ways, because prolific criminals seek their thrills not just in burglary and mugging, but by taking drugs, assaulting people, joyriding in cars and turning their neighbourhoods into jungles. They play their music very loud, and tell their neighbours to f*ck off when they're asked to turn it down. They smash up phone boxes after arguments with girls. They drop litter and scrawl graffiti and urinate in shop doorways. Of course, the ordinary people who live in these areas tend not to be *Guardian* readers, or university criminology lecturers, or MPs, judges and senior police officers, so they don't know much about the theories of crime. All they know is that they're delighted when our recidivists get sent away.

I met a lady yesterday who had the locks on her car damaged with a screwdriver some months ago. She lives in one of our rougher neighbourhoods, and she accosted me as I walked back to my car after spending an hour negotiating with a man and his ex over a broken TV remote control. Her face was radiant with joy.

'Oh, well done!' she said. 'Well done!'

I'm not accustomed to members of the public thanking me very often but, on the occasions it happens, I usually know what they're thanking me for. I was clueless. 'Sorry?' I said.

'Johnny Merchant!' she said. 'You've finally got him sent to jail!'

'Ah!' I said. It all became clear. Merchant was one of the infamous 15 and he'd been sent down for several years the month before for his umpteenth street robbery. 'Nothing to do with me, I'm afraid. All down to my colleagues.'

'Well, please pass on my thanks to them,' she said. 'Things are much quieter already.' Then her face fell, slightly. 'Mind you,' she said. 'I suppose it won't be long before his brother Terry will be out?'

'Well, we'll be keeping an eye on him when he's released,' I said.

Does prison work for the nominals once they're inside?

Maybe not.

Will they re-offend once they get out?

Most of them, I'm sure, but that's because they are criminals.

Frankly, though I wish it was different, that's not our problem. Our job is to protect the weak and the vulnerable and the law-abiding.

So if Terry Merchant wants it, he knows where to come looking.

IN THE TRADE

DURING STATION TEA BREAKS, officers who are not reading something more entertaining can be seen flicking through a copy of *Police Review* magazine, or perhaps an issue of *Constabulary*.

They are the most widely-read trade magazines for coppers – probably because they have job adverts in the back. But there is a new kid on the block. The latest addition to parade rooms across the land is *The Sharp End*. It says it's free, which is a superfluous announcement if ever I heard one; no-one would actually pay for it. It is published by the Home Office and carries no advertisements so the cost is therefore borne by the Home Office. Or, more accurately, by you, the taxpayer.

The Sharp End is government propaganda for the *'Loaded'* generation, the difference being that *Loaded* magazine's writers, being part of a huge, international, journalistic free market, are talented and have a sense of humour. *TSE* contains faintly worrying 'good news' items dealing with our ever-increasing powers and also lots of 'helpful advice' for frontline officers.

I picked up a dog-eared copy the other day (I'd missed the back issues of *Maxim* and *FHM* which were floating around) and found a piece full of useful tips about dealing with forensic evidence at crime scenes.

Why is the Home Office giving me advice about securing a crime scene? I thought. If I need advice about crime scenes, I'll contact the duty Scenes of Crime Officer, thanks. If I need advice about how to create pointless statistics and generate waste at huge expense, then I'll ask the Home Office.

The most bizarre story in the magazine was the introduction of 'Top Trumps'-style cards, featuring local police officers. The idea is that they will distributed by bobbies and collected by children, with the aim being to raise the profile of the featured officers and stop the little urchins smashing up bus shelters. This issue featured PC203

Nick Dadd, whose card tells juvenile CROs that he is 1.73 metres tall and has one commendation. His slogan is, 'Be a good citizen. Consider how your behaviour will impact upon others.'

In case you are interested, my slogan is, 'Go away. You're drunk.'

POLICE STATION PROCEDURE

IF YOU WANT TO know where all the police officers are, they are indoors. Many are in offices doing, er, important police work and the rest are in other people's houses taking statements. A few are in cars driving from the office to the complainant's house or back again.

Like most of my colleagues, I spend lots of time in custody, dealing with prisoners and their solicitors.

This week I arrested a lad called Kyle Ball for criminal damage. He turned up at the police station with his mum after I had convinced her over the telephone that the game was up. I arrested him, then brought him into the custody block and, after an hour's delay (caused by a colleague getting in just ahead of me), I began the booking-in procedure.

The booking-in procedure is similar to checking in your luggage prior to getting onto an aeroplane, only it takes longer and no-one asks if you're carrying electrical items or suspicious fluids.

Kyle's detention was authorised and he was asked about his general physical and mental health. He was searched and asked if he would like a solicitor. His mum said that he would, so Kyle was put in a cell and I went upstairs to wait for the brief to come down from Weatherby.

When the solicitor arrived, she inspected the custody record and then we went into a room for 'disclosure'. I don't like disclosure. Disclosure means telling the defence solicitor certain facts about the reason for, and the evidence relating to, her client's arrest.

In Kyle's case it was fairly straightforward. We had eyewitness evidence from two people who'd seen him methodically kicking out the glass windows in a bus shelter; one of them knew Kyle and the other had provided a good description. As they do, the solicitor then fished for other details. These tend to include things like who your witnesses are, the seriousness of any injuries (in cases of assault) and the exact nature of any forensic evidence you have, if any.

After disclosure, the solicitor, Kyle and his mum went into a private consulting room within the custody area for a meeting. In these meetings, the solicitor tells the suspect everything that I've told her in the disclosure and this enables them to cook up a good story.

That's often when we get our first sight of the pathetic farrago of lies (sorry, the defence) that the suspect will pin his hopes upon during the trial.

'I borrowed the car.'

'I didn't know it was stolen.'

'It was self-defence.'

My personal favourite is: 'I only went into the house to get a drink of water. I didn't burgle it.'

Disclosure and subsequent consultation both serve to make the interview a waste of time (particularly in the petty cases I deal with) and I can pretty much write out the summary of what was said on the interview even before the interview has started.

Sometimes I summarise before the suspect has actually got to that point in his story. 'So, John, what you're saying is, is that you did hit your ex-wife but it was self-defence because she threw a plate at you?'

The solicitor interrupts. 'My client has not said that!'

'My apologies. John, what happened?'

'I hit my ex-wife because she threw a plate at me.'

'Thank you, John. So it was self-defence?'

'Yes.'

I'm not saying that denying the expectation of privacy in a police station and stopping disclosure to solicitors would necessarily be a good thing. It might help the police in simple cases, it might not, but it would certainly save at least an hour in time spent in custody and it would make the interviews a lot more fun.

The interview with Kyle lasted 12 minutes. To his credit, he coughed the lot and he and Mrs Ball were out in about two hours. That's what I call efficiency. Kyle likes to pretend he's a bad boy when he's with his mates, but this will be his first time in court (he's received the reprimand and final warning before). Whether or not it makes any difference will probably depend on what sort of sentence he gets for smashing up the bus shelter.

In the expectation of a guilty plea at court, I put together the thinnest of files and spent the rest of the shift (three hours) on patrol.

TRIVIAL PURSUITS

'BLIMEY,' SAID MRS C this morning, as she flicked through the pages of her newspaper over breakfast. 'It says here that the police in Bath refused to follow some yobs who'd stolen a moped because they weren't wearing helmets. It says they were worried they might crash and hurt themselves.'

She looked at me in amazement. I carried on eating my marmalade on toast. Tell me something I don't know.

This sort of thing may not be force policy – yet – but ACPO is certainly getting very chary about police officers pursuing people who are in stolen vehicles.

The problem is, we crash too often and sometimes people get hurt. Sometimes even innocent people. In one force I know of, pursuits will only be allowed under the following circumstances:

1. Only suitably-trained officers in suitable vehicles (ie Class 1 drivers in Volvo T5s and Vauxhall Omegas) can be involved. (Pursuits in dog vans and the like are forbidden.)
2. There must be at least three such vehicles in a division/territory to allow for swift use of T-Pac (a manoeuvre carried out to box-in vehicles) or Stopstick (a three-foot-long Toblerone containing small spikes that is supposed to burst tyres and stop fleeing vehicles). Cross-county runs to help out are not acceptable.
3. The weather is good.
4. The pursuit is on an open road and is not heading towards an urban or residential area.

What are the chances of these criteria actually being met at the time a pursuit starts?

ACPO is now moving towards a policy of absolutely no pursuits at all, in any circumstances, and Mopedgate reflects that.

As with so much that ACPO produces, and in common with all bureaucracies, this is shot through with the law of unintended consequences.

It's a terrible, awful tragedy when a small child is hit and killed by a police car pursuing car thieves and we should do everything we can to minimise those risks. But if we stop pursuing these people we're effectively agreeing to car theft and maybe worse: what about a bank robber who makes his getaway on a motorbike without a helmet? Can the police in Bath chase him or not?

Most criminals aren't widely read, and they're not that big on the news, but things like this don't take long to get around.

Brace yourself for open season on all cars and motorcycles.

One more thing. These sorts of people don't tend to drive that carefully themselves. So the streets of our cities and towns will be full of teenage joyriders racing each other in other people's BMWs and Mercs, in a real-life game of Grand Theft Auto.

I wonder how safe pedestrians will be in this brave new world?

LEGAL EAGLES

THE FIGHT AGAINST CRIMINALITY, or at least stupidity, continues: shift after shift of meeting strange people in my Burberry Hogarth town to whom I only speak to because I'm being paid to do so.

No matter how hard I try, I cannot seem to get into the swing of policing in the value-free way I am supposed to. I maintain my own bourgeois values of thrift, education and respectability; during my hours of work it feels like I am on a different planet, dealing with an alien race with enlarged vocal chords and very small brains, the minimal activity within which is devoted to feeling aggrieved and searching for justice.

Hogarth's subjects were off their faces on gin and debauchery; now gin has been replaced by WKD, debauchery has become the norm and the solicitor has entered upon our happy scene to provide advice, guidance and counselling to the underclass; all at a price, naturally.

The rise of the defence solicitor has been enabled by the introduction of legal aid and the enactment of the Police and Criminal

Evidence Act 1984. PACE was designed to safeguard the rights of suspects in police custody, but its requirements are so onerous and its procedures so complex that it's really a lawyer's job creation scheme-stroke-criminal release charter. So much so that the small town in which I work is able to support several different firms of solicitors who specialise in criminal law and who all wear very nice suits and drive expensive cars.

Prior to PACE, if a suspect requested a solicitor, he was put back into his cell until he changed his mind and, when he did, he dictated his version of events to a police officer who wrote it out so the suspect could sign it. That's a much better system, if you ask me – as long, that is, as you want guilty people locking up. Today, a solicitor is summoned immediately the suspect requests it and, if the suspect is sober, one usually arrives within an hour or two.

I went to university with one or two of our local legal eagles, and I enjoy the opportunity to reminisce and ponder upon how we got where we are. Watching middle class lawyers shift uncomfortably in their seats as they deal with clients from an entirely different social milieu never ceases to amuse me. I particularly like to observe the first meeting between the two parties, usually at about 09:00hrs on a Sunday: the solicitor smiles at the client and then immediately recoils as last night's lager is exhaled all over him. The good ones even shake hands: 'Hello, Mike Smith, from Smith and Jones Solicitors. Sign here.'

They go off for their consultation, the solicitor carrying a briefcase and the client a plastic cup of tea. The officers in the custody block momentarily feel sorry for the solicitor: at least they don't have to pretend to like the suspect.

Lots of police officers don't like defence solicitors, either. Personally, I take the view that they do a job and represent their clients and try to get them off using whatever trick they can. They also want the business, so it is important that they are well respected within the criminal classes.

Solicitors' tricks include:

1. Making up stories in the consultation room prior to the police interview. Most suspects will make up stories to cover their tracks and a good solicitor will help them to fill in the blanks. (I

think this is against Law Society guidelines). Another service defence solicitors offer is that of offering a good excuse, so that, in interview, the suspect denies the guilty knowledge required to prove the offence. For example, if chummy's fingerprints are found inside a stolen car, the solicitor might ask the suspect (in the privacy of their consultation room), 'Chummy, are you sure you didn't just get a lift in this car and have no idea it was stolen?'

2. Going 'No comment.' If you've beaten up your wife and have intimidated her into withdrawing her complaint, a 'no comment' interview might just tip the balance when you go to court. Result!

3. Making pointless representations to the custody sergeant when the suspect is refused bail, in an attempt to get him to change his mind. This is done to impress the client and intimidate the sergeant. I've never seen it do the latter, but the former never fails.

4. Offering 'Free Gifts' to suspects. Solicitors dish out trainers and cigarettes to clients in exchange for repeat business. It all effectively comes out of the legal aid budget and is therefore paid for by you, the taxpayer. Remember that next time you get burgled.

5. Intimidating younger officers. A quick glance at the collar number, the solicitor will stop the interview, call you oppressive, accuse you of breaching PACE and threaten to make an official complaint.

6. Being all nicey-nicey in the disclosure with the officer, then turning into Perry Mason in the interview room when with the client. You only get to do that once, Mr Solicitor, and if you represent another of my suspects I have a feeling the next cup of tea I make for you will taste a bit funny.

Defence solicitors are not saints. They are in it for the money, and probably the challenge. They are clever people. But, clever as they are, they cannot prove that you have pissed in their tea, however much they might suspect it.

SUITABLE ADVICE

JUST WHEN MY THOUGHTS were turning towards home, and the fish pie Mrs C was making for me today, my radio crackled in my ear.

'... attend 14b Edwards Road and speak with a Maxine Ellis. She's asking to speak to an officer about her ex. The log is very complicated.'

Very complicated, eh? I cut to the chase: 'Is it a crime?'

'No.'

'Good.'

Dealing with domestic incidents is so much easier when there isn't a crime to deal with and all I have to do is complete a bit of paperwork and make sure nobody has been murdered.

The immediate signs were as I imagined: two walls painted a lurid pink, back when Maxine first moved in and before she got bored. Photographs of her numerous children from various relationships and a glacier of fast food packaging flowing from the top of the kitchen bin and out into the hallway.

Maxine was seeking advice about her latest ex, who was giving her 'hassle'. Non-specific, proletarian hassle, as it turned out: texts, telephone calls and personal appearances at inconvenient times, demands for money and arguments about their offspring. Unfortunately, you can't just listen for two minutes, point out that this is a pile of crap and leave (see 'Complaints'). So I started fishing.

'Do you have any formal arrangements regarding access to the children?' I asked.

'How do you mean?'

'When does he come and see the kids?'

'He turns up whenever he likes, which is no good for me or the kids.'

'What made you split up in the first place?'

'He's just a waster. He started doing drugs and having his mates over. I said he couldn't do it and we had a massive row.'

I had some sympathy for her position vis à vis the drugs and the mates, but there really wasn't much I could do. Maxine had got herself into this mess in the first place, and quite when it would end was anyone's guess. Still, at least she was sober and had sent the kids out of the house for my visit, so there was hope.

'He's not violent, is he? I asked.

She shook her head. 'No, he's not like that. He's never laid a finger on me. He knows I'd kick the sh*t out of him if he did.'

She looked like she could do it, too.

'Hmmm,' I said. 'Well, I wouldn't do that, if I were you. Apart from him being a bit irritating, what's the problem, then?'

'It's the kids,' she said. 'Like I say, he just comes round when he feels like it and then don't turn up other times when he says he will.'

I sat back in the chair and briefly closed my eyes.

'Maxine, you need to sort something out between both of you about the kids, something formal. An agreement you both stick to.'

'How do I do that?' she said.

'Speak to a solicitor.'

'Can't you do anything?'

'Not really. I mean, he hasn't done anything illegal. Tell you what Maxine, I'll keep an eye out and if I see him, I'll let him know we're on to him.'

Then I left. That was what is known in the trade as giving 'suitable advice'. We're not just in the business of apprehending criminals, you see. We're also referees in the game of life, as played in the lower echelons of society.

I generally dispense 'suitable advice' to two different, but not mutually exclusive groups.

Firstly, the insane (this includes those driven temporarily insane by alcohol, we call them 'drunk'). Here, three different types of advice are given:

1. Don't drink so much.
2. Go to bed, things will look better in the morning.
3. Are there any friends you can talk to?

Secondly, slum dwellers. In a generation or two, huge swathes of the English working classes have lost the traditional qualities of the stiff upper lip and self-control that once characterised them, and many have now been reduced to moral penury. With no obligations, or any that they take seriously, many behave like children. I advise them accordingly:

1. Don't drink so much.
2. Get out more.
3. Develop an interest or hobby
(watching television doesn't count).

I know such advice is unlikely to change anyone's life, but I have long realised the limitations of being a policeman and I no longer believe it is within the power of the Newtown constabulary to change society. Certainly, working in the urban nightmare that is the Church Road Estate, I feel uniquely unqualified to offer 'suitable advice' to people like Maxine, although I do it, obviously. Mrs C and I spend our evenings together with a game of Scrabble and a glass of wine with dinner, and finish with a mug of Horlicks and a book. How on earth can I advise an alcoholic single mother who 'self harms' and has a boyfriend with a heroin habit?

STOP PRESS: Quote of the week, uttered by a liberal arts student who was home for the weekend and whom I placed under arrest for criminal damage to a motor vehicle.

PC Copperfield: 'You're under arrest for criminal damage to a motor vehicle.'

Liberal Arts Student: 'I know, but I don't care! The truth will always set you free!'

PC Copperfield: 'Er... not in this particular case.'

THE DISCLOSURE OFFICER

LAST NIGHT, MRS C forced me to watch part of a bizarre television police drama. I can't recall the title, but one of the characters was a peculiar-looking Detective Sergeant called 'Havers' who worked for a Detective Inspector.

I enjoyed the denouement, where the villain, a uniformed constable with a beard and a rural accent, 'blasted' someone from close range with a shotgun. Havers leapt in, threw a drinking glass to distract the shooter and enabled a firearms unit to run in and save the day.

Complete fantasy, on several levels.

Why would a police officer so close to retirement start shooting people?

What was a DI doing out of the office?

Why didn't the firearms unit wait three hours until their risk-assessment was completed?

How can a murder enquiry be conducted with only two people?

Has anyone told Notts police?

I know there has to be an element of gloss applied to the average policeman's daily life in order to turn it into a gripping, prime-time drama, but come on. Let's have a bit of realism, at least.

In case any TV types are reading this book, I've come up with my own idea for a police drama. It's called '*The Disclosure Officer*' and it is terribly gritty and true-to-life. The central character is Brad Strong, the eponymous Disclosure Officer, who is responsible for viewing all the material in relation to the case.

In episode one, we see the difficulties Brad has in completing the MG schedules and the battles he does with his own tortured soul as he writes 'There is nothing the disclosure officer feels will undermine the prosecution case' on the MG6e.

Episode two revolves around secondary disclosure and includes a funny scene where the whole team gather round to read the defence statement. The situation becomes more serious when Brad realises that some CCTV has become lost in the property system and cannot be recovered.

The back story is that Brad likes gardening, going to the pub, playing darts and drinking pints of lager top.

There's a lot more I could put in, like how our hero struggles with the photocopier and tries to get the CPS to make decisions. If you're interested, get in touch via the publishers.

POLICING IN A MODERN SOCIETY

RECENT CHANGES IN shop-floor management have suddenly created a new spirit amongst our little team.

The changes (at the level of sergeant) have made things a lot more 'fun', and we are beginning to target known criminals. This is proving quite a new experience for those who laboured for months under the old system, where we were ordered to take care of even the most minor item of administration before being allowed out onto the streets. There is no end to administration in the police if you want to look for it, so we were always in the office, noses and biros to the grindstone (there must be something in the Human Rights Act about the amount of writing we have to do).

Things will, inevitably, change back in a week or two, once we slip behind with the paperwork. But we're enjoying the fresh air while we can.

We aren't the only people experiencing a new management broom, as I found out during two visits to our local DWP (Department for Work and Pensions) Jobcentre Plus office this week.

The visits threw up amusingly different scenarios.

Whenever I can't find someone who I need to bring in for questioning, I've always wandered in to the back office there for a chat. Everyone was very helpful and the staff used to relish the opportunity to nail some of their own unpleasant customers. I arrived on Monday, knocked on the door and was met by a new manager.

'Sorry, this is for staff only,' she said, in flat tones and with a dead-eyed gaze.

Fair enough, if a little abrupt. I proceeded with the enquiry.

'When's Andrew Kelly next in, d'you know?'

'Why?'

'Well, I need to speak to him.'

'What about?'

'No offence, but that's between him and me. The thing is, I can't find him at the moment and I know he always comes in here.'

'We're not allowed to divulge our clients' personal details.'

'I know that, but if you could just tell me when he's next in?'

'We're not allowed to divulge our clients' personal details.'

'Well, these aren't really his personal details, are they? I probably know more personal details about him than you do. I just want to know when he'll be in here.'

'Look,' said the new manager. 'People come here to collect their benefits, NOT to get arrested.'

Blimey, that told me. As luck would have it, the very next day we received a call to visit the Job Centre where a benefit claimant was 'kicking off'. I don't know about you, but if I was on benefits

I think I'd be very grateful for every penny I was given. It doesn't work like that with our local underclass; they complain bitterly about everything, and will explode at the drop of a hat.

When I arrived, the youth was still there, abusing and threatening the staff and making a general nuisance of himself.

We put the cuffs on him and led him out and, as we did so, the new manager hurried over.

'Thanks very much for that, officers,' she said. 'He was being *very* abusive.'

'Funny, isn't it?' I replied. 'I thought people came here to collect their benefits, NOT to get arrested.'

DOMESTICS

THE BUREAUCRACY ASSOCIATED with the government's recent Domestic Violence, Crime and Victims Act has had an impact on the weight of my briefcase: I now have to use the shoulder strap.

Domestic violence is something everyone can agree on: there should be less of it.

I have done my bit and I can think of several abusive and nasty men who have gone to jail as a result of my investigations. However, for every clear-cut case of domestic violence there are any number of 'rows'. When attending a domestic incident, I try to keep in mind several things. First of all, there is the widely-quoted statistic that women are victims of domestic violence 35 times before they actually decide to call the police. Then there is the fact that most murders are domestic in nature. I am, therefore, naturally anxious to help the victim and prevent serious injury or even death.

Weighing heavily on my mind, though, is the belief that people have a right to privacy and that if they both want to argue loudly it is really no concern of mine (unless they are my neighbours). Some people's domestic arrangements are a complete mystery to me, but I don't feel that gives me the right to start bashing their doors in if I feel like it. Even when I have gained entry to someone's house, I have to ask questions of a very personal nature and I am often surprised that more people don't tell me to mind my own business.

The nightmare scenario is when a concerned neighbour rings the police. 'He's beating her up again,' they say. 'I can hear shouting and screaming and things being broken.'

We rush round, usually at around 02:00hrs, and knock loudly on the door, demanding to be let in. Most of the time there has been an argument, some crockery has been smashed and both parties are drunk. Nobody has been assaulted and neither party really wants the police there.

It is entirely possible that the female has been injured and we cannot see the injuries.

It's possible that she has been a victim of psychological violence for years and has never had the courage to speak out.

It's possible that the male is putting on an act and has actually been stabbed by his wife and we can't see the blood.

It's possible that the two children, asleep upstairs, are being abused by the stepfather.

Although all of this is *possible*, it's also unlikely, and, anyway, attending officers are not going to be able to get to the bottom of the matter at 2am, when both the man and the woman are smashed and just want to go to bed.

New legislation is forcing officers to make arrests (usually for violence, and usually the male) even if the victim does not want her partner arrested. If the officer does not arrest someone he has to justify why he didn't.

The following example, which didn't happen on my shift, shows what can happen when we're not allowed to use common sense when dealing with domestic incidents.

Officers were called to a feuding couple following a child's birthday party. The couple, both middle class professionals, had had a blazing row which had resulted in a bit of pushing and shoving. They'd been drinking, but only a couple of glasses of wine, and in the course of the 'struggle', the tiniest of tiny injuries had been caused to the husband's face. The police were called, but not by the couple, and by the time officers arrived it had all calmed down.

One of the officers asked the man how he got the scratch on his face. He said his wife must have done it. She was arrested, taken to the local station and offered legal services, which she declined. She admitted that she might have caused the scratch, but said it was during the shoving and was pushing back in self-defence. The officers said they would have to arrest her husband.

She did not like the thought of this, as the kids would have to be farmed out somewhere while he was brought in, so she agreed to a caution (in itself unusual, since we almost never caution in these cases) and was allowed home.

Had she refused and asked for a solicitor, hubby might have been nicked, too, but the CPS would probably have dropped the matter eventually when each party to the marriage refused to support the prosecution.

So, all in all, this was a bit of a result for us.

For her, not so much. A police caution stays on police records and is disclosable to future employers for five years.

Given the circumstances outlined above, does *anyone* think this is a sensible way to proceed?

These are precisely the kind of incidents that are difficult to deal with. The officers attend and see someone with injuries and evidence of a struggle. Force policy demands an arrest, so the officers do their duty and take one party off for questioning.

'The thing with all this,' said one of my colleagues, a female officer with 10 years under her belt, 'is that people assume this is all about stopping domestic violence. It's actually about covering senior ranks' arses in the face of media and political pressure.'

She had a point. Would you end serious domestic violence even if you equipped every house with CCTV throughout? No. Some people would ignore the cameras.

Most domestic incidents are trifling matters that are over the following day, a few are serious and almost none result in murder. Many couples are happy, quite a few are unhappy, some actually like arguing and others never have a cross word. Treating every domestic squabble as though it's World War Three does mean we tick all the right boxes, but I doubt it does much to reduce the murder rate, and asking personal questions about people's relationships will not encourage them to telephone the police when they really are in trouble.

SAME SH*T, DIFFERENT DAY

AS NEW TECHNOLOGY drops in price and becomes simpler to use, it eventually becomes so cheap and easy to operate that even the underclass can avail themselves of it, and they do so, mainly, to upset each other.

Many years ago, mobile phones were used only by businessmen and email was so complicated and required so much equipment that its use was restricted to big universities. Nowadays, almost every slum dwelling I enter has a computer connected to the internet, a games console and a large plasma television that covers half of one wall. To stay in touch, each 'house resident' (to say 'family member' would be politically incorrect) has a mobile phone for the rare occasions when they step outside (eg to go to the chip shop).

You might think that given the extraordinary amount of information at their fingertips, the underclass would see what they are missing and revolt. With things like the National Geographic Channel, the History Channel and 24 hour news coverage at their fingertips, they should be better educated than ever.

This is not the case: anyone with any experience of dealing with those at the deprived and alienated margins of society (that's the bone idle and work-shy to you and me) knows that they only want to torment each other and then call the police to tot up the scores when they get bored.

Email and text messages are but the latest way they have found to argue and settle old scores. The police are involved like another plotline in a soap opera.

A few months back, a young woman called Kimberley had been receiving abusive txt msgs. I went round.

'I told them I was gonna call the police,' she said. 'It's fat cow this and fat bitch that, and I've had enough.'

'Well, here I am,' I said. 'Now, how do you see my role in all of this?'

'Eh?'

'I mean, what do you want me to do?'

'Make them stop.'

'How?'

'By arresting them.'

'Who are "they"?'

'It's next door.'

Not unusual; the modern British underclass are so lazy that they can't even be bothered to get off their fat backsides and walk next door for a slanging match.

'Right,' I said. 'Have you thought about discussing it with them? I mean, you're a grown-up, they're grown-ups… can't you sort it out between you without involving the police?'

Apparently not.

So began a two-month long enquiry aimed at confirming the source of the offensive messages. It's an enquiry made more complex and long-winded by recent legislation called the Regulation of Investigatory Powers Act (RIPA), the aim of which is to ensure that we don't overstep the mark and start tapping people's phones willy-nilly. At my level, it simply means another form has to be filled in, signed off, sent in, returned for one reason or another and then re-sent.

Anyway, yesterday I finally got the data back on Kimberley's phone and it proved, as she had claimed, that it was her neighbour who was sending the text messages. To celebrate, I went to see Kimberley to let her know that my investigation had progressed that little bit further.

However by this time my slum-dwelling friend had forgotten the whole thing.

'Oh, that,' she said, when I explained why I'd returned. 'I'm not bothered about that any more. They've moved out.'

Of course, in the constant fight against boredom, she had found a new enemy. 'While you're here, though,' she said, 'my ex has been emailing me these pictures.'

Of course, it's not all about hi-tech unpleasantness. From Kimberley's, I was directed to a ground-floor flat that had had some excrement pushed through the letter box. At last, I thought, old fashioned nastiness. There was cat and dog excrement on the floor inside – honestly, it's not at all uncommon to find several piles of animal faeces lying on the floor in these sorts of homes – and it was next to impossible to tell where the home-grown stuff ended and the new lot from the front door began, but I persevered, or at least was reasonably sympathetic.

'I want you to find who put sh*t through my letterbox,' said the injured party, a chain smoker in her 40s.

'Certainly, madam. Do you have any ideas who it might have been?'

She thought for a while: I could almost see her thumbing through her mental Rolodex. At length, she took a drag on her fag, and shook her head. 'Nah, but can't you do a DNA test on it?'

THE PEOPLE'S POLICE

ANOTHER DAY IN NEWTOWN POLICE, or, as I prefer to call it, the 5th Battalion of the Newtown Regiment of the People's Motorised Bureaucracy.

I spent much of the day driving a car, visiting people who didn't want to see me (and that's just the victims) and hoping to solve crimes that could have been prevented had I not been on hold, on the phone, to police liaison at the Halifax Building Society, trying to find out what time a dodgy cash machine withdrawal took place.

I have already talked at length about the absurdity of working on cases where the victim has expressly said that they do not want any further police involvement, so I'll keep this brief. Today, almost my entire day was taken up with taking statements from people which finished with those immortal words: 'I do not wish to make a formal complaint in this matter and I will not assist the police further with their enquiries. I will not attend court.'

Often the most infuriating thing about wasting your time on this sort of rubbish is that other people, whom you perhaps could help, stop you to ask you things and you simply don't have time to speak to them at any length because you have to rush round to the next time-waster.

Some people who call the police want a crime solved and will work to help in that endeavour.

Some people know it never will be solved and need a crime number for the insurance.

Some people are just a bit mad, or bored.

One of my calls today almost left me with a sudden death on my hands when I met an old lady whose fence had been damaged in a wanton act of vandalism. I knocked, and after a great deal of shuffling and shooting of bolts, she opened the door.

'Good Lord!' she said, looking faint and clutching her throat. 'A policeman! I hope I haven't done anything wrong!'

'Not at all, madam, it's just that you reported some criminal damage,' I replied.

'Eh?' She peered at me and cupped a hand round one ear.

'NOT AT ALL, MADAM, IT'S JUST THAT YOU REPORTED SOME CRIMINAL DAMAGE.'

'Oh, yes. But you needn't have come out. I just thought you'd like to know.'

SMOKING HAS BEEN BANNED! HOORAY!

HOW ABOUT THIS for an easy detection.

'Hello, is that the police?'

'Yes.'

'I'd like to report people smoking in a public place because I'm really worried about my unborn child and the effects of cigarette smoke.'

'How many can you see smoking?'

'About 10.'

Call-taker gleefully generates 10 new crime numbers. 'We'll send a patrol down immediately.'

'Oh, thank you so much, that's wonderful.'

'Caller, would you stay on the line until the police arrive, in case any of the smokers make a run for it?'

'Oh, yes, certainly.'

The police arrive and issue tickets for the offence of smoking in a public place. Ten tickets issued, ten crime numbers and ten detections. A 100% detection rate! So even if there are two domestic burglaries and no-one gets nicked for those, the detection rate will be a massive 83%! Long live statistics!

(Don't worry. This is satire. Smoking in public is a civil issue, not a criminal offence. Yet.)

NEW IDEAS

AS I'VE SAID, I work at the cutting edge of new ideas, and most of them are rubbish.

In the police, new ideas can be divided into three categories.

The first is Technology. There is a belief in the senior ranks that technology will be able to make up for bad management. This is wrong. If the police had designed email, each email would cost £1 and take a week to be delivered. Meanwhile, a printout of the email would have to be sent via the Royal Mail to a depot, where it would be filed with accompanying forms and statements.

For instance, 'Can you fax me a copy?' is something I hear every day. I've even heard it from the 'Hi-tech Crime Unit', despite the fact that faxing is only one step up from sending a telegram. Say I need Authorisation for Something. I can't just ring someone, or even email them. No, I have to print off a form, fill in the blanks with my trusty biro and then fax it off for the required signature. The faxed version is signed and then faxed back to me giving me the required written authorisation to do whatever it is I need to do. In order to file this chain of paperwork in the archives of the police station, I then have to photocopy the fax with the signature so that it is A4 size (faxes are always slightly longer than A4) and attach it to the other paperwork.

If I happen to gather some useful intelligence, I have to enter it into the relevant computer system and then, using my pen, write in a log that I have made an entry into the intelligence system. When I write a summary of a crime, I have to do it three times: to the CPS, to my sergeant and for the court file, each person requiring slightly different pieces of information. This brings me on to the second category of bad ideas.

Which is: Management. 'Fit for Purpose' is a phrase often used by engineers that means that something is robust or effective enough to do what it has been designed to do. Lately it's been adopted by politicians, who litter it pompously throughout their conversations, with other phrases like 'best practice', Gold Standard and 'It may be my parents' house, but what's that got to do with anything?'

If you are unfortunate enough to work in the private sector as a manager and you don't get it right – if, for instance, your products are not 'fit for purpose' – your company will fail and you will have to seek alternative employment. The success of the company depends on making the right decisions; making the wrong decisions will bring disaster.

In the police (and the public sector more generally), the exact opposite is true. There are no bad ideas, only good ideas that fail because of a lack of resources. For example: 'It is impossible to implement effective policing because of a lack of funding.' This is a lie. The truth is: 'Look, leave me alone, I want to collect my pension as soon as possible.'

Police management is much more about the management of inactivity than it is about reducing crime, the real challenge being to do as little as possible, take as much credit for any successes as possible and blame the rest on society. This brings me on to the third rich seam of bad new ideas.

Which is: Liberalism. 'Nothing makes any difference: crime occurs for a variety of reasons and the police and punishment can make no impact on the way people behave.'

We in the police have enthusiastically embraced the liberal vision of heroin-addicted burglars making good and repaying their debts by tidying up the gardens of their elderly victims. Many new police officers with degrees in criminology, sociology and psychology have been indoctrinated with this view and it has become accepted, so we stay in the police station and fill in forms and complete our investigations while the junkies don't turn up to do their weeding.

ARE YOU RELATED?

ANOTHER DAY, ANOTHER neighbour dispute. This time a Mrs Hall called the police because her neighbour (from down the street) drove by and stuck two fingers up at her daughter.

Sometimes, this sort of thing can be recorded by our police call centre as a crime, but today sense prevailed and it was recorded as a 'neighbour dispute.' (As I've said, we in the police don't restrict ourselves to dealing with crime. We also go out to try and settle neighbour disputes and even help out in civil matters, the assumption being that early police intervention in such incidents will prevent them descending into massacres, rather than mere farces.)

On entry to the premises, I found the mother and six screaming children. I found a clear space to sit down. 'So tell me what happened, Mrs Hall,' I said.

It was very hard to hear what she was saying over the noise of the children and Girls Aloud, but what gradually emerged is that this was all part of a long-running court case in which her partner was one of the witnesses and the neighbour, a Mr Jones, was a defendant. The Jones family are one of those large extended families that think that they can do whatever they like on an estate and the police won't do anything. Often, they're right.

A number of other things had been bothering her, including:

1. Mr Jones boasts of being a drug dealer, don't he?
2. Mr Jones' partner has been shouting at her in the street, yeah?

Her initial account went on for some time, as she had to keep getting up and hitting children to stop them vandalising the house. Needless to say, the child who was the subject of the drive-by V-ing was vandalising and screaming away with the others, not in the least traumatised by her unfortunate encounter.

'Are you related to Mr Jones?' I asked.

The answer was, of course, yes, though the relationship was one of those peculiar to the English slum; he's the girl's 'uncle', this being a non-blood euphemism for one of mother's previous short-term sexual liaisons.

'OK, Mrs Hall,' I said. 'What do you want me to do about it?'

This is always a bit difficult, because we can't actually arrest someone for making rude signs to a third party. (I know this sounds like behaviour likely to cause a breach of the peace, but in this case the behaviour likely to cause the BoP had now finished; I needed a victim who felt upset, or threatened, or something, but there wasn't one. Worst of all, because no crime had actually been committed, in that the victim clearly does not feel insulted or offended even if the person admits to sticking his fingers up, I couldn't get that all-important detection.)

'Look,' she said. 'Can you just make sure he can't come round here bothering me and my kids?'

'Hmmm,' I said. 'The thing is, this is still just about a free country and we can't really ban people from places if they haven't actually committed a crime.'

It fell on deaf ears. 'I don't want him near here,' she said.

Finally, I came up with a course of action. I would speak to the other party without taking official action.

I went and spoke to Mr Jones and suggested that he watch himself in future. Naturally, Mr Jones knew why I was there and said he could produce seven witnesses to say he was elsewhere at the time of the alleged gesturing. He also had some concerns of his own. These included:

1. Mrs Hall had accused him, in public, right, of being a drug dealer, which he weren't.
2. Mrs Hall had been gobbing off at his partner in the street, yeah?

'To be honest,' I said. 'I'm not really interested in the detail, I just want you to leave each other alone.'

Against the advice of his partner (Maureen), Mr Jones decided to leave the matter there and, after spending only two hours in the two properties, I resumed my patrol and the ceaseless and remorseless search for real criminals.

A further two hours later, I heard over my radio that Mr Jones and Maureen were at the police station and wished to talk to me. I attended and saw that Maureen had been crying.

'We've been thinking about what you said,' said Mr Jones. 'And we want her (Mrs Hall) done for defamation of character.'

Yes. *This* is why I joined the police.

ROBERT PEEL AND VERA'S WINDOWS

AS YOU KNOW, it's rare for me to get out and about on foot, 'interacting' with the public. I'm not sure why those in charge don't have us doing more foot patrol. They know very well that deploying lots of policemen on foot in bright yellow jackets is the best method of deterring criminals – otherwise, why do they have us all wandering round like that in the town centre of a Saturday night? Cops in luminous clothes do make a difference: even some drunk people think twice. (Obviously, it doesn't always work with drunks, There are those who will gaily expose themselves in public, or urinate in shop doorways, or fight each other whatever you're wearing. Some of them will even do it inside the police station after being arrested.)

Anyway, if the high-ups know it works (largely) on a Saturday night, why don't they have us doing this at other times and in other places? Why is the theory of 'high visibility policing' not practiced in, say, our vast, social dumping grounds, the council estates?

This question was posed to me yesterday by an 80-year-old lady called Vera who is unlucky enough to live in a maisonette in the Church Road Estate.

Someone had broken two of her windows with stones and I'd been sent round to investigate. She was a lovely old woman, whose house was immaculate (a pleasant contrast to many of the surrounding properties I have been into). I had some tea and a Happy Shopper chocolate digestive.

In the course of the conversation, it emerged that the broken windows were merely the latest in a long line of incidents which had put the fear of God into a harmless pensioner. They were incidents which, although relatively minor in their own way, had combined to create a fear of disorder which kept Vera stuck at home after about 5pm.

'What I don't understand,' said Vera, 'is why there aren't more police round here.'

'Hmmm,' I said. 'I don't understand that either, Mrs Parker.'

The majority of people living on even our worst council estates are completely law-abiding, in my experience. Yet their lives, like the lives of many of the poor and vulnerable in society, are dominated by a fear of disorder.

Disorder was a high priority for Robert Peel, the founder of the modern police service. Peel was born in 1788, the son of a wealthy industrialist and MP. He went to Harrow and Oxford and, at the age of 21, entered politics, buying a seat in the House of Commons in 1809 and becoming Home Secretary in 1822. Peel was concerned about the problems of law and order in London – even without alcopops and violent DVDs, it was a rough place to live – and in 1829 he set about reforming the system of policing. Up to that point, there'd only been an informal arrangement of night watchmen between you and the wrong end of a footpad's swordstick.

In the process, he created the new Metropolitan Police force, who became known as 'Peelers' or 'Bobbies,' under the first Commissioner of the Metropolitan Police, Sir Richard Mayne. The system of beat policing that was devised existed continuously from 1829 right up until the 1960s.

Peel developed nine principles of policing:

1. The police exist to prevent crime and disorder.
2. The ability of the police to perform their duties is dependent upon public approval of police actions.
3. The police must secure the willing co-operation of the public in voluntary observance of the law to be able to secure and maintain the respect of the public.
4. The degree of co-operation of the public that can be secured diminishes proportionately to the necessity of the use of physical force.
5. The police seek and preserve public favour not by catering to public opinion but by constantly demonstrating absolute and impartial service to the law.
6. The police use physical force to the extent necessary to secure observance of the law or to restore order only when the exercise of persuasion, advice and warning is found to be insufficient.
7. The police, at all times, should maintain a relationship with the public that gives reality to the historic tradition that the police are the public and the public are the police; the police being only members of the public who are paid to give full-time attention to duties which are incumbent on every citizen in the interests of community welfare and existence.
8. The police should always direct their action strictly towards their functions and never appear to usurp the powers of the judiciary.
9. The test of police efficiency is the absence of crime and disorder, not the visible evidence of police action in dealing with it.

Peel's principles, beautifully written and elegantly clear (even, I hope, with my minor editing), at once point to a bygone age and show us where we are going wrong. Would Peel recognise our modern police service? I suspect he would at first be horrified at the shoddy standards of dress adopted by most officers (myself included) – particularly the facts that we rarely wear our helmets and that our luminous jackets make us look like a cross between lollipop ladies and road workers. He would be amazed at the vast amounts of money that are spent on the police (or on computer systems, civilian staff, cars and buildings). Going out on patrol, he would be delighted with the general wealth of the population and horrified by the moral poverty of so many of them. I suspect that Sir Robert would be familiar with many of the problems faced by officers today. He would be impressed with the average officer's level of education and ability and his honesty (corruption was always a problem in the old, old days). He would be amazed at the lack of uniformed officers on the street and the numbers inside the police station.

What are the modern equivalent of Peel's principles? Sadly, we have to contend with so much bilge about equality and diversity that it's difficult to find clear, crisp guidelines similar to Peel's. The best I can do is reproduce the 'Mission' of the modern-day Met:

Working together for a safer London.
Working together with all our citizens, all our partners,
all our colleagues:

• We will have pride in delivering quality policing. There is no greater priority.
• We will build trust by listening and responding.
• We will respect and support each other and work as a team.
• We will learn from experience and find ways to be even better.
• We are one team – we all have a duty to play our part in making London safer.

Somehow, I prefer Peel's philosophy. A while ago, I printed off his principles and stuck them in my briefcase, so that they can provide some guide for my conduct as I fight crime in the deepest thickets of political correctness and bureaucracy. I cannot see myself doing the same with the Met's Mission.

STREET BAIL

ONE OF THE PROBLEMS a uniformed officer has is managing his caseload – a paper tsunami of crime.

A single officer might be dealing with 20 different matters, ranging from credit card fraud, through nuisance telephone calls, to a fight involving a crowd of people on a Saturday night. This means that the individual officer has 20 sets of problems: 20 witnesses to see, 20 people to arrest, 20 interim crime reports to write and 20 sets of comments from supervisors, saying, 'Why hasn't this been dealt with yet?'

In June 2006, the government introduced 'Street Bail'. Arresting someone only takes a minute or two: it's the booking in, interview and other enquiries that take hours. Street Bail means that I can now arrest someone on the street for a crime and say, 'I'm bailing you to appear at Newtown police station on Thursday at 10.00am. Failure to appear is punishable by prison or a fine.'

I can then carry on with the rest of my day, safe in the knowledge that the person I have just arrested will be coming into the police station next Thursday at 10:00hrs for an interview and (probably) a charge.

For once, this is a good idea. If I can get my offenders coming into the police station at, say, three hour intervals I'll be able to plan my day better and spend less time hanging around the custody suite waiting for solicitors, interview rooms and all that stuff. In theory, I'll also get to spend more time out on the beat on other days.

Having said that, it's very early as yet and I'm sure something will go wrong with it, probably related to paperwork or Human Rights.

The problem of scheduling-in offenders is mirrored with witnesses and even the victims of petty crime. Because the police service is free (like the NHS), its customers (victims and offenders alike) like to use it to settle scores and get one over on their former lovers or neighbours. They don't feel the need to meet a police officer at a given time, but instead expect to be waited on, hand and foot. After all, they've paid their taxes (a few of them have, anyway).

Here's an example (I've got hundreds). A week ago, I visited a house on a council estate on the edge of town to see a Sharon Smith who'd been assaulted by another female.

I walked up the concrete path towards her front door, stepping over the toddler's trike and numerous piles of dog faeces, all the while squinting as the sunlight bounced off the fridges and washing machines sitting on the lawn.

It didn't take long – about five minutes, I'd say – before the IP appeared at the door. I hadn't recognised the name, but as soon as she opened the door I realised it was the same Sharon who I had spoken to before about sending text messages to Kelly Broxholme. (Having the same cast of characters involved in more than one of your ongoing cases is quite common; often they'll be an offender in one case and a victim in another, and sometimes their status changes as the enquiry develops.) A fat, peroxide blonde with bad teeth and a drinker's nose, she was still in her dressing gown – well, it was only 14:00hrs – and she didn't look overwhelmed with gratitude to see me.

'Hello again, Sharon,' I said, my face a picture of concern. 'I'm PC Copperfield, I spoke to you a few weeks ago about those text messages, do you remember? Anyway, I gather you've been assaulted now?'

'Yes,' she said. 'Have you arrested the bitch yet?'

'Which bitch do you mean, Sharon?' I said. Then, before she could answer, I said, 'Anyway, I'm not going to start arresting people before you give me a statement. I just wondered if we could perhaps get that out of the way now?'

'No way,' she said. 'I can't do it now, I'm busy. How about next Friday, in the afternoon?'

'Certainly, Sharon,' I said, through gritted teeth.

Back into the police car and off on another waste of time.

Today found me on her doorstep again, at around 16:00hrs.

'Hello Sharon, it's me again.'

She was crammed into a ridiculously tight pair of white jeans and a white top emblazoned with the word 'SLAG' picked out in gold glitter. Her midriff wobbled as she spoke.

'You've caught me at a bad time,' she said, swigging from a bottle of Bacardi Breezer and taking a huge drag on a Lambert and Butler. 'I'm just off out for a night with the girls. And tomorrow I'm off on holiday for two weeks. You'll have to come back next month.'

Back to the car, and away we go.

I wonder whether, if Sharon was paying for the crime to be investigated (not in the way taxpayers do, I mean in cold hard cash, say £25 a call-out), she might think twice before cancelling appointments and being too busy. Other people might also think twice before calling the police for minor incidents when they were so drunk at the time that they can't really remember what happened.

I'm not suggesting for one minute that victims of crime should have to pay to have their complaints investigated, but it's worth thinking about next time a uniformed policeman or woman calls at your house outside of business hours. He or she is one of a small number of highly dedicated and determined officers who, despite everything that is put in their paths, still want to try to help people. Don't make it any harder for them.

THE PUNISHERS

I LIKE GOING TO give evidence at Magistrates' Court. It gives me a chance to read my book and it's even better when, as so often happens, I'm actually on a rest day, because then I'm being paid double time to be there.

Magistrates are the first line of defence, courts-wise. They're unpaid lay people and something like 98% of all crimes that go to trial are heard before them, as opposed to judges in the Crown Courts. They don't have much power – maximum jail terms of six months, and so on – and sometimes they don't have much clue, either. But they're a well-meaning bunch.

Apart from doing my bit to interrupt the criminal career of the odd violent drunk, my only experience of magistrates is swearing out search warrants. To get a search warrant, you have to get a magistrate to sign it. The procedure is fairly straightforward and the last time I did it the magistrate was advised by the clerk (the clerk is the legal adviser to the magistrates). The conversation went a little like this.

Clerk: 'What's the source of the information?'

Magistrate: 'What's the source of the information, officer?'

Me: 'The suspect's brother.'

Clerk: 'Are there likely to be any young children at the address?'

Magistrate: 'Are there likely to be any young children at the address, officer?'

Me: 'No.'

We continued like that until the warrant was signed with the words, 'Do let me know how you get on, officer.'

I suspect the magistrates like having the occasional police officer in the witness box as well: someone wearing a collar and tie (if only a clip-on one) and able to speak sense. It must make a pleasant change.

As it happens, I was at the Magistrates Court this week.

It was the case of Paul Sykes, juvenile thug of our parish (and the book was *Stalin: In the Court of the Red Tsar*, a revealing account of the life of Stalin and those closest to him. One cannot begin to imagine what the victims of the purges had to go through before and after the show trials. Victims at the lower levels were selected by lottery and the confessions of senior party members were obtained after weeks of torture.).

Sadly, my reading was interrupted by the victim, a taxi driver whose takings he last saw in the hands of young Sykes. These days, waiting rooms specifically for police officers have largely disappeared so we share a small room with everyone else. Inexperienced and nervous, the driver hadn't brought a book in with him so he had to make do with the small selection of Woman's Weekly magazines.

'What will I have to say?' he asked, a worried look on his face.

'Just tell them what happened, if you're asked,' I said.

'What about the bloody scumbag who robbed me?' he said.

'Well, we do have an open system of justice,' I replied. 'He'll have to hear what you have to say about it. It's only fair. But his mates won't say anything and if they do they'll be thrown out or arrested.'

In my experience, the visitors' benches are usually empty, though occasionally, a few yobbos do come to offer support to their friends or relatives. They usually arrive in their best tracksuits and sometimes stop smoking. Despite their best efforts, though, the ushers are often unable to prevent them wearing their baseball caps. (Incidentally, the link between smoking and crime is never more apparent than outside the court, where crowds of dole-claiming thieves and their chums gather around shared packets of Lambert and Butler; literally, taxpayers' money going up in smoke).

'Will it be in the papers?' the cabbie asked.

'Possibly,' I said. There's sometimes a lonely court reporter in the press benches but they don't cover everything that happens.

'What do you reckon he'll get for this?' he pressed on, oblivious to the fact that I was trying to get on with Stalin.

'Assuming he's found guilty, probably a supervision order,' I said. 'Maybe a short sentence.'

The driver nodded glumly and walked off to find the toilets.

As someone who approves of the early and frequent incarceration of offenders, I think the sentences passed down by the magistrates are insignificant: a fine here, a supervision order there or maybe a conditional discharge. Sometimes, a court will release someone on conditional bail. The conditions might, for example, include not going anywhere near Mrs Smith or anywhere in Church Street. I was reading the local paper the other day and would like to say I was surprised to find that someone 'was released on bail by the court, on condition that he kept to his bail conditions this time.' But I wasn't. It's quite common for the magistrates to impose a driving ban on a banned driver who was found driving a car.

As I sat back and tried to find my place, the CPS lady popped her head round the door.

'I've had a quick word with the defence and they're happy to accept your written evidence,' she said.

Marvellous, that was: almost the definition of a very good day. A three-hour wait, and I could go home and enjoy the rest of my day off, having been paid, twice over, for the full nine hours.

DERBYSHIRE POLICE

A FEW YEARS AGO I was on holiday in the States and spent the day with police officers in an area with a very high murder rate.

I arrived in the morning with my host and was introduced to the Captain.

'Y'all a bobby from England?' he said, looking me up and down.

'Yes, a bobby, that's right.'

'Y'all have guns, right?'

'No. No guns at all. Just a baton and some CS.'

'Sheee-it,' he said, whistling. 'Ah wouldn't do this job without a gun.'

Without further ado, I signed the necessary forms to say that I wouldn't tell anyone what I saw and that if I was killed I wouldn't sue the city. Then I put on a bullet proof vest, and went out on patrol, with approximately four different varieties of small arms in the car.

Our first call was to an alarm at a bank. In Newtown, the clerks lean on them by mistake and then wonder why a police officer is standing in the foyer a few minutes later. Here, I was about to go into the bank when my host drew his shotgun and pointed it at the door. He didn't seem to be taking any chances. 'You guys have shotguns right? Could be some guy in there with one right now.'

I slipped away back to the car and began to regret signing the forms.

We don't have that many crack-related machine gun homicides in my force – though it's only a matter of time – so a day spent with us would be far less interesting. But it's not allowed, anyway, because of public liability insurance considerations.

In Derbyshire, however, if you would like to spend a day with a police officer and you are a resident of the county, you can. You do need to fill in four application forms, though.

Four forms? Now *that's* what I call giving someone an insight what the police do all day.

For real authenticity, though, the forms would have to be returned to the applicant a couple of times with a note attached saying things like, 'Please complete this correctly. You have omitted the date of birth of your brother-in-law.'

YOU ALL LOOK THE SAME TO ME

TODAY WAS A GOOD DAY. It always is when I'm conducting house-to-house enquiries in the area of a crime.

There'd been a domestic burglary and, after nosing around and chatting with the victims, I knocked on next door. It opened to a reveal a man who goggled at me as though I was an alien. It's funny, but the unannounced presence of a uniformed copper on your doorstep seems to do this to some people.

'Hello there, sir,' I said, all cheery-like. 'There was a burglary next door and I wondered if you knew about it.'

'I wasn't here.'

'When weren't you here?'

'When the burglary was.'

'When was the burglary?'

'I don't know, but I wasn't here, so I don't know when the burglary was.'

'Fair enough. What if I tell you when the burglary was, and you tell me where you were at that time?'

'But I didn't do it.'

'I'm not saying you *did*, I'm just asking if you may have heard anything or seen anything suspicious.'

'No, I didn't.'

'But how do you know if I haven't told you when it happened?'

'We're always having problems with kids round here.'

I took a deep breath, looked around and bludgeoned him to death. I went inside, wrapped his body in Clingfilm and stored it in the bath. I'll be returning every day to collect a piece of it, which I will place in the property store at the police station, knowing that, once booked in, it will never be noticed again.

The other problem I'm often faced with is that we all look the same in uniform (my North Korean tiepin is a detail too far for most of the sociopaths with whom I deal).

After doing my bit to rid the world of burglars and idiots, I thought I'd call back at Mrs Smith's today – she of the peroxide hair, red nose and assault complaint – and see if she was back from her fortnight away.

I noticed she'd added a floral-patterned armchair to the front garden; its stuffing was erupting from the top and cascading onto the weeds and bare mud. After several knocks on the door, she appeared; fatter, blonder and redder.

'Hello, Sharon,' I said. 'You look like you've had a jolly good holiday.'

She looked at me, suspiciously.

'I just wondered if we could have that chat? About your assault complaint?'

'Have you found the people who smashed my Tracey's window in yet?'

'No.'

'It's been over a month now.'

'Well, the wheels of justice do grind exceedin' slow Mrs Smith.'

'Eh?'

'These things take time.'

'Time?'

'Hmm. Anyway, that's not one of my cases, I'm afraid, I'm here about...'

'It was you that went round there.'

'Mrs Smith, it really wasn't, it must have been a colleague of mine.'

'No, it was you.'

'Look, I don't know anything about your Tracey, or her window. I don't know who she is, where she lives or what she looks like. I don't know about her window being smashed, which window was smashed or who did it. The first I knew about it was when you told me just now.'

'You definitely came round her house last week in August.'

'I was in Scotland that week.'

'Well, it must have been your friend, he had black hair.'

'Don't tell me Mrs Smith. Did he arrive in a white car with "Police" written on the side?'

'Er... anyway, I've been getting these phone calls.'

SEVEN MINUTES WELL SPENT

MEMBERS OF THE PUBLIC are forever reporting suspicious people: door-to-door salesmen, reps getting a few minutes' kip in their cars, delivery drivers, child molesters, that kind of thing.

Today, a woman called to report a drug dealer in her street. I drove round there, but he wasn't a drug dealer at all; in fact, he was just a bloke waiting for a lift to work. I was quickly able to establish this.

'Excuse me,' I said. 'Are you a drug dealer?'

'No,' he said. 'I'm just a bloke waiting for a lift to work.'

I often find that the direct approach is the most effective. If I had thought he really was a drug dealer, I might have searched him immediately. Where possible, contrary to what you might have read about stop and search, and the evil pigs who delight in frisking law abiding people for no reason, police officers tend to avoid it. If I stop and search you, I am obliged to give you a written record of the fact. The written record is a postcard-sized piece of paper containing all your details (name, address, date of birth, vehicle details, racial group and so on) as well as the grounds on which I stopped and searched you, the legislation I used, various other bits of information and space for you to sign (if you want to). NB: every time I stop and search, I have to fill one of these in.

As of 1st April 2005 (April Fool's Day, as it happens), recommendation No 61 of the Stephen Lawrence enquiry came into force. The effect was that almost anyone I talk to in the street, never mind search, has to be given a similar written record. According to the Metropolitan Police, this record takes seven minutes to complete. So, if I go to an incident and see a group of four people and wish to ask them their names and addresses, it takes me about half an hour. Later, I will also have to enter the details on a computer, a process that takes a further half an hour (drive back to the station, wait in line for the computer, enter in the details). Called 'Stop and Account', I predict that this procedure will turn out to be a lesson in making something quite straightforward into another chance to fill in a form.

If you want to see more police officers out on the street, this may appear insane.

However, if you are a senior police officer it may appear the best thing that's ever happened for you, career-wise. Ask yourself the following questions:

> 1. If crime goes up will I lose my job?
> Answer: No.
> 2. If one of my officers is accused of being a racist,
> will I lose my job?
> Answer: Hmmm. Possibly.

Unless, that is, you have a bureaucracy to fall back on: a written record of every stop by every policeman and woman, a written policy on the matter, a system of complaint and redress, all monitored by other senior officers. A system, in other words, of shifting the responsibility to the lowest possible level: Me.

So, you see, whether it takes seven minutes or 70 minutes, it's time well-spent from the point of view of those who run the police service. As the system goes through the various committees and bureaucrats, it becomes more and more complex, and the form itself becomes longer and longer, so in the end it actually may well take 70 minutes to complete. I'll carry two pens with me from now on, just in case.

As I drove away from the bloke waiting for a lift, another call directed me to another man lingering by a lamp-post a couple of streets away. I was there in a minute or two and pulled up alongside him.

'Hello, there,' I said. 'Sorry to bother you, but we've had a couple of calls from neighbours who seem to think you might be up to no good. I'm sure that isn't the case, but would you mind telling me what you are doing?'

'Just waiting for another mate to come and then we're off to work,' he said, slightly defensively. I got out of the car. How about that? Two suspicious incidents in the space of five minutes, and both near-identical. But something about this chap didn't seem quite right. He wasn't wearing what you might describe as work clothes, for instance: stout boots and a bright yellow bib, for instance.

'Oh yes?' I said. 'Where are you off to, then?'

He wasn't able to say exactly where he was going, or what they'd be doing when they got there. I engaged him in conversation until his lift turned up, whereupon I searched both lads and the vehicle. I didn't turn up much beyond a small amount of drug paraphernalia (a bent spoon for boiling heroin up in and some citric acid which is used to help dissolve the drug) which I couldn't do anything about, anyway. In the end, I didn't make any arrests but the two lads in the car probably were up to no good and I entered the fact that I had seen them together and that they had the use of the vehicle, into our intelligence system.

Thanks to the government, as I say, it now takes forever just to ask a couple of lads what they're up to.

If, like some people, you resent the very idea that the police ought to be able to make this enquiry of someone, that may be a good thing.

If, like most people, you understand that it's a basic prerequisite of the effective interdiction of crime, it may not.

I BET YOU THOUGHT I MADE ALL THIS UP

I CAME ACROSS AN interesting little news item on the internet while Mrs Copperfield was cooking my tea this evening.

It was a news story from some time ago, and it concerned one Ryan Hughes, 18.

As I say, in the twilight world inhabited by most police officers, the dividing line between victim and offender is often quite fine. This is why I always warn victims of assaults that the chances are I'll be arresting them as soon as the person who assaulted them makes a counter-allegation. I'm rarely wrong.

Tragedy is never very far away from the police officer, either, unlike holidays, which always seem a long way off, and here is a good example (of a tragedy, not a holiday).

It falls to the unfortunate Ryan to tie these two seemingly disparate threads together. He stole a motorbike (offender) but was hit by a silver Rover (victim) and died (tragedy).

Interestingly, the silver Rover with which he collided was also said to have been stolen. In the words of Harry Hill, 'What are the chances of that?' With apologies to honest Merseysiders (I'm sure there are a *few*), I would say the chances are possibly greater in Liverpool – where this unfortunate occurrence happened – than in other parts of this sceptred isle.

The driver of the car 'did a runner' as, surely, we all would if we hit and killed a teenager on a motorbike. Running off like that was an offence. You can never say for certain, but there's a fair possibility he was known to the police so the chances are he will have been nabbed. I hope he was.

Anyway, as in all these things, it's an ill wind that blows nobody any good. Given that the motorbike Ryan Hughes was riding was stolen, he either stole it or received it and either way he committed a crime in so doing. A crime, moreover, which the Scouse bizzies will be able to file as 'detected', even though the thief is dead.

Long live the war on paperwork!

I BET YOU THOUGHT I MADE ALL THIS UP, TOO

IT'S RARE TO FIND a police force so proud of its in-house bureaucracy that it actually boasts about it in the public domain.

Staffordshire Police says it leads the world in 'The Ethical Recording of Crime.' I suppose it must be easier than leading the world in 'The Solving of Crime.'

A suspect died on our patch the other day. He was wanted for a couple of minor offences but the Grim Reaper got to him first, which was a shame. His death in itself wasn't related to anything criminal (unless you count the long-term injection of lots of illegal drugs) and CID dealt with the matter while I unrolled the police tape and sat in the car for a few hours.

As with young Ryan's untimely end, above, the death of any suspect presents a golden opportunity to 'solve' the crime for which he was a suspect (on the one hand, you won't get him before a court but, on the other, he's hardly going to appeal against an 'administrative detection', is he?)

Of course, this being the British police, it also presents a whole new set of bureaucratic problems.

Thankfully, in the case in question, our detectives dealt with them. But imagine if Staffordshire Police had got involved?

Among their 'world-class ethical recording practices' (or mindless police bureaucracy, as I like to call it), here's what a uniformed officer in Staffordshire has to do if a suspect dies (or, in police jargon, what happens when they're dealing with a 'D1').

The officer must do the following:

–   Provide statement/s of evidence outlining the incident.

–   If the suspect was interviewed prior to his death about a given offence, supply details of the interview with the suspect (this entails filling out either MG15, or copy TR2 including brief details of offender's account in the officer's report). I think a TR2 is some kind of form to do with interviewing a suspect but, whatever it is, a summary of an interview is going to run into a couple of pages or so.

–   If no interview was conducted with the suspect, or no admission was made on interview, corroboration of whatever the offence was will be required in the form of either witness evidence to the incident, or (in the case of an assault) of any injuries sustained by the victim that would tend to support their account of the incident. (Do not overlook the evidence of the officer initially attending the incident. Details of the scene and demeanour of the parties involved may be sufficient to corroborate the allegation, if no witness or injury evidence is available).

–   Some form of confirmation of the death of the suspect is required. (This could be the contact details of the Medical Practitioner or Coroner's Office, as appropriate.)

–   Accountability Form to be completed and countersigned by Supervising Officer, prior to submission to the Crime Audit and Investigation Standards Unit.

In other words if you're dealing with a minor crime and your main offender dies, you can't just write: 'The suspect is dead, case closed.'

You have to complete all the above steps, and for *what*? To satisfy the victim? No: to satisfy the bureaucrats at the 'Crime Audit and Investigation Standards Unit.'

That's not the end of it though; there are seven other disposal codes – D4(1), D4(2), D5, D6, D7(1), D7(2) and D8 – that have been devised by the Home Office purely so that police forces can file crime in the 'detected' box without actually bringing anyone to justice.

In a further example of bureaucratic lunacy, D5 is all about crimes committed by children under the age of criminal responsibility. If they're under 10 you can't prosecute them, but you still have to complete four or five forms to get the job filed. All eight disposal codes naturally require the submission of reports and statements by uniformed officers who might otherwise be dealing with members of the public who are actually alive and/or at least 10 years old.

KEY WORKERS

WITH ALL THE PANICKING going on these days – bird flu, international terrorism, tsunamis (unlikely to affect us on home soil, but you can't be too careful) and the like – the government has thoughtfully set up the Civil Contingencies Secretariat. I know it sounds a bit Soviet era, but stick with it. The idea is that you log on to the website (www.pfe.gov.uk) and find helpful tips, such as 'If you find a dead duck in your garden, don't eat it' and 'If terrorists set fire to a nuclear power station near you, run like buggery'. OK, I made those up. But it's of that sort of order: as the site itself says, a lot of its advice is based on common sense and may seem obvious. Having said that, I have absolutely no idea what 'karnal bunt' is but it sounds horrible, so there's one thing worth reading up on.

I bet the whole enterprise cost a few million quid, but at least another load of Whitehall backsides have been covered. And if we do all end up dying of avian influenza, we won't be able to moan about a lack of information on the disposal of dead sparrows, that's for sure.

Of course, in the event of such an emergency, 'Key Workers' will be straight into the front line.

I've never been happy with the concept of 'key workers', even though I probably am one. Key workers are people who, in the eyes of the government, are essential for the continuance of civil society. They include teachers, health care professionals and those in the emergency services.

One of the major benefits we key workers are entitled to is a cheap loan to buy a house should we work in London. This particular scheme was devised by the Department of the Environment (and I bet bureaucrats in the Department of the Environment are also considered key workers; if not, sorry).

The thing is, I don't feel like a key worker. Which parts of my 'work' are 'key', anyway? Is it the taking of staples out of reports and the stapling together of other reports, in the correct order, for filing? Is it the administrative 'solving' of crime? Is it hours on the phone to banks asking about credit card frauds? Or maybe waiting for a solicitor is the highest expression of a civil society?

No, key workers, as far as I'm concerned, are the people who deliver biros, printer ink and photocopier toner to my nick and thousands like it. If martial law is ever declared, who's going to guarantee the supply of forms, or keep fax lines between different departments of a single police force open? If they can't struggle out of their subsidised housing and brave the superbugs or meteorites or alien invaders, I'll effectively be redundant.

Not that too many people would notice, which is the funny thing about 'key workers'. For such vital cogs in the engine of the country, they do seem to take an awful lot of time off sick each year. And yet, to my constant amazement, society seems to tick along nicely without them!

I haven't received my pack from the State about what to do in the event of a civil emergency, though one must be on its way.

However, I have had some training about what the responsibility of the emergency services will be, and how they will respond. Having listened to it, my advice is:

- Buy a gun.
- Buy a first-aid kit.
- Buy a fire extinguisher.

As the website puts it, with rhetorical whimsy: 'What is resilience?'

HE HIT ME WITH THE LEMON

IT NEVER CEASES to amaze me how complex people's lives are.

Take domestic violence.

You might think domestic violence is a simple matter: man hits woman with lemon, woman sustains injury, police called, man arrested, goes to court, matter dropped because woman refuses to give evidence.

Last week, I attended just such a routine domestic incident at the small, terraced house of a woman called Linda.

On my arrival, I found Linda standing outside in the garden with the contents of her kitchen around her feet. A bellowing sound could be heard, and more objects occasionally flew from the open window and landed near us. They were being thrown by her estranged husband, Ray.

Linda was upset, as she often is. She works for the council, something she fits in around her main hobby which is meeting up with Ray and fighting. She's in her late 40s and whenever I see her she's always in tears, either worrying about Ray because he's about to go to court, or apologising to the police for withdrawing her complaint. She is quite an emotional person and, she says, a spiritual one, too; by way of evidence, she will point out a collection of fantasy dragons she keeps on the top of the telly.

'What's going on?' I asked.

A cucumber sailed through the air and missed me by six feet. 'You make me f*cking sick,' shouted Ray.

Andy, another officer, arrived and, while he spoke to Linda outside, I had a pre-arrest chat with Ray in the kitchen to see if I could get him to say anything incriminating.

'What's been going on?' I said.

'We've had a row,' he said, breathing hard.

'I can see that Ray. What about?'

'It's my day to see the kids, so I've come round to pick them up. I'd even been to Tesco and done some shopping for her. Soon as I walked in, she had a go at me. I know I've had a drink, but it's like this all the f*cking time. Every time I come round she has a go at me and this happens.'

'Come on, Ray,' I said. 'Have you hit her again?'

'I just threw that out the door, and the shopping with it.' He pointed to an upside down table and several bags of groceries lying in the front garden.

'Hang on here, Ray,' I said, 'while I have a quick word outside.'

Andy filled me in. 'She's saying Ray chucked the shopping at her and some fruit has smacked her in the head. She reckons it was a lemon but she can't be sure.'

About right for this estate: the only fresh fruit for miles around, and it gets used as an offensive weapon.

So it was back to Ray for the magic words. 'Ray, you're under arrest for hitting Linda again.'

The rest of the afternoon was spent gathering evidence and dealing with Ray.

The whole thing was going nowhere, of course. Linda withdrew her complaint the following day. As it was a domestic, and because Linda had called the police out loads of times before (and was therefore, in statistical terms at least, a possible future murder victim), the CPS thought they would run a case against Ray without her (a so-called 'independent prosecution'). I therefore got asked the following questions:

1. Why did you not call SOCO to get the lemon fingerprinted?
2. Can you get a statement from the child? (There was a suggestion that a neighbour's child had witnessed the incident, or at least seen Ray chucking the contents of the fruit bowl about).
3. Get a statement from the neighbour. She will need an interpreter, please organise one.
4. Why did you not ascertain exactly where the offender had been drinking prior to the incident?

I spent today gathering the relevant statements in preparation for Ray's trial (and, let's face it, acquittal) in a couple of months' time.

DAVE'S LAW

A RULE OF THUMB I have developed over the years is that the importance of an incident is in inverse proportion to the amount of work required to bring it to a close. For example, arresting a murderer might take 15 minutes but sorting out a marital disagreement over who chooses the channel on the television could easily take several hours. It's incredible how quickly some adults can regress to juvenile spite and bickering.

Yesterday, I was called to an incident where a man and a woman were outside a house shouting at each other. It was the man's house; his ex had recently upped sticks but she'd come back to retrieve the TV and some other audio-visual equipment. Ownership had been disputed with a healthy vigour, and it was all well underway by the time we arrived.

The man had called round a friend with limited DIY skills to change the locks. This bloke was leaning on the bonnet of his van, butting in from time to time in an attempt to pour oil on troubled flames.

'Get in that van and stay there,' I said to both of them. 'And could you please come with me, madam.'

I went into the house with the woman and her two small children, who were watching wide-eyed. The kids distress me a bit in these cases, so I try not to look at them too much. She had her sister with her to provide moral support and incorrect legal advice.

'Right,' I said. 'Whose television is it?'

'Mine, he gave it to me.'

'OK. Wait here.'

Back outside, the two men had disobeyed my instructions to stay in the van and the locksmith was measuring up the door.

'Why can't you just stay in the van until we've sorted this out?' I asked.

'It's my house, officer.'

Deep breaths, Copperfield, deep breaths.

'Right. Whose TV is it?'

'Mine. She bought it for me for my birthday but now she wants it back. Why have you let her in my house? Why can't you get her out and tell her to leave my telly alone? I just don't understand why you can't do that.'

And I don't understand why you can't piss off and come back after 18:00hrs when I've booked off duty, I nearly said.

'Right. You wait here. And keep quiet.'

Back inside.

'OK, he says the telly's his.'

'Well, it ain't and I want it back.'

'I can't just make him give it to you, I'm afraid.'

The girl's sister butted in helpfully. 'Our uncle Paul's in the police, and he told me we'd be able to get the telly back,' she said. People do this to me a lot, as if the fact that they have a brother who's a sergeant in the CID somewhere changes the law in some way.

I went back outside. 'Look,' I said, to the man. 'She reckons it's her telly. Why don't you just let her have it, for a quiet life? They're only fifty quid second hand anyway.'

'It's my bloody telly,' he said. 'You've got the power to go in there and tell her that. My brother's in the police, he said so.'

Oh God, not another one. 'Well, perhaps if you can get him and her uncle Paul down here, they can sort this out between them and we can go?'

'You're just taking her side because she's a woman. What's your number?'

'Please would you remind me why you called the police, sir?'

'Because she's trying to steal my telly,' he said. Now he was shouting.

'Please calm down, sir,' I said. 'We don't want this to get out of hand, do we?'

'I'm sorry,' he said. 'But this is a bloody disgrace.'

With neither side actually looking to murder each other (and thereby save me a lot of time), I tried to find a solution. I didn't particularly like either party: the man was thick and awkward and the woman was trying to use the police to get her hands on electrical items that probably weren't hers. After an hour, we arrived at a truce. He would keep the 'Digibox' and the DVD player, and she would take away the TV.

For this, I was accused of 'taking sides' and of being ineffectual and rude.

The only way of dealing with domestic incidents – ones which haven't turned properly nasty, anyway – is to allow the idiots to bore each other almost to death before coming to a solution which is equally unsatisfactory to both parties. Sadly, you can't just bang their heads together and clear off: it's impossible to leave potentially explosive situations without being open to the charge of neglect of duty, especially when there are children involved. Of course, if an offence has been committed it's much easier to deal with: you can arrest one party and deal with the other at your leisure.

There's a crucial difference between dealing with domestic incidents and criminals. Most of the time, the criminals know what's going on. Once you say, 'You're under arrest' to a well-handled criminal, he knows the game is up; it's a hazard of his chosen profession. Parties in a domestic incident are always full of righteous indignation and they just know they haven't done anything wrong ('Can't you just tell her, and let me get my stuff?'). Underlying the situation are potent feelings of sexual jealousy and rejection which make it difficult for either party to see sense.

Imagine how it feels for the ordinary police officer, often on his own, with two groups of people shouting at each other and accusing him of not doing anything. Children are crying, but ignored. The temperature is going up all the time. People will not move into separate rooms as they are told. There are kitchen knives within reach and, if it does all go pear-shaped, assistance is a long way off.

All this over a plasma TV and a DVD player.

Later on, and with only a couple of hours of the shift left to go, I received a call involving an incident involving two areas of law which any self-respecting police officer should leave well alone: tenants and threats to kill.

The law surrounding the rights of tenants is particularly complex and extends across the criminal and civil fields. Investigating threats to kill is like trying to wade through treacle: slow and dispiriting. Combine the two and you know you'll be there for a while. And we were.

To summarise, the tenants had turned the house into a rat-infested slum and not paid any rent, and the landlord had got so fed up he had threatened them.

'Look officer,' said the landlord. 'They owe us for six months rent and you can see the damage they've done.'

There was cat food all over the kitchen surfaces, the carpets were stained, there was food on the walls and the bathroom was caked in grey, soapy dirt.

The tenant was unapologetic when I spoke to him alone. 'He's been harassing us,' he said. 'He's told me he's going to kill me if I go out of the house and my missus is up the duff.'

'Are you taking the piss?' I said. 'You've not paid any rent.'

'That's no reason for him to keep threatening me.'

'Well, why don't you just pay the rent and keep the place tidy?'

'I know my rights and he just can't keep threatening me.'

We argued some more, while the lad's long suffering and enormously pregnant girlfriend sat quietly in the squalor. I went back to the landlord to ask for some clarification.

'Don't you have to serve some sort of eviction notice or something before you can get rid of them?' I asked.

'We've tried that, but I just want them out. I've had enough officer.'

'But you can't just threaten people and kick them out.'

'I haven't threatened anyone.'

So the standoff continued: the landlord and his cronies wouldn't go away and the tenant had nowhere else to go. My mobile rang and my wife asked when I might be home.

'Er… later,' I said.

WASTING POLICE TIME

HOW MUCH TIME do I actually spend doing anything that people might consider it appropriate for a uniformed police officer to do?

The Home Office is confusing the issue by including 'case file and report preparation on incidents' in front-line activities. I read about all this in my lunch break today.

It was a brief respite from the rest of the shift which I had spent deterring crime by maintaining a constant presence on the street. Constant from 11:00hrs to 12:00hrs, that is.

I'd started the day by typing up a couple of crime reports and arranging the papers in the required order.

I then caught up on emails: other departments sending me information on how to deal with the threat from Al Qaeda and the

Continuity IRA, reminders about completing domestic violence logs correctly, the latest news on our partnership arrangements and new force policy on dealing with illegal immigrants.

An email from our CPS liaison department told me that Bus Shelter Kyle had, amazingly, gone bandit (decided to plead not guilty at court), so I spent an hour preparing the additional required paperwork for that.

A couple of hours on the phone followed: getting addresses of naughty children and chasing up a couple of things that had been sent for forensic examination.

I then tried to get some information from a bank customer who had been defrauded of £200; this took half an hour.

Next my sergeant handed me an accident report from a few months ago with a request that I interview the driver. He lives at the other end of the country. This will involve faxing copies of the relevant sections of the accident report and a request to the relevant force to carry out the interview on our behalf. I'll have to do this twice, because they'll lose the first lot.

A couple more completed forms and a copy of a custody record for our CPS liaison department and I was almost ready to resume mobile patrol. Started shift at 08:00hrs, ready to go out at 11:00hrs.

Once out and about, crunching good, honest gravel under my Doc Martens (until I reached the car, that is), I was immediately sent to deal with some 'nuisance youths'. I stopped a group of five children who vaguely fitted the description I'd been given: white males wearing baseball caps and hooded tops (is there any other way to dress these days?). I asked them to account for their movements: BIG MISTAKE. In each case, I have to complete one of those seven-minute forms and hand a copy to the subject. The form asks for all the usual details, including ethnicity (as defined by subject) and ethnicity (in the opinion of the officer) and requires that the officer detail the reason(s) for asking the subject to account for his whereabouts or behaviour (in this case, suspicion that one of them had kicked a plant pot and smashed it). The good thing is, the form proves we're not racist. Thirty five minutes and a brief area search later, I took a statement from the victim of the vandalism (terracotta pot, £2.50, B&Q sale, I might get one for my geraniums) and reported the crime over the radio. Which brought me to 12:30hrs, and break time.

At 13:15hrs, I found a sergeant and asked him to sign a form so that I could show a witness photographs of a possible plant pot vandal. He agreed, so I returned to the witness and showed her the photographs and completed the rest of the form.

At 14:00hrs there was a report of a shoplifter detained by staff at Boots. I did a quick calculation. If I take this job, I can book the thief into custody, search his house, take the witness statement, write my arrest statement, brief the solicitor, interview the shoplifter, charge the shoplifter and complete the file (because I'm very quick) all before 17:00hrs, and home time.

By my reckoning, I'd been on the streets for about two hours, and that includes time spent taking witness statements.

Time spent actually trying to catch criminals: probably 45 minutes.

Some senior officers have argued that we should become 'super-cops', with teams of administrators to help us with the routine tasks. That's not a bad idea. What is less clear to me is whether most of the 'routine tasks' should be done at all. I wonder, too, whether the public would be happy with a vast proportion of the police budget being spent on clerical assistants?

Whatever the exact proportion of my time is spent dealing with nonsense, there is a tipping point where the job of being a policeman shifts from 'law enforcement' to 'administrator': at some point, so much of a constable's time is spent administrating that it becomes the whole point of his existence, and catching crooks becomes something we do if we have a spare minute or two.

CHASING PEOPLE

IT'S RARE THAT I GET to chase people any more, which is sad because it's why I joined in the first place to be honest. By the time a call comes in and is routed to the nearest unit, the offender is usually long gone.

Nowadays, I just turn up with my briefcase and take a statement.

To be honest, we usually know who we're looking for in most cases, like domestic violence, or when the victim and offender know each other, so there isn't really the incentive to go charging through broken windows and over fences anyway.

Having said all that, I do still occasionally get the chance to go running after someone and the other night I did just that.

Some lunatic had smashed the window of his local and then gone on the run. The landlord gave us his name and a rough idea of where he lived. As luck would have it, I'd dealt with the same fool only last week so I knew his exact address. These people tend not to be criminal masterminds, and you usually find the place they've gone on the run to is their house. Working on this theory, my colleague Kate and I rushed round there.

'I bet his missus answers the door looking like we've just woken her up,' said Kate.

Sure enough, she stood there on the doorstep, yawning and rubbing her eyes like a very B-movie actress. 'I don't know where he is,' she said. 'I've been asleep the whole time.'

Then we heard the back door slam. I excused myself and legged it down the entry. I didn't catch the offender, of course, I just got a glimpse of him running through the fence at the end of the garden. But it was good fun calling out to him to give himself up and shining the big torch in peoples' back gardens, jumping over walls, that sort of thing. It's funny in these situations how common sense departs and the only thing left is the hunting instinct.

Having missed him, I'll have to change tactics: I think I'll just pester his wife into giving him up. I'll knock on the front door loudly at 08:00hrs every morning, when I'm on dayshift, and 21:45hrs when I'm on nights. (You may be wondering why I don't just go round at 05:30hrs, or 23:45hrs, and really inconvenience them? Well, you won't be surprised to know that it's against force policy to do this. Routine arrests can only be arranged between 08:00hrs and 22:00hrs. You probably won't be surprised, either, when I tell you that my force has determined that arresting people outside these times contravenes their human rights under Article 8 of the Human Rights Act, which confers the Right to a Private Life.)

Despite the obstacles to me arresting him, most of them imposed by senior police officers, I'll allow him a week or so to give himself up before calling his employer and telling him I want to speak to him during working hours. So he either talks to me next week or loses his job. I don't suppose I'm allowed to do this either, technically.

THE AMERICAN WAY

AS I'VE EXPLAINED, when I interview a suspect about a crime I first meet his solicitor and tell the solicitor what evidence I've got.

The solicitor then tells his client what we know and they cook up a story together.

I then interview the suspect with the solicitor present.

Note: I'm not allowed to talk to the suspect about the crime if the solicitor isn't present.

If I even evidence into the interview without having first told the solicitor about it, the solicitor stops the interview, sometimes very pompously, and 'consults' his client.

This all makes for a tortuously long process; each stage of the interview is recorded on sets of three separate tapes, and each set has to be separately exhibited, labelled and transcribed.

As well as being long, it's also mad. I understand the need to protect the innocent, but what our system really does is give the guilty the best possible chance of creating a plausible fairy tale with legal assistance (trust me, we only actually arrest guilty people for proper crimes, most of the time).

I was reading up about the US legal system last night (I'm fascinated by what goes on in other countries) and I came across a case heard before the appeal court in Richmond, Virginia.

What had happened was, a chap called Curtis Hilliard had been arrested on suspicion of murder after an Anthony Robinson Jnr had been shot dead in a car. Hilliard was at the police station with detectives White and Kochell when the following discussion took place.

HILLIARD: 'Can I get a lawyer in here?'
DETECTIVE WHITE: 'Do you want to do that?'
HILLIARD: 'I already have a lawyer. I mean, I can talk to you, don't get me wrong. But I just want to make sure I don't just jam myself up. And I'll tell you everything that I know. This is my word.'
DETECTIVE WHITE: 'OK. That's fine.'
DETECTIVE KOCHELL: 'That's fine.'

HILLIARD: 'I'm not saying that I will say anything other or… just because he's in here. I just want to, you know, make sure I have… I'd feel a little bit more comfortable.'

DETECTIVE KOCHELL: 'That's not a problem. We tried to provide you with a comfortable atmosphere here. And, like I said, it's not the stuff that you see on TV dealing with Sipowicz, OK, where he takes a guy and throws him up on the wall. That's not what we're about.'

HILLIARD: 'I will say, I will go as far as to say this. Probably what you all got in that book ain't nowhere near.'

DETECTIVE WHITE: 'Anywhere near… of what we know of why it happened?'

HILLIARD: 'Yeah.'

DETECTIVE WHITE: 'Well, that's why we want to hear from you, because we know there's a bigger picture there. OK? You know what the problem is, Curtis, is that you got caught up in it.'

HILLIARD: 'Yeah, I did. I was there. I'm going to just say that, I was there. But before I say anything else, I mean, I already talked to you before we go to court.'

In case you missed it, what Hilliard just did was admit he was at the scene of the murder without having his attorney present while he was talking. That admission got him convicted of murder and landed him with a total of 63 years in jail. Result!

His appeal was based on whether he'd had his rights read to him properly, and whether this admission should have been allowed in evidence. The judges dismissed his appeal, on a majority.

Should any US members of the 'law-enforcement community' be reading this book, you'll be scratching your heads and thinking, Sounds OK to me? Those of us here in the UK are thinking, You guys actually get away with that? If it happened like that in this country, the case would be binned by the CPS as soon as the prosecutor saw the video of Detective White saying 'Do you want to do that?' in response to Hilliard's request for a lawyer.

If, instead, he'd managed to keep his gob shut until we got him in an interview room with his brief, the brief would butt in the moment Curtis started to incriminate himself.

And a murderer would be back out on the streets, instead of sitting in a cell until he's about 85 years old wondering why he had to open his big mouth.

CHASING MY TAIL

HAVING FAILED TO CATCH my pub window smasher the other day, the matter goes onto my workload. If it had been a serious job (like a burglary or a murder) I would have been able to hand it over to a specialist squad of detectives, but it isn't so I can't.

It will join the other nonsense I am dealing with, the highlights of which are Kelly and Sharon's threats (which will probably never go away), a shoplifting in which two steaks were stolen by a man in a hooded top, Dave Dodgy Geezer being on bail, a playground fight where one of the kids lives in Weatherby and Sharon's complaint of assault. In total, I'm currently investigating about 10 cases, but it can be as many as 20.

Each file consists of a front sheet and a copy of the computer printout which generated that particular crime. Also attached are original statements from injured parties and/or witnesses, as well as all the other paperwork that crime generates.

It is basically down to me as the Investigating Officer to gather evidence and bring the offender to justice. Each patrol officer has his or her own workload and it forms the basis of their daily activity.

Sometimes, it's fairly simple: arrest the offender and interview him at a mutually convenient time. Then he is charged and bailed to a court and you prepare the file to go with it.

However, it could be that the offender has an alibi which you have to check. In that case, he is bailed to reappear at a later date when he will be charged or not, depending on whether the alibi is honest or just some cock-and-bull story he's cooked up with his mates.

Even if the offender is charged, the CPS often asks you to make further enquiries, so sometimes the paperwork never seems to end.

Often it's complicated: there might be CCTV to gather and examine, other witnesses to see or banks to telephone (in the case of frauds). Sometimes witnesses have to be shown photographs. In some cases (pub fights, for example) there are multiple offenders, all of whom have to be arrested and interviewed and bailed or charged.

Some crimes are crimes in name only: the injured party does not wish to make a complaint. Even in these cases, the offender has to be spoken to because it can be filed as a detected crime and human rights laws mean that if an allegation is made against someone then they have the right of reply.

Here, various forms have to be filled in to 'get the detection.'

In any case, a full report has to be written up by the officer detailing all the efforts he has made to trace an offender. This report can be a couple of pages long, but it must satisfy the sergeant and then the crime audit desk before it can be filed away.

This system necessarily entails patrol officers spending much of their time taking statements in peoples' homes, filling in forms and writing long reports.

Furthermore, each investigation must be completed in a specified period of time or a report has to be prepared outlining the reasons for a longer-than-usual investigation. It is vital that an officer's workload is 'in date'. The bureaucratic burden created for officers is, as you can see, quite large. It's even worse for sergeants – so much so that each shift has two or even three sergeants, one or two supervising the officers on the streets, the other sat at a desk monitoring the paperwork.

Naturally, all this has to be done in between responding to calls from the public, an activity which creates yet more crimes to go onto my workload.

So next time you wonder why your half-brother has not yet been arrested for hitting you last Saturday night, you know why: I've got nine other people, all wondering the same thing.

GLAD TO BE GAY

I'VE DECIDED to be gay.

Don't tell Mrs C, or she may resort to long silences or extended visits to her mother's. It's been a difficult decision but, having read an interesting piece about it in *The Guardian*, I really must do something about getting promoted.

The story concerned the large number of black and Asian officers being promoted faster than white officers, simply (it's suggested) because they are black or Asian.

There is a suspicion that people so promoted are incompetent or unqualified, but I have always maintained that most senior officers are either incompetent or unqualified, and often both, so race has nothing to do with it.

Anyway, the first thing I have to do is join an under-represented minority. I can't become black, much as I might like to, so I might as well try gay for a while. If I start early enough, it might be good for my career. The Gay Police Association envisages a four-phase 'roll-out' of the monitoring process:

Phase 1: Include a voluntary question in non-attributable staff surveys/cultural audits.
Phase 2: Consider the introduction of a sexual orientation question in all new application forms for those joining the pilot Forces.
Phase 3: Introduce sexual orientation data along with other information in personnel records.
Phase 4: Advise ACPO, Staff Associations and other interested parties accordingly.

There are a couple of ideas that I like here: asking all new recruits whether they are gay or not and keeping a record of the officer's sexual preferences along with his personnel record. The GPA has a FAQ section (just how 'f' are these 'q's' being asked?).

I know that there are a lot of you straight people out there who have old-fashioned ideas about privacy and such. You think us gays are just saying we're gay because we want to make Inspector before we hit 40, but that's just a disgraceful slur.

JOHNNY FOREIGNER

THE TOWN IN WHICH I work contains a large number of people who are not British and do not speak English.

As a police officer (and, therefore, a racist, Nazi thug) this creates problems for me, especially if they are criminals or they drive cars. As I've said, we have a particularly large number of Iraqi visitors, who are mostly economic migrants. We're told they're asylum seekers but most of the young men I talk to are here to work and have a good time, until they are able to bring their families over in a few years' time or go back home with enough money to buy a house and some land (probably after the inevitable civil war over there has come to an end).

As you know, I have a soft spot for most of them though I do find it disconcerting to see how quickly they acquire traditional English requirements and customs: big plasma TVs, satellite dishes, a love of chips and many bastard offspring. Just as quickly, they learn the patois of the slum, uttering words and phrases like 'That's assault!', 'I know my rights!' and 'I've just sent off my provisional driving licence to the DVLA, so I haven't got one at the moment.'

Today, I've been mainly stopping Iraqi males and asking them to produce their documents. (I know this might offend some people, but I only had two hours and I wasn't going to waste time stopping people who looked like everything might be in order, so I stopped older cars being driven by young men in a less salubrious part of town; as it happened the vast majority were from Iraq.)

In the UK, if a police officer wants to see your driving documents he can require you to produce them immediately. However, more often than not, he'll probably give you a slip of paper (called a 'producer') that you have to present at a police station of your choice within seven days, along with said documents (driving licence, insurance and certificate of road-worthiness for the vehicle).

So, what happens with Iraqis? It usually goes something like this.

'What's your name, sir?'

'Ali Kameer.'

'And is this your vehicle, Mr Kameer?'

'Yes.'

'Do you have a driving licence?'

'I've just sent off my provisional driving licence to the DVLA, so I haven't got one at the moment.'

'Do you have any insurance?'

'I no understand.'

'Have you ever passed a driving test?'

'No unnerstan'.'

'Oh, dear. Your English appears to have deserted you, sir. Have one of these.'

I give them a producer, safe in the knowledge that I'll never see them again. It's all rather farcical, to be honest. I suppose I could arrest them, because any offence, however trivial, is now arrestable, but do we really want a police station full of foreigners who haven't got their MOT certificates in the glove box?

'... WOULD LIKE TO SPEAK TO AN OFFICER.'

OUR DISPATCHERS QUITE OFTEN say this to us over the radio.

It's a sure sign that some trivial matter is worrying someone and that the police are the only people who will be able to help (because there's no-one else in the area with an IQ above 'fairly stupid').

In a consumer society like our own, where people expect service immediately, they are unwilling to accept anything less than the best. In the police service we are dedicated to providing excellent QoS (Quality of Service), so if you wake up in the middle of the night and realise that your aunt has been harassing you for the past five years, naturally you should be able to ring us and expect a prompt visit.

'Not at all, Mrs Hughes. If you're worried, you should give us a call. No, it's not right that she should be sending emails calling you a mad bitch. Yes, Mrs Hughes, I have trouble sleeping sometimes, too. No, I don't think you're completely insane, you just need some rest. Me? Sometimes I take the whole bottle.'

Two hours later, Mrs Hughes will be going out of her mind with worry about something completely different.

Still, it pays the mortgage and, if it wasn't for the mad (or at least educationally subnormal), I'd be out of a job. That's the thing about policing: you're always dealing with people who inhabit a slightly different planet to yours.

Like the elderly woman who insisted that her former husband had disappeared. Disappeared from the spirit world that is. He needed collecting with a vacuum cleaner.

'Sorry, officer,' she said. 'Didn't they tell you that? Well, the nice young man who came last time didn't mind.'

Or the young man who insisted that the law in England allowed him to play 'hard house' music until the early hours, unlike the law in Wales, under which it had to be turned off at 22:00hrs during the week and by 23:00hrs at weekends.

Alcohol plays a large part in my professional life. Many people I meet are under its influence. I heard the other day that Russian police officers simply hose down their drunks and release them back into the community. What? Without referring them to any outside agency? Unbelievable!

Amazingly, consumption of alcohol seems to give people an almost encyclopaedic knowledge of the law. 'You can't arrest me!' is something I often hear from drunks, as I arrest them for damaging their neighbours' property or beating their women. Women are responsible for lots of crime. Indirectly, of course: it's their menfolk who actually commit the crime, but it's usually in the name of the women in their lives. When called to a domestic assault, I like to ascertain the facts in the following way.

'Did you hit her?'

'Basically, I really love her, but she just pushed me too far this time.'

'I see, so you didn't really mean to do it?'

'No, I just lost it, I really love her.'

'So you say. Are you drunk?'

'Well, I've had a few.'

'So, you're a violent drunk?'

'You're twisting my words.'

'And you're under arrest.'

Strike one for justice.

Returning to take the statement from the battered female, I ask penetrating questions.

'How long have you been together?'

'On and off for 18 months.' (Somehow, it's almost always 'on and off' in these cases).

'Has he always been violent towards you?'

'Yes, pretty much.'

'And at what point did you decide he would make an ideal father for your child?'

'Well, it just sort of happened.'

So there it is: beer, women and insanity.

We'll do drugs next (not literally).

IN HIS DEFENCE, HE TAKES HEROIN

I HAVE READ THAT 90% of acquisitive crime in my town is committed by drug addicts.

I am unable to comment as to the accuracy of this statistic. However, my own experience leads me to conclude that 100% of acquisitive crime, indeed 100% of all crime, is committed by criminals (OK, some people do inadvertently break minor laws).

Criminals are not all the same: some are just starting out, some are experienced, some are part-time, some are good at it, some are incompetent, some are violent, some aren't. Many are irritating: they whine and complain and constantly push the 'call' button in their cells. (it may or may not surprise you to hear that criminals who are booked into police custody, following an arrest, are given their own, en-suite cells, with a button to push should they require anything from the custody sergeant. I have stayed in far worse seaside b&bs.)

Drugs certainly play a large part in the lives of acquisitive criminals, particularly, and young criminals generally. Drugs are fun and they make you feel good, and that's the extent of it. They do not 'cause' crime, though, any more than the existence of DVD players causes burglary, or the existence of short, ginger children causes bullying.

The failure of the criminal justice system to deal with illegal opiates is the same failure that has allowed crime to rise more generally, namely:

– Not making individual criminals responsible for their actions.

– Not giving criminals sufficiently onerous punishments, chiefly involving incarceration.

In respect of the first problem, we have created a system in which regular use of illegal substances is a factor in mitigation. For example, you or I might prosecute a burglar by saying to the magistrate, 'Not only has he broken into the house, sir, but he also admits to taking heroin on a regular basis and he is, therefore, guilty of two offences.'

In a real-life court, the defence will actually say, 'He is a burglar but, in his defence, he regularly takes heroin.'

This brings us on to the second problem: punishment. The assumption is readily made that the burglar is not in control of his own actions. The burglar is therefore sentenced to a rehabilitation order, the (politically correct) view of the magistrates being, 'If only he was not taking heroin, he would not be stealing.'

Such a view is fundamentally flawed: crime is a moral problem, not a chemical one. Crimes like theft and the use of illegal drugs are committed by people who wish to break the law. They break the law because stealing is easier than working and taking drugs is fun.

Smaller police forces long ago came up with an ingenious solution to the problem of drug crime – have a very small drugs squad (or, better still, don't have one at all). If you make fewer drug arrests, surely you've got a smaller problem?

The bigger forces tend to talk a lot about 'going after the dealers'. I think this means joining the DEA on a cruise around the Caribbean, which is more fun than bashing down the doors of local crack houses. I can see the sense in this – stopping the drugs at source, or as close to the source as possible, is obviously the logical thing to do. But it's also very hard to do and it doesn't address the everyday issues that concern most people. If you have been the victim of acquisitive crime, or you spend your life dodging the detritus of drug users in your local park, you know exactly who you want targeting and they don't live on yachts. They live next door and they burgle and rob anyone they can, they batter old ladies for their pensions, steal benefit books from the mentally handicapped and extort money from kids.

They have no respect for anyone and yet they are free to go about their business virtually unchallenged. Meanwhile, there are four speed cameras for every vehicle on Britain's roads*.

*This isn't *strictly* accurate, but it can't be that far out.

THE ENEMY WITHIN

THE MAJORITY OF AN average patrol officer's work is of no benefit to the community.

For example, two weeks ago I was sent to a house on the outskirts of town to meet a worried mum. Her nine-year-old son was being bullied at school, things were getting physical, she'd had no response from teachers and was at the end of her tether. He'd been beaten up again that day and, in desperation, she had called the police.

A crime number (for assault) was issued and upon my arrival I met a genuinely worried parent.

She welcomed me into her living room, plumped up the cushions and I sat down. 'Thank you for coming officer,' she said. 'I'm sorry to waste your time, but I really don't know what to do. I don't want to make an issue of it but I wonder if you could speak to the children who are doing this and ask them to stop?'

How would you deal with this?

The parent and child had my sympathy, certainly. I wanted to spare them the indignity of youth courts and so on, but I had no idea if the named offenders were guilty or not. I could, technically, arrest the alleged offenders even without a formal complaint from the victim, but in these cases it can do more harm than good. I took a statement from the bullied child and then went to speak to the offenders (cautioning them, advising them of their right to legal advice, ensuring the presence of an appropriate adult and recording my questions and their answers verbatim in my pocket book). They naturally denied everything. Nevertheless, I warned them of the consequences of such behaviour, particularly as they got bigger and stronger and became able to inflict real damage.

So far this had taken about two hours, but I felt I had achieved something: putting the fear of God into a couple of young bullies, putting a young victim on his feet and satisfying the reasonable request of assistance from a troubled parent.

That should have been the end of it: victim happy, police officer happy, probable offenders suitably chastised. I filed the statement and the interview and wrote up a report for my supervisor with a warm glow of self-satisfaction.

But, wait. Remember the crime number that was allocated for assault? That crime is now officially undetected, or unsolved, because the offenders denied it. Government targets have to be met and each crime has to be solved; the number of 'detections', or solved crimes, is crucial. That is why we have Crime Auditors. Two weeks after the bullying incident, I got the file back from the Auditors, together with a typed note telling me I had missed a crucial piece of evidence: the victim had mentioned in his statement that he was with a friend at the time of the incident. This friend could provide corroborating evidence that the assault took place and the crime could then be filed as (administratively) detected (even though no-one would be charged).

This meant I had to contact the friend and get a statement. Furthermore, I also had to get proper statements from both offenders, because they might technically be witnesses.

Earlier, today, a further two weeks later, I finally tracked down the witness (aged 11) and spoke again to the offenders, this time recording what they said in statement form, rather than as a Q&A as I did first time around.

Naturally, they had all taken my advice and were now the best of friends.

My presence, so long after the original incident, was an irritant and I got the distinct impression it might undo all the good work of before.

My warm glow of self-satisfaction has disappeared, but at least the crime can be filed.

Do I serve the community? Or the victims? No, I serve the bureaucrats who go by the name of Crime Auditors.

IRONIC RINGTONES

'COMMUNICATION'. IT'S VITAL in today's police service. Like all good bureaucrats, we like to have things written down so all emails are printed off and filed, computer printouts are photocopied and filed and forms are accompanied by other forms, 'just to be on the safe side', and filed.

The purpose of communication in a bureaucracy is to apportion or shift blame down the organisation as far as possible. Dealing with crime takes a back seat to the all-consuming task of filing, and making sure you are not in the firing line.

As you'll by now be aware, the easiest way of ensuring you get to retirement without having any complaints made about you is to join the ever-growing army of 'vital' support staff performing 'vital' work in offices, dealing with 'crime prevention' or working on 'best-value' and 'best practice' strategies. Their contribution to crime prevention tends to be an 09:00hrs to 17:00hrs, Monday to Friday kind of thing. They're big on modern communication: they send a lot of emails to front-line officers criticising them for not giving out appropriate crime prevention advice to a given punter. In the Police Service, this constitutes 'support'.

The 'Domestic Violence Unit', for instance, might 'support' front-line officers by ordering them to get statements from six-year-old children about incidents that happened two months ago. Unfortunately, we don't have a form for Go and get it yourself.

A month or so back, I had a run-in with this lot.

I'd visited a house where the male had attacked the female and given her a couple of black eyes and a split lip. He was a nasty piece of work, and putting the cuffs on him and leading him down the garden path with all the neighbours watching was a pleasure (though I was sorry for his wife, who was probably mortified).

A week or so later, I got an email from the DVU. 'Is there any CCTV evidence in relation to the assault which occurred in Mrs Carter's kitchen?'

'Is there any CCTV in your kitchen?' I emailed back.

This was an 'inappropriate' response, apparently.

Mind you, modern communications are not all bad. Indeed, I have found a way in which they can brighten up the bleakest day.

It's all because of downloaded ring tones. I have mine set to play D-Ream's classic Things Can Only Get Better. I'll be at a 'serious incident' involving a member of the underclass, and Ms X will be mid-rant: 'My boyfriend's just smashed up my flat, and I haven't got anywhere to live. My dad's gone off with my mate's girlfriend, and she called me a dirty bitch and I can't cope, wot with the kids, shut up you f*cking kids, or I'll lose it, I…'

Suddenly, the Copperfield Nokia sparks into life: THIIINGS CAN ONLY GET BETTERRR, CAN OOOONLY GET BETTER WOOH-OOOH.

Well, it cracks me up, anyway.

SMALL VICTORIES IN THE WAR AGAINST BUREAUCRACY

I'D LIKE TO THANK YOU, the taxpayer.

You're always at the back of my mind, as I respond to emails, fill in forms and photocopy them and write reports.

As the wait for a solicitor goes into its second hour, or I spend an afternoon driving round trying to find a bail address for a prisoner to avoid remanding him, I think of how lucky I am to work for such understanding people.

It's not just me, though; last Saturday night, all four of us were thinking the same thing, though your generosity didn't extend to teabags so we had to buy them ourselves. Even so, we couldn't quite believe our luck.

You each spend about £316 a year on our Criminal Justice System. (This isn't strictly true; it's £316 per head of the population so, when you take into account kids, pensioners and the bone idle, taxpayers actually fork out a lot more than £316. But let's not complicate things unnecessarily.) The total is £19 billion per year.

So, using these figures, a family of four hands over £1,264 per year to be spent on the criminal justice system. In my town, of 60,000 people, that gives a total of almost £19 million to spend on the apprehending, trial and punishment of offenders (obviously, only a proportion of that is spent on the police, the rest goes on prisons, courts, legal aid and so on).

Are you getting value for money?

I'm sure the two boys involved in the bullying/racial incident I dealt with last week would say it's all marvellous: 22 pages of A4 paper, five hours' work, no prosecution.

The drunk and disorderly chap would probably agree: the attention of six police officers and four hospital staff, with a report running to 10 pages of A4, and all for the price of a £50 fine.

The street robber who had three victims certainly got value for money from the courts: he was only charged for one and the other two were 'taken into consideration' (ie ignored).

I'm not sure the elderly street robbery victim I had last week would see things the same way, though. She waited in the station for two hours, her handbag was never found and there was no conviction.

How would *you* spend the money if you were given it yourself, instead of having it taken from you in the form of taxes?

On a three-day diversity course? On a youth liaison worker for the kids? Would you pay for a visit from a crime prevention officer or lots of nice victim support letters? Maybe you would get together with the neighbours, and send a young offender on an 'Enhanced Thinking Course'?

I thought not. So what would you favour? Short or long prison sentences?

Part of the bargain we make with the State is that the State will protect us if we behave and will punish those who do not. A civilised country needs police, not vigilantes. Punishment is handed out fairly, by the State according to laws developed by its citizens. Justice is not dispensed summarily, by private individuals, but by judges acting impartially, based on the evidence before them. If you think the State is spending your £19 billion per year wisely, sit back, relax and stick the TV on. Even supposing you've got this far, you shouldn't be reading this book anyway.

My petty stories are replicated throughout the country, and the effect is that the guilty go free and the innocent don't go outside.

BIG IDEAS

THERE'S BEEN A LOT of talk, recently, about replacing the 43 police forces of England and Wales with one big, national organisation. It's been bubbling away for ages, this idea.

I remember a speech poor old David Blunkett made to the Superintendents' Association a few years back.

I remember it for two reasons.

First, because he made the revelatory suggestion that the more contact people have with the police, the more dissatisfied they become. I thought that was my line – I've been saying it for ages: don't call the police, we won't make you happy.

Second, I remember it because Blunkett floated this idea of one super-force. What a cracking suggestion. After all, we've had massive success with large, nationalised industries in this country before… all those glorious names, like British Leyland, British Coal, British Steel and British Rail.

The idea came back recently (and with the government's mania for centralisation and control freakery, it's no surprise) before it then died down again. I wouldn't write it off for good, though.

Assuming it happens one day, what would we call this new Super Service (let's leave acronyms out of it, for once)?

We'll probably have to spend a few mill getting some branding experts in, but I'll just throw my own hat into the ring first: what about 'The People's Police'? I like it, it's a bit Lady Di and suitably New Labour, and it gets the message across very well I feel. We could rebrand the country while we're at it. How does 'The People's Republic of Freedom' sound?

They'll probably go with something boring like 'The State Police of New Britain'.

Anyway, I can quite see why the Superintendents would like the sound of all this. One big force would give lots more job opportunities to ambitious senior ranks. They could put in for transfers to the seaside, and the Lake District, or the Cotswolds, and there'd be no local accountability at all. Their only boss would be the Minister of State Police. As long as they kept him happy by pandering to the demands of the liberal establishment at the expense of the electorate, it would all be tickety boo.

The State Police probably wouldn't be any more successful at catching criminals, but that's a side issue.

Superintendents, who haven't been out in the streets for a while, are always coming up with big ideas. I remember another recent one. They were much exercised by the fact that people find it hard to get hold of a particular copper when they need one. I can sympathise on this score. On the one hand, we are expected to be at the end of a phone if someone needs us but, on the other, we are expected to be out and about (the obvious solution is mobile phones, but that can't be done; I don't know why, it just can't). As well as being on the beat, the average bobby has to deal with emergency calls, routine calls, the continuing investigation of current cases, continuing inquiries on behalf of the CPS and injured parties who are requesting updates or wishing to complain about him. Furthermore, he will have to schedule arrests and interviews of suspects in ongoing cases, as and when he can find the time. Finally, there are reports to be written about ongoing cases, as well as court files and emails to be answered. Make no mistake, I'm not complaining, I'm simply explaining why it will be some time before I can get round to you.

The Superintendents' great solution to all of this is Call Centres. 'Clients' would be able to phone up and be given a realistic time at which they could expect an officer to arrive at their house and carry out their wishes. My guess would be, sometime in the next two days.

This is a great scheme: as my colleague Mike pointed out, if you set up the call centre in India and called all the employees 'Police Staff', you'd kill two birds with one stone (the other being you would meet all your diversity targets overnight).

Alternatively, people could always continue to turn up to a police station and have their lives sorted out that way. My advice to people going to a police station and wanting to see an actual police officer is: bring plenty to be getting on with. Like a jigsaw, or a big book.

REAL CRIMES

I WENT TO A BURGLARY TODAY.

I've touched before on the thorny subject of what to do if you catch some toe rag rifling through your drawers (answer: nothing, if you know what's good for you) but let's assume you slept through the whole thing.

Next morning, you're left with me, bumbling along in the wake of the thieves. Whenever I go to a burglary, and I go to a regrettably large number of them, whatever the Home Office might say, I reach for the modern English policeman's weapon of choice: the photocopier (double sided, black and white, 40 copies per minute).

I print out leaflets to put into letterboxes asking if people saw anything at about the time of the burglary. I usually do about five houses either side of the attacked property, ten on the opposite side of the street and any other properties that may be significant (shops, garages etc). I also take a detailed statement about what has been taken, the layout of the house, any damage caused and I give the crime number to the injured party. Scenes of Crime Officers will arrive (if they're sure they can finish up before it gets too late) and try to recover things like footprints and glove marks. Finally, I leave a leaflet offering the services of Victim Support and advise the homeowners to take better security precautions in the future.

The victim's faith in the police restored (or not), I leave to return to the police station to write a detailed report of my actions. Then the whole thing gets handed over to the burglary squad. That sounds impressive, but isn't.

In this case, the thieves had left vast amounts of electrical items and so forth and instead stolen bottles of whisky, which was odd and might have pointed the detectives somewhere I suppose.

I probably shouldn't say this, but the thing about burglary is that if you wear gloves and nobody sees you you've pretty much got away with it. There's the odd occasion when you find the property and some evidence pointing to an offender, but that's rare. Most burglaries aren't 'solved' in the traditional sense of the word: they're solved when someone has been arrested for one burglary and confesses to a load of others in order to wipe his slate clean prior to a stretch inside.

Having said that, at least it's a proper crime, with real victims who are distressed and pleased to see you, so I don't mind attending and doing what I can.

It's the fake crimes with idiots treating you like some sort of agony uncle I'm not so keen on.

I'd not been back at the nick for long when a man called Tony Giles came into the police station. The lady who was looking after the front office told me he'd been in yesterday but nobody had been available to see him. In fact, she said Tony had been in about five times before to complain about his ex-wife, Angela. I looked at the incident log. It revolved around a letter he had received from Angela which he thought was quite threatening. After a good five minutes, in which Tony went on about how he kept having to explain his whole marriage to a different officer every time he came to the police station, I read the letter. It wasn't particularly threatening, to my eyes, but then I'm not the sensitive soul that Tony is. Still, the job had a crime number attached (for malicious communications) and I was never going to get Tony to sign something to say that no crime had been committed, so I took a statement and promised Tony I'd be speaking to Angela before too long.

I seem to spend at least half my life on this sort of nonsense.

As I say, I don't mind dealing with honest victims of crime; it's those people who want the police to sort out their lives who really irritate me, mostly because they cut down the time I've got to work with the others.

THIS IS RACISM, MAN

CAN ANYONE TELL ME of any truly successful, truly multicultural society anywhere in the world? I don't think there is one. I don't particularly celebrate this fact, and I'm sure you don't, either. You're an intelligent, thinking person – you wouldn't be reading this book, otherwise – and you have little, if any, interest in the race, religion or 'culture' of the people you rub shoulders with. As long as people keep their music down, obey the law of the land and are generally pleasant, you couldn't give a monkeys whether they're from Bradford, Brazil or Bratislava.

But, sadly, not everyone is as intelligent as you and there are plenty of people in sections of all communities who positively loathe their neighbours. It's all going to end in tears, I fear.

In the meantime, my fond hope is that, one day, I may be able to do my job without being called a Nazi. Today I went to a fight.

A description was passed over the air along the following lines: 'Offender is an Asian male, twenties, yellow T-Shirt, 5ft 5in, medium build, injuries to back of head.'

So I go and have a look and... blimey! There he is!

I stopped him and spoke to him.

'Would you mind just waiting there a second, sir? Only we've had a report of an assault and, well... control, can you repeat the description of the offender, please?'

I made sure the youth was listening in. After it had been read out (and I mean he matched the description to the letter) he said (and I quote), 'This is racism, man. Why aren't you stopping any of those English people?'

I suspect it will be some time before the Police Service adapts and becomes less PC, and realises that this vast social experiment is doomed to fail.

Earlier on I had visited just a nice, liberal-minded person. She was a social worker, and a *Guardian* reader (nothing wrong in that, some of my best friends are *Guardian* readers). As part of an ongoing enquiry, I had to show her the photographs of some offenders. The witness did her best and looked though the snaps, and, inevitably, we fell to discussing the causes of crime.

She furrowed her brow. 'I suppose drugs form a large part of it, wouldn't you say?'

'Criminality forms the largest part of it, Ms Proctor,' I replied. 'That and the fact that they know they can get away with it.'

WHY BRITONS NO LONGER TRUST THE POLICE

I KNOW IT'S NOT FASHIONABLE, but I like some of the writing of Peter Hitchens. I was flicking through an old paper lying around in the canteen the other day when I came across a typically forthright piece.

'How and when did the police become social workers in uniform, drivelling the language of political correctness, soft on crime, obsessed with race and sex equality and hostile to the middle class?' he wrote.

I don't know exactly, but one thing's for sure: the priorities of the police are very different from those of the public.

I often fondly remember my days at training school, where we spent four days on 'Diversity' and about two hours doing burglary (basically, the difference between sections 9(i)(a) and 9(i)(b) of The Theft Act).

During the diversity training, the atmosphere of the course was that of a North Korean Re-education camp, with each person having to make a full and frank confession of his own prejudices.

A list was put up on the board – homosexuals, blacks, Asians and gypsies (socialists, environmentalists and animal rights campaigners were not mentioned) – and we all had to write down traits we associated with each group.

Naturally, at the end of the exercise the instructor then crossed out each word and said, 'Well, they're not all like that.'

Even then, I couldn't think of a more ridiculously simplistic and fatuous exercise.

The course then moved on to discussing how we should all live together, how all forms of behaviour (except racism, child abuse and wife beating) are acceptable and how, with a little give and take, we could all get along just fine.

I maintained my resistance to the idea, saying that certain ways of life were probably incompatible with others and that we probably wouldn't want a society where some people were living under Sharia law in the name of diversity. However, I don't think I made any progress.

The funny thing is, in all my service, no victim has once mentioned diversity, or asked if they could please have a police officer of a different sex or colour. They've usually waited long enough by the time I get there. All they want is their property back and the perpetrator bought to justice.

DEATH DOESN'T DISCRIMINATE

UNLIKE CRIME. Crime discriminates against the poor, with both the perpetrators and victims generally coming from the underclass.

On the estates in the town in which I live, both parties often live next door to one another, and occasionally swap status depending on the day of the week.

A classic case of this arose this weekend.

On Friday night *Shelley* was the victim, having been punched by Sandra in a nightclub.

On Sunday morning, *Sandra* was the victim of Shelley's rude and threatening text messages.

Both victims (who are *also* perpetrators) naturally see the police as the only solution to their problems.

Shelley and Sandra will provide work for me and other officers for many months. I've photographed Shelley's injuries, and in the next few days I'll set aside a morning to interview a friend of hers who was with her in the nightclub and witnessed the assault.

It will take a couple of hours to fill out the form that needs to be sent off with Shelley's phone in order that we can recover the list of text messages for analysis. (Unfortunately, it's not enough just to write down the text messages. For evidential reasons, an analysis has to be done of the phone and the data [the text messages] extracted by a qualified professional.)

How has it come to this?

A once trusted and popular police force that actively patrolled Britain's streets on foot is now driven to investigate the petty personal lives of the underclass. Driving from one set of crime numbers to the next, being careful not to offend or discriminate against anyone, we divide people into either 'Offender' or 'Injured Party'. Even those words are carefully chosen; whatever happened to 'criminal' and 'victim'? The choice of words reflects the widespread liberal belief that 'offending' is understandable because the whole Criminal Justice system – indeed, the whole of society – is a bourgeois creation designed to protect the rich against the poor.

Now those poor are reaping what the liberal elite have sown. Vicious criminals run our council estates, while I delve into the personal lives of sad, bored people like Shelley and Sandra, a uniformed Nero with a paperwork fiddle.

Death, on the other hand, allows the ordinary constable a glimpse into the lives of respectable people. Many people in this country have never spoken to a policeman in their lives (though sadly, as the

State becomes more and more powerful and invasive, more and more people will fall foul of new laws); the only time they do so is when a close relative dies suddenly.

Sudden death is rarely a happy event, although it is often tinged with relief when an elderly person is its subject. For the attending officer, however, it is a not altogether disagreeable experience. He is immediately afforded the respect of those present (a respect he willingly returns) and is able to offer some useful help and advice to people genuinely in need of it.

A man in his late 70s had died suddenly and I was sent out. He lived in a village just outside the town and had been a farm manager for 20-odd years. His wife and children were very polite and grateful that I'd arrived.

'Thanks very much for coming,' said the son.

'Would you like a cup of tea?' asked the wife. 'Alf always has a morning cuppa.'

'Had, mum,' said the daughter.

'Yes, please,' I said. 'I'd love one.'

'Here, mum, I'll make it,' said the son.

'You sit down,' chided his mother. 'I'm perfectly capable of making a cup of tea.'

One thing I have noticed amongst the elderly is a fierce self-reliance that is almost totally lacking amongst the underclass. Naturally, that self-reliance is often tempered with years of illness, but one still detects an independence born out of hardship and making-do.

The modern British underclass, however, has a firm belief in the primacy of its own rights at the expense of everyone else's. It has few needs, beyond the possession of a large television and other shiny electrical baubles and the jingle and rustle of sufficient funds to pay for large quantities of high strength lager each night.

Can these people ever be shifted from the notion that the world owes them a living? I doubt it, or not without a good deal of pain.

SICKNESS

ANOTHER DAY, ANOTHER STATEMENT. Today, a woman called Lorna has called the police because she is having trouble with a male who may well be her ex-partner. I kick things off in the time-honoured fashion. 'What appears to be the trouble, madam?'

'Well, right, what it is, right, is my ex... had enough, see? On drugs... violent in the past... off work... slapped me about... new boyfriend... want my CDs back...'

I drift off, but pick up enough to know it's a domestic registering 2 on the risk assessment scale (no immediate danger).

'What's your full name?'

She tells me.

'Occupation?'

'On the sick.'

'Really? That's a surprise.'

'Yeah, I'm off long term with nerves.'

Are you a 'chronic asthmatic'? Are your children suffering from 'ADHD'? Would you describe yourself as 'on the sick'? Or are you 'off long-term, with stress like'? If you think any of the above applies to you, stop reading this and go back to watching the television. If any of them apply to any of your neighbours, sell up and move house, immediately.

Research shows that the health of the underclass is poor, probably because they have a poor diet, they smoke and drink too much and they do very little exercise.

The nature of health, and particularly poor health, has changed. TB, smallpox and cholera used to stalk the slums, picking off the young and the old alike. Now life expectancy is higher than it has ever been, the food supply is no longer uncertain and medical care is supplied free by the state.

Are we gambolling in the leisure centres with our new-found health? Are we happy and making the most of our longer, almost pain-free lives? Lorna isn't, I can tell you that.

The strange thing is that she doesn't look that ill. She's not particularly fat or nervous (if being nervous is the symptom of the condition known as 'nerves') and she's even wearing a tracksuit and trainers. But she does have a lot of time on her hands, and this is her real problem. Looking on the bright side, advances in medical science mean that Lorna is able to choose from a variety of diseases from which to suffer (in her case, she's chosen nerves although I suspect it's mild depression). Lorna's children have also been diagnosed with a medical condition to excuse their laziness and disobedience: ADHD (Attention Deficit Hyperactivity Disorder), or 'naughtiness' as it used to be called.

The state has also conveniently invented a whole host of new diseases and, through sickness benefit, it actually pays people to have these diseases. How stupid is that? Pay people to be ill, and they will be ill. Pay people to get pregnant, and they will have a baby. Give them a flat, and they'll be at it like rabbits.

After taking Lorna's complaint, updating the log, completing the domestic violence report as well as the (separate) crime report, and then returning to the station to make an entry in our intelligence system, I took my chances with another crime. As luck would have it, it was another interesting response to the government's efforts to improve the health of the nation: Criminal damage to a new health centre.

A *health centre*, can you believe it?

I could understand it, almost, if they were breaking in to steal the contents, but meaningless criminal damage to a social amenity like a health centre? I wonder what would happen if the government of a third world country decided to bring a health centre to a remote village, and some children were found damaging it. They would be lucky to escape with both hands. In Britain, today, they were cautioned.

NEW OFFENCES

AS THE GOVERNMENT becomes increasingly unwilling to punish the guilty, so it develops other offences for which, it feels, it might actually be able to convict people.

Anti-Social Behaviour, for example.

Anti-Social Behaviour is stopped by an order, an Anti-Social Behaviour Order or ASBO. People commit a number of offences and eventually they become the subject of an ASBO, which means that they are not allowed to do certain things, walk in certain streets, visit certain people and so on. Acceptable Behaviour is brought about by an Acceptable Behaviour Contract, or ABC.

I explain these things because they are part of the government's war on Anti-Social Behaviour.

(Enthused by all of this, I suggested my own, very innovative, solution to crime to my chief inspector yesterday. 'Tell you what, sir,' I said. 'Why doesn't the government bring in "Crime Orders", or "COs"? We could use these to ban people from committing crime. Then if someone breached his CO we could, say, lock him up, or something?' 'Are you being sarcastic, Copperfield?' asked the Ch Insp, looking at me with narrowed eyes. 'Or have you been drinking?')

Luke, a rat-like youth for whom the term 'feral' might have been invented, is probably more familiar with the whole ASBO process than I am. His bad behaviour keeps several people in work: his social worker, the people at the children's home where he lives, the psychologist he goes to see occasionally and, of course, me.

In his brief but destructive criminal career, Luke has committed hundreds of offences, as he's happy to admit off-the-record. But he has only been caught for a few (and has been convicted of even fewer).

Today, he's nearly blinded another child with a BB gun, but the victim is too scared to do anything about it and there are no witnesses so Luke will probably get away with this one as well.

Needless to say, I'll have to speak to him at some point, but scheduling his appointments is a nightmare.

Monday's out because he's mountain biking with a youth worker, Tuesday morning is education, Wednesday afternoon is spent with the child psychologist and after that I'm on nights (and as Luke is a child, he can't really be arrested after 22:00hrs).

Surely, the best place for a persistent offender like Luke is jail?

Don't get me wrong, I'm not totally unsympathetic to him. While I'm no pinko liberal, even I can see that a lot of this is probably caused by his dreadful upbringing. If you're alternately ignored or beaten by your parents and then abandoned to the 'care' of the State, it's almost inevitable that you'll turn out rotten. So, given that he's still a young lad, the jail I'd send him to would be designed to introduce some discipline and basic education into his life, and it would do so in a reasonably pleasant environment.

But the main thing is, Luke wouldn't be able to shoot any more children, push any more dog mess through old ladies' letterboxes or spray his 'tag' on any more walls. For a while.

ASBOs, ABCs, Identity Cards, Restorative Justice and the rest of it are all symptomatic of our failure to understand the concept of 'just deserts' ie if you commit a crime, you will be punished, preferably (if you're a bit older than Luke) by having a very unpleasant time in jail.

Jail is totally misunderstood by liberals. 'Look at the reoffending rate,' they say. Yes, criminals reoffend (though they reoffend more after community sentences than prison). They reoffend because they are criminals. They are greedy and lazy people who enjoy breaking the law.

If someone is thrown into jail and they don't reoffend when they come back out, great. If they do reoffend, put them in jail again – only, this time, for longer.

Honest people go out day after day and earn a pittance without breaking the law. Why don't liberals try to 'understand' this behaviour?

SHE'S HARASSING ME/I JUST WANT TO TALK TO HIM

IMRAN HAD BEEN WAITING for half an hour in the front of the police station, while I sat with my head in my hands, preparing myself for yet another examination of some fairly obscene and/or mildly threatening text messages. Eventually, I girded my loins and went to the front desk.

'Have a seat, sir.'

'Right, what it is, right, officer, like, I've been getting these texts off my ex…'

As we progress, it becomes obvious that Imran's real problem is that his ex is white and that his devoutly Muslim parents did not know about, and would not have approved of, their union. Since he broke off their relationship, the sheer weight of the text messages is mounting and he's worried her next move might be a visit to the family home.

'Basically, right, she's harassing me.'

There are a number of factors that make a police officer cry when he hears the word 'harassment':

1. People have generally done nothing to sort out the problem themselves.

2. Because crime numbers get issued at the drop of a hat, the matter cannot be solved without pages of bureaucracy.

3. The people who are being harassed aren't whiter than white in the first place, and are usually harassers themselves. This means that their neighbours/ex-partners/work mates/cyber-buddies will make a counter-allegation of harassment, with all the hassle that entails.

Crying about it won't help me, of course. Here in the UK we have a law against harassment. It was set up with all the best intentions after, to be fair, a couple of quite nasty cases of stalking, and the original intention was to target violent and frightening cases like those. Of course, it's broadened well beyond that now. Nobody likes receiving rude, abusive or threatening text and/or voice messages. But – outside very serious cases, which we actively like to get involved with – is it really a matter for the police? We can't magically improve the quality of your text messages, or stop the rain which must fall into every life, even yours. Many aspects of life which were previously thought of as 'unpleasant' are now 'illegal'. This means that nuisance neighbours and nuisance calls take up as much time as burglary and robbery. Somehow, we need to regain our sense of proportion, the ability to see that nasty texts from an ex-girlfriend are less important than the gang of youths hanging around the old peoples' sheltered housing.

As luck would have it, after a half hour chat, Imran appeared to share my views on the whole affair.

'Look, I don't want to make a big thing of it, like, and get her arrested,' he said. 'That'll just send her mad. Can you just have a word, like?'

I took her details and, when I get a moment, I'll go and threaten Imran's ex with legal action if she doesn't stop.

I'm taking odds in the station as to what she'll say.

3/1: 'It weren't me. Anyway, if it was, I never meant them things.'

2/1: 'I love him and I just want to talk to him.'

Evens: 'He's the one who's been calling me, the bastard. I want him done.'

CURRENT AFFAIRS

HERE ARE TWO OR THREE things I saw or heard recently that I think will prove to be important in the future.

1. Channel 4 News had a story all about obesity. Apparently, it's dangerous and the government isn't doing enough about it.

My solution: Make obesity a crime. I'm a bit short on detail at the moment, but I've sketched out the basis of an idea. I suggest we set up a special police squad, equipped with bathroom scales, forms, a tape measure, more forms, some fat-measuring equipment, some additional forms and a stapler. This squad would be backed up by new 'Stop and Weigh' legislation and they would be able to either arrest you for being fat or issue 'Fat Bastard' tickets which would give you a week to lose weight.

2. File on Four was all about private security firms in Iraq. Quite good, but a bit boring towards the end. The programme clearly wanted a classic left-wing solution to the problem. Britain leads the world in providing security, mainly because of the excellence of our armed forces and our liberal labour laws. At last, something we're really good at. So what do the liberal elite (well, the team at File on Four) want? Why, they want to regulate it out of existence, of course. Get the ex-British Army squaddies out and replace them with disciplined, restrained… er… Russians? Angolans? Bolivians?

And, finally, I loved the story about the female officer who had to organise a trip to a Sikh temple. She wanted to get the people to the temple and at the same time make clear her concerns about the food served at the establishment. Needless to say, this meeting of Health and Safety on the one hand and Diversity and Community Relations on the other was never going to end happily. The poor girl did her best with the following advice: 'Go to the temple, but don't eat the food.' And for that, she was disciplined.

If Political Correctness doesn't get you, then Health and Safety will.

Welcome to the police, and mind how you go.

A QUIET NIGHT

LAST NIGHT WAS FAIRLY QUIET: 15:00hrs till midnight, single-crewed all shift, and finished on time.

I finally got round to speaking to Lorna's hyperactive son, who had witnessed his mum being slapped about by her boyfriend. The boy seemed quiet enough to me but was hopeless as a witness. I took a statement anyway, which didn't really add much to the case, but at least I can't be criticised for not completing all the enquiries.

Then I went to a 'family incident' involving a recovering alcoholic mum (she was on one litre of vodka a day) and her heroin-addicted daughter who, in turn, has a four-month-old daughter by an absent father. Needless to say, all are housed and paid for by UK Taxpayers Ltd.

I always know I'm in a council property because:

a) they have a kind of fuggy, overpowering warmth that you only get if you're not paying the heating bill; and
b) there's always a massive plasma TV and Sky+ box in the corner, permanently on.

Predictably, the heroin addict denied being a heroin addict, saying she had stopped for the sake of her baby, and the alcoholic denied being an alcoholic. I tried denying that I was a police officer, but that didn't work. I've actually forgotten what the problem was now, but it's usually along the following lines: 'Thank God you've come. Our lives are in a right mess. Please can you sort them out in half an hour?'

My answer is usually something like this: 'No, but if I have to come back again tonight one of us will be arrested. And it won't be me.'

Firm but fair, firm but fair.

Finally, I visited another of life's unfortunates, Tracey Kelly. Tracey is a bulimic who is also alcoholic. She had been out boozing all day with her brother, Paul, and he had assaulted her after an argument or, as we say in the police, 'following a verbal altercation'.

She had quite a nasty bruise and was drunk when I got to her flat to take her statement.

'How much have you had to drink, Tracey?' I enquired, genially.

'What's that got to do with you?' she said, with a rather truculent air.

I persisted and she eventually cracked. 'Four glasses of wine, but I've had nothing to eat. I'm bulimic and the only calories I can get are from alcohol. You just don't understand my condition.'

Four glasses of wine? I thought. I meant all day, Tracey, not in the last half hour. I probably should have waited to take the statement, but she was never going to be sober anyway so I pressed on. About an hour (and a couple more glasses of wine) later, I had written everything down and listened to all her family difficulties.

I had also worked out how much carpet I would need for my stairs and hall. About 30 yards, since you ask. I'll probably go for a good quality underlay because the cheap ones are a false economy.

I was trying to get away, but she kept saying, 'I want him arrested now… I'm really scared he might come round after you go.'

I wanted to say, 'Shut up, you mad idiot, you're giving bulimic alcoholics a bad name.'

What I actually said was, 'Don't worry… if he comes round, dial 999.'

Later, I checked our computers and found Tracey been arrested three times before for assault and had made three other complaints to the police following arguments with ex-boyfriends.

THE POLICE ON TELEVISION

WHEN I'M WORKING NIGHTS, I like to watch the reality police shows on TV, like *Street Crime UK*, *Police Beat* and *Extreme Police Brutality*.

Street Crime UK consists of four or five fly-on-the-wall vignettes, usually showing the thin blue line arresting someone for being drunk and disorderly.

Police Beat is similar, but set in the USA and presented by a fat man who holds a cup of coffee. It shows different crimes and a short aftermath (usually an offender being led away in handcuffs).

If you watch these two one after the other, *Street Crime UK* can seem quite embarrassing. In *Police Beat*, all the cops are armed to the teeth. In fact they've got so many guns they can't carry them all, so they have to leave some behind in the car (usually the shotguns). They're all built like brick sh*thouses and they have more computer power in one of their cars than we do in our entire police station. Best of all, though, they don't take any nonsense: they handcuff within a couple of minutes, at the most, and that's an end to it.

On *Street Crime UK*, by contrast, we see the police endlessly negotiating with drunk members of the public, warning them again and again about their language and rarely using the handcuffs, except when there's no alternative. To be fair to the UK bobbies, they know that if they arrest someone, it's going to take three or four hours to process (if it's anything more complex than a Section 5 POA), so that's them off the street for the duration.

I'm sure US officers will tell me I'm wrong, but I think at least part of the reason for this discrepancy between our two systems is that they work in 'Law Enforcement' whereas over here we're all softly, softly.

Guns play an important part too: even if you're drunk, you'd think twice about taking the piss out of a well-built, 6ft 4in 'law enforcement officer' armed with an automatic pistol or a shiny new Remington 12 gauge. I think the gun sends out a message, and that message is this: We are here to enforce the law. We are not wardens. We are not here to sort out arguments between girlfriends. We are not here to be sworn at and we do not warn people – we arrest people, we put them in jail and then we come out again for the rest of you.

MR AHMED AND HIS SON DON'T ALWAYS SEE EYE TO EYE

IN MY POSITION, I'm able to observe the striking gulf between the first and second generation of British Muslims. Through my work, I come into contact with the best of the former and, and all too often, the worst of the latter.

I greatly admire the way that – in common with other Asian groups – older Muslims have such strong family ties and powerful work ethics. Unfortunately, more and more of the younger generation (the men, anyway) appear to be aping the worst of the West: they seem actively to want to lead wasted, dissipated lives of drugs and alcohol, benefits and multiple children by different mothers.

Only the other day I had to visit the Ahmed family in their neat, terraced house on the edge of town. Mr Ahmed had worked in a local factory for nigh-on 40 years after arriving here as a young man. 'Not one day off sick,' he told me, proudly.

Mrs Ahmed had stayed at home and brought up three sons and a daughter. The daughter and the oldest two boys were married off and doing well; the younger boy was causing them, and us, much trouble.

My unfortunate business on this particular occasion was to inform them that he had been arrested for being drunk and disorderly. It clearly pained them both.

'I'm ever so sorry, Mr Ahmed,' I said. 'All I can say is that he'll be out in the morning.'

'I do not understand,' he said. 'You know it's against our religion to drink?'

'Well, yes, I understand that, but your boy had definitely been drinking. Quite a bit, actually. He was causing a nuisance and he started shouting and swearing at the police, so we had no choice.'

'He doesn't work, he doesn't help in the house, he does nothing,' said Mr Ahmed. 'He will never be allowed out again.'

Above the fireplace was a sepia photograph of an old man with his uniform on and a row of medals on his chest.

Mr Ahmed saw me admiring the photograph. 'My grandfather,' he said. 'He came here once.'

'He looks like a good man, Mr Ahmed. Did he like England?'

'Hated it,' said Mr Ahmed, starting to laugh. 'He completely hated it. He stayed here for one month only, then said he never wants to come back. People all rude and too busy.'

I could hardly argue with that. 'You ever take your boys back home?'

'Ha!' he said. 'They are too soft now. They all tell me they miss their friends.'

Mr Ahmed's wish, he said, had always been to make his money, then return home but he'd never quite got round to it. After I had delivered the unfortunate news about his son, he told me he wished he had.

'Would you like something to eat, officer?' asked Mrs Ahmed. 'I was just going to give my husband his dinner.'

I was due a meal break. 'That would be very nice, Mrs Ahmed,' I said. I sat and chatted to them both for the next half hour or so, while we ate a delicious lamb curry. Looking around their tidy front parlour, I couldn't help contrasting the gentility and courtesy with which they had greeted me with the usual reaction of the white trash who inhabit the outer reaches of our society.

Speaking of white trash, I found Tracey Kelly's bother, Paul on my way back to the police station to deal with Mr. Ahmed's son. He told me pretty much what I had suspected: Tracey had drunk herself into a stupor on bright blue WKD and cracked her head when she fell on the steps of the nightclub. I'll check the CCTV tomorrow.

WHERE DOES ALL THE MONEY GO?

I ARRESTED LORNA'S BOYFRIEND today and after speaking to the CPS they decided not to prosecute on the evidence of a woman with no injuries and 'nerves', and her hyperactive son.

What a waste of time and money. It got me thinking. P. J. O'Rourke likes to quote Milton Friedman to the effect that there are four ways of spending money:

1. Spend your own money on yourself.
2. Spend your own money on other people.
3. Spend other peoples' money on yourself.
4. Spend other peoples' money on other people.

In the police, and in the rest of the civil service, it's always Type 3 and Type 4, so those doing the spending don't really give a toss how it's spent.

I bet a lot of it goes on stamping out stealth racism. Don't laugh. Following the huge success of 'Institutional Racism', the race relations industry has now launched a new brand on to an unsuspecting public: 'stealth racists'.

The CRE has produced a report identifying the failure of the police to deal with racist officers. Apparently, the action the police have taken since the Macpherson Report into the Stephen Lawrence killing has simply driven racist officers 'underground'.

So: stealth racists are real racists who are just pretending to be nice. They live amongst us, they are the bottom-dwellers of the oceans of our life, a hidden enemy which must be exposed. Nobody is safe from them and their influence, which is bad.

Where are they? Everywhere. Look at that police officer who just drove past you in his patrol car. Is he a stealth racist? He might be. What about that female officer, the pretty blonde one. Is she one of them? We are now at war with these stealth racists and it is the duty of every one of us to inform the authorities if you suspect anyone.

You've heard this nonsense before? I thought so. As with any scare story it has three key elements:

1. Villains who are undetectable.
2. An unknown number of villains.
3. Villains who are in positions of power.

What kind of radar are these 'stealth racists' avoiding? The liberal radar. So what kind of radar is liberal radar? One which detects warm, fuzzy feelings emanating from a true liberal, no doubt. But, according to the report, libdar is easily confused by stealth racists because they know what to say (words like 'inclusive', 'diversity', 'tolerance' and 'multicultural') and what not to say.

Here are a few of the report's highlights:

'Just as worryingly, evidence from an informed source suggested that many officers had gained little knowledge from their probationary module. Examples included those who did not understand the term "institutional racism", or the difference between prejudice and discrimination and direct and indirect discrimination.'

No? Really? Fancy, a trainee police officer not knowing the difference between prejudice and discrimination. What a scandal. Read on.

'... an officer who claimed never to have heard of the Stephen Lawrence Inquiry Report; another apparently unaware of any legislation on discrimination; and others who could not recall any coverage of diversity in their probationary training or who could not say what it had covered. One former trainee claimed that the trainers had hardly referred to religion, another said they had not gone beyond definitions of racism.'

The plot thickens... this is really making me angry now.

'... another said they had only given out notes, and yet another that he had not bothered with diversity because there were no examinations on it.'

That last bit sounds like me, actually – or anyone who has ever been on a course in their lives (but of course nobody at the CRE, an organisation composed almost entirely of saints).

The report mentions the bureaucracy in the police.

'In November 1999, two police officers were on duty in a police car. One of them was alleged to have said to another motorist, "So, you're deaf as well as black". A complaint was made and after a disciplinary investigation, misconduct proceedings were brought, and the police officer making the comment, and his colleague (for not reporting the offensive remark), were both found guilty and fined. We were shocked to find that the investigation report had 62 pages of attachments, 20 pages of witness statements and 172 pages of interview transcripts. It took over a year for the force to investigate and to refer the file to the PCA and the CPS, and the misconduct proceedings were not concluded until June 2001.'

OK, so the 'deaf as well as black' remark was crass and probably offensive, but 62 pages of attachments, 20 pages of witness statements and 172 pages of interview transcripts? Yep, sounds about right for the British Police. And as for taking just over a year and a half to investigate a complaint? They obviously rushed things because it was a high profile case.

For the record: I'm not a racist – in fact, I'm married to a woman whose skin colour is considerably darker than my own, and whose family roots lie thousands of miles away.

I don't like criminals and I love locking them up, whatever their colour. I do like law abiding people, and I consider it my duty – and my pleasure – to protect them and their property, whatever their colour.

I don't know of any racists among the police officers with whom I work.

I do know a lot of people who find this stuff maddening and time-wasting to the point of distraction.

SIMPLE SHOPLIFTING

'SHOPLIFTER AT HMV… not causing any problems.'

In Newtown police, we grade detained shoplifters as 'priority' calls, and while some officers don't like them, I've never found them any problem. It helps, of course, if you have an English speaking adult who will admit the offence.

As soon as I got into the back office of the store, I knew I wouldn't be having any trouble. It was Pete Wright, Newtown's most honest shoplifter. While Pete sat in the chair, the security guard and I looked through the footage. Pete was standing in front of the display looking around for a minute or so, then he took the computer game off the shelf and scraped the security tag off the underside before slipping it in his jacket and making for the door.

'Did you do it Pete?' I asked him.

'Of course I did, you can see that on the film.'

'Come on then, let's get going.'

I briefly searched him and turned to the security guard.

'Can you do your own statement if I get this lad interviewed?' I asked. He nodded, so I left some paperwork for him and went off to custody.

I wrapped the whole thing up in about three hours, the only slight hiccup being Pete's request for a solicitor. Not a bad way to spend an afternoon, really.

FROZEN TO THE CORE

AS YOU WILL have gathered I'm suspicious of the Commission for Racial Equality (as I am about most publicly-funded quangos). It's not that I don't think there is racism in British society. Sadly, I do. It's not that I don't believe in equality. I do: in fact, I believe in meritocracy, which is surely racially blind, plus the deployment of good manners and general niceness to everyone until they exhibit reasons for behaving otherwise (and even then, I'd rather absent myself from their company than get involved in any confrontation).

As I've said before, if you're a white criminal I'll take delight in locking you up and if you're a black victim I'll try my level best to get you the justice you deserve.

No, the thing about the CRE which worries me is that they have a vested interest in uncovering yet new evidence of racism. I'm not sure how much Trevor Phillips, the 'chair' of the CRE earns, but I bet it's not far shy of £100,000. I don't know how many people are employed by the CRE or what its annual budget is, but I bet the answers are 'a couple of hundred' and 'around £17 million'.

If they cease finding evidence of racism, we don't really need them any more and they all have to pack up and go and find other jobs elsewhere, which can be a bit of a pain.

Of course, the police are an easy target.

In December 2003, the CRE began an investigation into the police after the undercover Panorama documentary 'The Secret Policeman', which showed some quite stupid and unpleasant police recruits being racist. Last year, they finalised and released their report.

It ran to almost 300 pages and made over 100 recommendations.

One of the recommendations was the introduction of a new, police-only, offence of 'racial misconduct' but I've yet to see this appear in any weekly force orders and I have no idea what the definition of racial misconduct will be if it becomes official policy. It could be using racial epithets at work, perhaps. It might be articulating a certain point of view, perhaps that immigration is a bad thing, or that we seem to arrest and charge a disproportionate number of young VMEs (that's Visible Minority Ethnics, as we must learn to call them).

I suspect racial misconduct will turn out to be like Original Sin: we are all born with it, and it will only go when we have seen the multi-cultural light. I look forward to Soviet-style show trials, where police officers confess all their prejudices in public before uniformed juries.

Most of the report went on about how racial equality must be considered in every aspect of policing. So, if the chief comes up with a change in force photocopying policy, it's vital that the general duty to promote racial equality is at the heart of toner changing.

The report also highlights the problem of VME officers being disproportionately subjected to misconduct hearings, rather than being dealt with unofficially as most white officers would be. It's that law of unintended consequences again, though, isn't it? If you were a sergeant or inspector, would you dish out a good, old-fashioned dressing down to an errant female or VME officer, risking accusations of racism or sexism, or would you make it official at an early stage, have everything in writing and cover your backside?

One of my favourite parts in the report is the bit where the problem of screening racist recruits is examined.

It asks: 'Why do a disproportionate number of VME candidates fail the Respect for Diversity test?'

I don't know the answer to this for sure, but I suspect it's probably because white candidates with half a brain know they're the ones who are most at risk of failing it. So they're the ones logging onto the internet and mugging up on the attitudes and phrases required to pass.

We then come to the question, 'Is it possible to screen out racists?' To which most sensible people would say, 'Probably not.'

The report says:

'The question we first sought to address – Does SEARCH [Author's note: Search stands for 'Selection Entrance Assessment for Recruiting Constables Holistically', a system of oral and written tests; why do these acronyms always have to make proper words?] screen out racist recruits? – remains a matter of differing expert opinions. The competency clearly tests general tolerance and considerateness more than attitudes to race equality, even with the revised text. There was broad agreement from within the Centrex E&A (Police Training, Examination and Assessment) section with the observation that the theory underlying this must be that there is a correlation between general "decency" and not being racist, sexist or homophobic etc. As such, it was conceded that the process would not identify a generally enlightened person who had just a particular prejudice, eg against Gypsies and Travellers, Germans or gay people (unless one of the exercises happened to be about that group) but it was stressed that no system is absolutely watertight. The contention that there could be a direct psychological test for racism was contested, and indeed Centrex is publishing a critique of a number of different psychological instruments which claim to be able to do this. There appears to be no objective way of testing whether any given scheme has screened out the right people, and only the right people.'

I think we might be moving to the kind of test where brainwaves are monitored by attaching receptors to the scalp as the candidate is shown reruns of Snatch and Das Boot and forced to read the works of Joe Orton: 'OK, that's covered gays, Germans and gypsies. Let's see how he responds to Cockneys. Nurse, switch on Eastenders.'

If you aren't yet in the business of advising the police about, or providing training in, race and diversity, I advise you to get in now, because the future's bright. Similarly, if you are actually in the police then you need to get in to a department responsible for implementing and creating race and diversity policy.

COMPLAINTS

LIKE I SAY, I don't have a particular animus against the CRE. I feel the same way about the IPCC.

When I received my first complaint, a wizened old copper took me on one side to impart a pearl of wisdom (time-served, silverback sergeants are always doing this to young bobbies).

'Dave,' he said. 'If people aren't complaining about you, you probably aren't doing your job right.'

That's as may be, but things are different these days. As far as the modern police service is concerned, complaints are filed in the same sections as mud (sticks) and smoke (none without fire). The complaint may be utterly without foundation and you might be completely exonerated but the faint whiff of trouble will accompany you wherever you go. It's doubly worse if the allegation was one of racism, sexism or homophobia, naturally. It's no exaggeration to say that a small series of complaints with no basis whatsoever in truth can harm your career.

Thus, most policemen and women – at least, those with any ambitions – tend to go to great lengths to avoid being complained about. The best way of doing this, of course, is to get yourself behind a nice big desk as quickly as you can. The thing to avoid at all costs is dealing with the public, face to face.

So, what do you think is the most common complaint made by the public about the police?

Racism? No.

Corruption? Hardly.

Brutality? Pah! Why would I want to beat a suspect up? To get a confession? What for? I won't get paid any more.

No, the main source of complaints is rudeness. The public hates incivility on the part of police officers more than anything else. It's funny, that, given that they're always calling us pigs and telling us to f*ck off, but there you go.

I try to maintain an outwardly respectful and cheerful demeanour at all times. I always call members of the public 'Sir' or 'Madam', if they're over the age of 21 and pay their taxes. You don't have to mean it, but a bit of old fashioned courtesy goes a long way. I also keep quiet wherever possible – just long enough for the other party to run out of steam or get bored with the sound of their own voice (which can take a while). After all, if you're not talking, you can't be accused of being rude (as long as you're not openly flicking the Vs). And I'll always phone back later to check everyone is happy with whatever it is I've done. I like to ask two or three times, just so that they remember. It only takes a couple of minutes and people appreciate it. It can be hard to be polite, though, and sometimes it's impossible.

Traffic accidents are a case in point. Police officers and other emergency crews put themselves at great risk when they attempt to block roads and divert traffic and members of the public are at greater risk when they approach such obstructions. A long, detailed explanation of why a motorist cannot proceed is not only unnecessary, it is also dangerous. When some bozo pulls up alongside me, tells me he's late for the office and demands to know what the hell is going on, obviously I would prefer to say, 'An accident has occurred ahead, sir. It involved a goods vehicle and a car. I do not know, at this stage, whether or not there are any casualties and, while I appreciate that you normally use this route for work, I hope you understand not only that the road has to remain closed for the paramedics and our investigation but also that you are in a dual carriageway and the traffic is moving very fast. You are in a dangerous position and you are putting my life, your own life and the lives of other motorists in danger, sir.'

What I actually end up saying is, 'Don't stop there, keep going.' If he argues, I say, 'Don't argue, or I'll lock you up. Now, move.'

Off he drives, fumbling with his mobile to get the number for the Independent Police Complaints Commission; orders given in loud voices by policemen are grist to the ever-turning mill of the IPCC.

Most complaints by the public are 'informally resolved' with some advice to the officer concerned being given by his Inspector and some sort of apology to the complainant.

Very few go all the way to IPCC hearings or, worse still, the courts (deaths in custody and fatal road accidents involving police vehicles spring to mind as exceptions). The whole discipline and complaints procedure is lengthy and complex so I don't intend to go into it here, but it's certainly thorough: the best detectives are always in the complaints department.

I had another complaint made against me a couple of months ago. It was entirely unexpected; I actually had to use the computer logs to jog my memory about the incident and then talk to a colleague who'd been there to work out if I'd been in the wrong.

'It was a domestic where the man drove off in her car. She reckoned we should have arrested him.'

'He wasn't there to be arrested and she didn't know where he'd gone, so what's the complaint about?'

'No idea. Speak to PSD.'

This was enough to bring me out in a sweat. I had to account for myself to someone from the Professional Standards Department (the police who police the police), which was difficult because I couldn't remember what I'd said, either. It turned out neither could the complainant – it was my general demeanour she objected to. It was all 'informally resolved' in the end, but it left a nasty taste in my mouth, particularly as I now have a black mark on my record when I've never actually done anything improper and certainly not illegal.

Of course, this won't worry the good folk of the IPCC. The organisation employs many people (over 250) at great expense (over £20 million per annum) and if it weren't for all those moaning minnies they'd all be looking for new jobs, along with the staff of the CRE.

The IPCC needs your support, so my advice is this: go ahead, and put it in writing. There is absolutely no quality control in police complaints, so yours will be looked at and, you never know, you might even get some compensation (if anyone knows the hourly rate for unlawful detention, let me know).

As for me, I'll be like 99% of all the other police officers I know: I'll remain placid and easy-going whatever the situation. Whatever pressure I may be under, I'll repeat the traditional mantra to myself: Think about the pension.

IT WASN'T ME, THE BEER JUST WENT MAD

THE GOVERNMENT NOW acknowledges the fact that young men in England love drinking beer and fighting.

Actually, that's not strictly true. What the government actually acknowledges is that 'binge drinking' is a problem in 'society'. That's great news for the police. We've **always** had a problem with binge drinkers, believe me. Now, at last, with Ministers, sociologists and academics on the case, maybe the problem will be solved?

One thing to bear in mind, first of all: apparently, the problem is 'extremely complex'. Don't make the elementary mistake of assuming it can ever be solved by punishing the guilty more severely, more often. Oh, no. What it needs is A Study. The results of the study will be published and a number of recommendations made. Any sensible recommendations will be ignored and young English males will still enjoy drinking beer and fighting.

For a taste of how complex the problem is, I direct you to Fiona Measham, a lecturer in Criminology at Lancaster University.

In the *Sunday Times*, she points out the following as causes of the problems of excess drinking:

1. A change from weak beer to strong beer.
2. New pubs designed for young people.
3. Long working hours.
4. People are more hedonistic than they used to be.
5. The growing sophistication of advertising by the drinks industry in response to ecstasy (the recreational drug which was perceived as a threat to their profits).

Does Ms Measham get paid for all this? By whom? Can I have some? The problem of excessive drinking has two causes:

1. People enjoy it.
2. People don't suffer the consequences of their excess, except medically and then only really in the long term.

DRIVING COURSE

I HAVE BEEN ON another driving course these last few weeks, and much fun it has been, I can tell you.

The thing about courses in our force, is that

a) they take about twice as long as necessary
b) the training department contains twice as many people as it needs to;
and
c) most of the courses are a waste of time and a statement of the bleeding obvious.

Still, if I'm not going to be called a pig or a bastard for a few weeks, and will be paid by the taxpayer to drive around the country enjoying the views, I'm not going to say no, am I?

I passed the course, which means I'll be able to get to an incident just after it has happened, rather than quite some time after it has happened.

I'm in two minds about police driving: on the one hand it's good to drive fast to a burglary in progress or an officer assistance call, but the rest of the time it's a waste of effort. Almost invariably, you get there and it's all over, leaving just the paperwork to complete and possibly someone to be arrested. -

The other thing about police driving is that you always seem to get drawn to vehicles rather than criminals.

For example: Car Tax. I don't doubt that it's an offence to drive a car without displaying a tax disc but, on the other hand, have we not got other things we could be doing? If the Inland Revenue want the tax so much, can't they can come and get it themselves?

I haven't been able to get away completely from work though. Modern technology means that wherever you are you can always pick up your e-mail and voicemail messages. On my return to the real(ish) world, I found a dozen or more voicemails – including some from Tony (about his ex-wife Angela) and Lorna (asking why her boyfriend won't be 'getting done'). Some problems just never seem to go away.

THE POOR ARE ALWAYS WITH US

ONLY NOW THEY'RE FAT and have DVDs and satellite television and gallons of lager to swim around in.

The Government is trying to convince us that if only they got out more this would help save the country money and stuff (I'm paraphrasing in my own ham-fisted way, of course). From a law enforcement perspective, I'm not so sure it would help all that much. From my point of view, people who are too fat usually can't be bothered to leave the house to commit crimes, especially if Noel Edmonds is on TV, and, if they do, I can catch them if they start running.

The lager thing is interesting, too. Sometimes it causes crime, other times it prevents it. This was brought home to me the other day when I was investigating another typical slum-crime, a trivial assault. They'd drunk too much but, at the same time, curiously, not enough. Enough to start fighting, not enough to just doze off.

I was getting a statement from a witness to the fight and asked her at what time the incident had occurred. She named the time with some certainty.

'Are you sure it was then?' I said.

'Yeh,' she replied. 'I know it was, 'cos Big Brother was just about to start.'

Television is the permanent backdrop to life in the slums, a kind of electronic anti-depressant.

Looking at my pocket book and the custody record, I see that this whole process took in excess of six hours.

I SEE NO SHIPS

A REFERENCE TO NELSON at last.

In particular, a reference to the fact that, despite being in extreme peril, facing the real possibility of defeat, and death, Nelson did his duty: he put his telescope to his eye patch and said that he could see no ships, even though the enemy were close at hand.

I'm sure that by now revisionists are hard at work proving that Nelson never actually said this, and that he was really gay ('Kiss me Hardy') and a cross-dresser, and a BLT or TLDG, or whatever the trendy acronym is this week.

If Nelson was in the British Police Service today and did a similar thing, he'd have been investigated for neglect. I can imagine the enquiry: had Nelson actually been on the telescope-handling course? Why were there so many white males in charge of ships? And was it really necessary to engage the enemy, anyway? Couldn't he have sent over a small boat with some trained negotiators?

Ultimately, I think that Nelson's blindness and single-handedness would have worked in his favour, and he'd probably have been exonerated. If he'd had two working eyes and two arms, though, he'd have been history.

All this got me thinking, and I have decided to create a special award for blindness in the face of farce, hereafter called the I See No Ships Award.

My first I See No Ships Award is to be jointly shared by Sally Davies, 'Community Contact Officer for the Eastern Sector of Peterborough', and Tom Lloyd, the former Chief of Cambridgeshire Constabulary (sacked in 2005 for misconduct), for the following press release which came to my attention:

'Dear All
The first Anand Mela (or joyous fete/gala) took place on the Embankment in Peterborough over the weekend.

The first event of its kind in Peterborough was organized by a number of Indian Community organizations, together with some statutory and voluntary organizations. The event had an array of stands, which celebrated such things as Indian fashions, cuisine, arts, sports and dance.

The Police also took the opportunity to mingle with organizers and the visiting general public and Police personnel manned a display stand, in order to answer questions and give out advice on a career in the Police Force.

Tom Lloyd, the new Chief Constable of Cambridgeshire Constabulary, also attended on the first day of the event, having spent the morning witnessing a number of new initiatives which have been implemented on the Welland Estate and paying a visit to the new mosque, which is under construction in Central Ward.

The visit by the Chief Constable gave him the opportunity to view at first hand some of the projects and initiatives that local Community Beat Officers have been involved in, in addition to meeting some of the key community representatives.'

Nice, I'm sure you'll agree. It's there in the first line: Mela = joyous fete-slash-gala.

But wait, what's this appearing in the *Daily Telegraph*?

Multicultural festival ends in punch-ups

A festival to celebrate a city's multiculturalism ended with rival ethnic groups involved in running street battles. The East of England Anand Mela festival was organised by the Indian community in Peterborough to demonstrate its culture, music and food. But about 90 Pakistani and Iraqi youths exchanged blows and hurled chairs on Saturday night.

When police broke up the battle, clashes continued in the city centre. Further fights broke out on Sunday. Police brought in reinforcements from other parts of Cambridgeshire and Essex. Tensions in the city have been running high between the long-established Pakistani community and recent immigrants from Iraq, mostly Kurds.

Jayshree Mehta, the festival organiser, described the trouble as 'a scuffle'. She said: 'Fireworks were displayed afterwards and it was a lovely day.'

So while Sally and Tom and were looking at saris and sampling the onion bhajis, bobbies from across the East of England were struggling to contain 'a scuffle', which sounds rather more like World War Three, with Iraq and Pakistan battling for supremacy.

The Anand Mela Website says 'East England Anand Mela went with a bang at The Embankment, Peterborough'.

Yes, quite.

Cambridgeshire Constabulary has its own Race Equality Scheme. The introduction says: The Race Equality scheme further conveys Cambridgeshire Constabulary's commitment to race equality. The CRE Leadership Challenge is being progressed and a whole range of other initiatives to mainstream equality are also being implemented. We will do whatever we can to achieve racial harmony.

My suggestion: Let's have more multicultural festivals. Sally and Tom can referee, and may the best side win.

AMBITIOUS HEROIN ADDICTS

I'VE MET MANY heroin addicts in my time.

There are two alternative reasons for the prevalence of these people in modern Britain. (They may not be apparent to you where you live but, trust me, they're like rats; you're never more than 50 yards from one. Or something like that.)

1. Ordinary people are being approached by evil drug dealers. These ordinary people are then plied with heroin. Once they have tried the drug, they find it irresistible and, in order to pay for it, adopt a life of crime.

2. Bored, easily-led, amoral, recidivist criminals enjoy the feeling they get when they take heroin. Such people have no interest in anything other than their own immediate pleasure. In order to get heroin, they commit crimes in the knowledge that they'll have a good long run before they get caught and that the punishment will be a joke.

Naturally, I favour explanation (2) over explanation (1).

Today, though, I had to put aside all my prejudices because Newtown's most honest (and most unsuccessful) shoplifter, Pete Wright, reported a crime against him. Pete's a nice enough chap, but will steal anything that isn't nailed down (and attempt to loosen anything that is). For that reason, I left everything I could in the car, taking only the essentials: a pen and some paper.

Although Pete's flat was a complete mess, with barely any surface free from dirt and rubbish, the roll of tinfoil was the only evidence of drug addiction. He chucked some stuff on the floor so I could sit down and pointed out the smashed window where he claimed the burglars had made their entry. Yeah, right. But with no evidence to the contrary, I took him at his word and recorded the details of this 'crime'. The general idea was that if Pete could persuade his paymasters at the Benefits Agency that his money had been stolen, rather than used to buy drugs, they would give him an emergency payment with which to buy more drugs (another good example of the police working in partnership with other agencies without consulting local taxpayers).

Pete is 23 and has lived in Newtown all his life. He has been on drugs for about five years now and has managed to stay out of trouble (and prison) so far. But his paler complexion and skinnier build were obvious signs that he was taking far more heroin than he used to. When I first met him, he had been dumped by a girl, lost his job and his parents were concerned about him. But he was still able to lie about the drugs, was still picking up some agency work and, living at home, was fed and looked after.

Now, Pete is at Stage Two of his descent into moral depravity. He still wears his baggy designer coat, designer trainers and the latest tracksuit. But he has lost all his non-addicted friends, his family have thrown him out and he's shoplifting.

Stage Three is burgling people's houses and Stage Four is prison.

With the formalities over, we started talking.

'Look, Pete,' I said. 'I can tell you now how this story will end if you don't pull yourself together.'

'What do you mean?' he asked, as though he had absolutely no idea what I was talking about.

'You're spending a couple of hundred quid a week on heroin, and you're only on benefits of £75,' I said. 'Shoplifting's one thing – not that I'm condoning it – but I've seen lads like you move on to stealing mobile phones off children or forcing your way into old ladies' houses. You carry on like this, you'll do something really stupid and then you'll be going to prison.'

He looked at me, wide-eyed. 'You've got me all wrong, Dave,' he said. 'I'm going to get back into catering.'

Like many addicts, Pete's powers of self-delusion are stronger than his self-disgust.

BORED? NOTHING MUCH TO SAY?

WORK IN THE POLICE? Then why not 'Send an email.'

As a patrol officer, I get an average of four or five emails per day, mostly of the 'round-robin' type ie they are sent to everybody in the organisation regardless of relevance. I make a point of deleting them en-masse.

Often they concern new legislation or force policies. Quite often, there is one that says something like, Did an officer deal with a Mr. SMITH in the Newtown area last week? Mr. SMITH wishes to make a complaint about the incident. Would the officer concerned please come forward.

Let's hope no-one gets killed in the cyber-rush for that one.

Another might be, Officers are reminded that the SHINING PATH is a South American Terror organisation. Any suspected members are to be reported to your local Special Branch.

Well, it's good to know we have a Force Policy with regard to the Shining Path. I'm sure you feel a lot safer in the knowledge, too, particularly if you're on our patch and you're a member of the Peruvian establishment.

Occasionally, you get an absolute gem. Some eagle-eyed fellow officer in another force sent me this one. Before you read it, remember that, because crime rates are falling so fast in the UK (no, really, honest, they are), we in the police have more time to think about other stuff like Health and Safety. In this particular force – which must regrettably remain un-named – a whole committee is examining figures in minute detail. Here is part of the email: 'This process [the examination of Health and Safety data] has identified that over a three year period, between July and October the number of accidents, incidents and assaults have increased in [this division]. The actual reasons for the increase are difficult to identify and are influenced by numberous (sic) factors. Would all Police Officers and Police Staff please be aware that accidents, incidents and assaults increase over the period July to October. Therefore, extra caution is required in carrying out our daily work activities in an attempt to DECREASE the numbers.'

What are the 'numberous factors'? Why are they keeping them secret? And what do they expect the coppers to do in these four unusually dangerous months? Drive really slowly to jobs? Only arrest people weighing eight stones or less? Be extra careful when tying their shoelaces?

CRIME REPORTING

THE MOST IMPORTANT part of any crime report is the section labelled 'ethnicity.'

The other day I met a young woman who had suffered a double misfortune.

First of all, she had been the victim of a crime. Secondly, she had reported it to the police.

She hailed from the island of Bali (why anyone would want to leave Bali for Newtown is *literally* beyond me) and had an Indian father and Malaysian mother. English was not her first language, but fortunately her English-speaking fiancé (a solicitor) was able to help with the translation. They made a delightful couple, and it was a pleasure to speak to someone with such an unusual and interesting background. All was well until we got to the section called 'ethnicity.'

We record someone's ethnicity to ensure that they are treated differently according to their needs. (Or is it, the same to ensure we don't discriminate against anyone? Or differently, to ensure that under-represented groups are encouraged to contact us? Or the same, to ensure that everyone receives the same treatment? I'm not immediately sure. Anyway, for me, it's a box that needs a tick.)

I tried a number of questions.

'What nationality are your parents?' and 'What country do you come from?' were my first gambits, but neither really got us close to defining her ethnicity.

I tried, 'How do you see yourself?' but failed to extract more than a quizzical look.

Eventually, the girl's husband-to-be threw his hands in the air and said, 'What colour are you?'

We filled in the form as O9 (other).

The government system of racial classification would be familiar to anyone with experience of South Africa under apartheid. The 'Pass Laws' classified people as (broadly) Blacks, Whites or Coloureds.

For the record, we classify people in two ways.

Firstly: Appearance as identified by Officer:

White
Black Caribbean

Black Other
Indian
Pakistani
Bangladeshi
Chinese
Other (I know it's only 8th on the list, but it's still 09)

You might think this is quite complex enough. Oh, no.
There is a second classification, namely Self-Classification by Victim:

White British
White Irish
Any other white background
White & Black Caribbean
White and Black African
White and Asian
Any other mixed background
Indian
Pakistani
Bangladeshi
Any other Asian background
Black Caribbean
Black African
Any other Black background
Chinese
Any other Ethnic group
Not stated – Declined
Not stated – Did Not Understand

I am happiest explaining this system to Kurds, of whom we seem to have an unusually large number in my town. They have lots of jolly patriotic folk songs which they not only play on their gramophones at high volumes, but also sing. I begin by saying:
    'Where are you from?'
    'Kurdistan.'
    'So what nationality are you?'
    'Kurdish.'
    'So how would you define your ethnicity?'

'Kurdish.
'I don't have a box for Kurdish.'
'I am Kurdish.'
'Right sir, the nearest I've got is O9 (other).'
'That is Kurdish?'
'Oh yes, it most certainly is, sir.'

CRIME REPORTING (II)

AND ANOTHER THING. In addition to the large racial element to police crime reporting, we also have to report how the victim and offender (and in many cases, as you know, there isn't a lot to choose between them) are related.

Here is the list of choices:

Partner – living separately
Partner – living together
Brother or sister
Step-brother or sister
Son or daughter
Parent or guardian
Work colleague
Friend
Acquaintance
School colleague
Stranger
Neighbours
Former partner of intimate relationship
Family – other
Same sex relationship
Forced marriage

Look closely, and you begin to realise just how poisoned by political correctness we really are. 'Marriage' is only referred to in context of it being 'forced'. The best you can hope for, even after years of wedlock, is 'Partner – living together.' Being a 'parent' gets the same tick in the box as 'guardian'.

Quite why any of this is necessary, anyway – any details relevant to the offence will be in statements – is anyone's guess. It couldn't be that we're collecting data for some huge social experiment, could it?

HEALTH & SAFETY

AS YOU MAY KNOW, this book sprang out of an online blog called, with dashing originality, The Copper's Blog.

It's had around 1.5 million hits since it started, so I must have been doing something right. People send e-mails and comments and most of them are positive. Those who don't like what I write, and there must be some, generally don't bother to read on or contact me, I guess.

There are those people who doubt my policing bona fides, however.

I recently logged on to a Police Forum called PoliceUK. It's a good site if you want to join the police, offering encouragement, tips and advice to new people, which can only be a good thing. On this particular day, they were debating me and my writing.

I can't resist repeating one post:

'I have read his "blog", and find it hard to accept that he is for real, because in my opinion (if found out) he would be in danger of being disciplined for one of potentially many offences against the discipline Code of Conduct ie "Politeness and Fairness", "Confidentiality", and the catch all – "General Conduct" (bringing discredit upon the service). Some of his comments depict the police in a bad light, and likely to cause offence to some members of the public. Regarding a burglary he says 'The thing about burglary is if you wear gloves and nobody sees you then you've got away with it, the only real line of enquiry then is if you use any stolen credit card and you can be traced on CCTV.' Pretty defeatist if you ask me. What about DNA, marks left by tools, footprints, modus operandi, stop check intelligence, use of informants? There is a wealth of actions you can take at the scene of a burglary. This guy sounds extremely lazy. If he is for real I would lock him up for

175

obtaining property (his wages) by deception. In light of most Police Forces in the UK having extremely skilled Computer Crime Units, I suspect his attempts at anonymity could be quickly unveiled and "Professional Standards Department" breathing down his neck, and I don't think the "NONE OF THIS IS TRUE, IT IS ALL FALSE" line at the top of the page will help him out either. And good riddance, too.'

Ha, ha, ha. I'm guessing that was written by someone at the Home Office.

A lot of people send me very funny things. One piece of correspondence concerned Health and Safety, a new religion in Government circles and something which has been worrying me a great deal. It all started when Mrs C was served a glass of white wine in a plastic pint glass at our local. The reason for this was that she had decided to drink it outside where there might be 'kiddies playing'. A chap called Mike sent me a fascinating story he'd picked up from the website of the Health and Safety Executive.

HSE staff burn payslips to protest over bad deal

Staff at the Health and Safety Executive will undertake a series of protests across the country tomorrow (Friday) following a decision by HSE management to impose its pay offer. Members of the specialist union Prospect will demonstrate outside HSE's London headquarters at Rose Court, Southwark Bridge at 9am, and St Hugh's House, Bootle at 11.30am, to burn their payslips in protest at the decision.

As Mike points out, 'Isn't burning payslips dangerous? What next, standing on chairs to change light bulbs?'

LITTLE TINKERS

IT IS WITH SOME difficulty that I manage to contain my joy at the arrival of another community of gypsies. 'Living the dream' is one phrase that springs to mind, as the odour of diesel fumes merge with the smell of freshly cut leylandii and used nappies at the itinerants' site.

'Diversity' and 'tolerance' demand that police officers accept those whose way of life is different from their own, and fair enough. If you want to live in a caravan, that's your affair (though I can't understand why, round by us at least, so many of them end up parked on industrial estates and waste ground. If I could go and park up anywhere, I'd park somewhere with a view of the sea).

Whatever, some gypsies do make it hard for us to tolerate their diverseness, a position shared, I imagine, by most people who choose to live in houses and pay their taxes. Without generalising, and I'm sure there are lots of honest travellers who pay their taxes, steal nothing and do a lot of work for charidee, the two main problems I come across with the wrong kind of gypsies are that they nick stuff and inadequately resurface driveways. I often wish that they were as good at the latter as they appear to be at the former.

The one thing you can say about gypsy criminality is that their lifestyle does give them a headstart when it comes to dodging the law.

I once arrested a gentleman of the road for stealing scrap metal off a building site. Because he gave his address as a caravan site hundreds of miles from Newtown, it was decided that the only way to ensure he attended court was to keep him in custody and put him before the court the next day.

The magistrates obviously took a different view. I arrived at work the following day to see the chap leaving court and getting into a Transit van. He was never seen again.

Magistrates have been on diversity courses and are sometimes reluctant to imprison people who appear to have a perfectly adequate address.

MURDERING BASTARDS

FIRST THING IN the morning, the sergeant hands out the assignments for the day.

Today, I got Ray the Lemon, via the medium of a thick folder of documents about him which flew across the room at me. Reading through, it appeared that Ray hadn't learnt about domestic violence from the last time I locked him up. He had got drunk and then smashed up some property belonging to his ex-wife, the eternally apologetic Linda. My job for the day was to fill in the blanks in the case of R v Ray and then interview him.

To add to the general excitement in the station, someone had been murdered and the suspects were in Newtown custody.

The arrival of a party of murderers always creates something of stir in my police station, so much so that the car park, always full to bursting from 09:00hrs until 17:00hrs on weekdays anyway, begins to look like a car supermarket, with people driving round and round trying to find a space. It was hellishly busy in custody, too. In contrast to the routine drunken domestic nonsense that I deal with, a murder means the arrival of squads of important detectives. Alongside them, there were armies of defence solicitors, all seeking 'disclosure' from the detectives and 'consultation' with their clients. Interview rooms, normally empty, were full and consultation rooms (where clients confidentially discuss things with solicitors) were hard to find.

Orchestrating the whole circus was the custody sergeant. He was busily ensuring the murderers were properly looked after and that their whereabouts within the custody block were monitored, as well as deciding on bail and reviewing evidence with the many detectives. Did you notice I said, 'the many detectives'? That's in contrast to the small number of uniformed officers: ie, me.

By about lunchtime, I had sufficient evidence to interview Ray and, after briefly speaking to his solicitor and running the gauntlet of detectives, I finally saw him in the calm of an interview room which had been temporarily vacated by the CID. He was familiar with the process; he'd been locked up numerous times for getting drunk and trying to 'discuss domestic matters' with Linda. So we were soon off through the preliminaries and into the details of Ray's accident with his ex-wife's water feature.

'So Ray,' I said. 'Tell me about this fountain.'

'I put it up years ago when we got married,' he said. 'It was broken so I thought I'd fix it.'

'And why did you decide that last night would be a good time to fix it?'

'Well, I'd had a few drinks and I saw her new boyfriend...' Ray tailed off.

Owing to the cans of special-strength lager Ray had drunk before smashing up the fountain (or fixing it, depending on your point of view), he couldn't remember the exact details.

'So, you were just fixing some things around the house... at midnight... in the dark?'

'Yeah.'

'OK, Ray. If you were just fixing the fountain, as you claim, why did you try and run off when the police turned up?'

'Well, I knew you lot would nick me as soon as you saw me. Look. She just winds me up, all the time. Even when I just go round to see her.'

After some further discussion, Ray changed his story somewhat and sheepishly accepted Linda's account, which was that he had deliberately smashed up the fountain prior to attempting to escape through a new wooden fence at the rear of the garden. The fact that he failed to escape through the fence is testament to his ex-wife's current partner's vastly superior skills in DIY, a bitter irony not lost on Ray. We signed the forms and with some regret, left the calm of the interview room for the whirl of the custody desk.

I told the sergeant what had happened on interview and bade farewell to Ray as he completed his legal aid forms.

As I left, I was accosted by a detective.

'Can you tell me where the interview forms are, chief?' he said. 'And your pens?'

'Third drawer down, second column from the right,' I replied, helpfully. 'Pens in the cupboard over there.'

Those murderers have had it now.

INFREQUENT FLIERS

IN CONTRAST TO people like Ray, innocent people are all too often involved with the police. My heart always sinks when I'm forced to deal with an innocent person, be they victim or (sometimes) alleged offender.

Regular victims like Linda know where to sign the forms, they know how to get an officer to attend their address and they know who their offender is.

Infrequent victims assume that the police only deal with major crime and that that's why we can't attend immediately.

The house of the infrequent victim is often hard to find because I simply don't go there all that often. But when I do go inside it's usually immaculate. Tea is served in clean cups and cake is consumed.

Yesterday I met Roger Johnson. Roger was a man who's never had so much as a parking ticket before. However, he is unfortunate in that he has a middle-aged multiple divorcee ex-girlfriend who is a lunatic. There are a lot of these about. She made an allegation of assault last month, but a pile of other cases has meant that it's taken until now to get round to dealing with it. The allegation is one of those 'either way' jobs, in that there's no evidence either way: she says it happened, he'll deny it, she has a very minor bruise which she could have got anywhere and he's never come to our attention before.

I spoke to Roger on the phone and he agreed to come in, but when I actually arrested him at the police station he couldn't believe what was going on.

'An "allegation of assault"?' he said. 'But that's ridiculous. Have you got any evidence?'

'Not really, no.'

'So why are you taking her side, then?'

'I'm not, it's just that she says you hit her.'

'Oh I see, so if I said she'd hit me you would arrest her, would you?'

'Yes, probably.'

'But that's ridiculous.'

'You're telling me. Look Mr Johnson, there's no evidence against loads of people I arrest. I wasn't there, I didn't see it with my own eyes, I'm just doing my job.' He stared at me. I pressed on. 'To be honest, not being personal, but I couldn't really care one way or the other. I just take the statements, arrest people and then someone else decides what to do. You seem like a reasonable person, just listen to what's going on and the sooner we get going, the sooner you can go home.'

In the custody suite he declined legal advice. I asked him why he was doing this.

Mystified, he said: 'Because I've done nothing wrong.'

Lots of people who are unfamiliar with police procedure do this and it sounds like common sense. You've not committed any crime, so why would you need a lawyer?

The fools! Have they no idea? Do they assume that common sense plays *any* part in police procedure?

INVOLVED IN A SCUFFLE? CALL US

I HAD A BUSY NIGHT last night, when I locked up two young men for brawling outside one of our less salubrious 'nitespots'.

It was the usual thing: they'd got tanked up on lager and WKD alcopops and then lost their senses of humour.

These days, this sort of thing doesn't just happen to the underclass.

A while back, Prince Harry – ie the Queen's grandson, of all people – was involved in a scuffle with a photographer outside a nightclub (I'm not saying Harry was drinking lager and WKD, by the way; I'm sure he'd been on the Pimms and Bolly).

All the elements were there for a perfect example of the kind of case I seem to spend most of my time investigating:

1. Fighting
2. Nightclubs
3. Drink
4. Photographic evidence

Both parties declined to complain to the police but, had they done so, the police investigation would have gone like this:

1. Harry complains of assault and makes a statement, crime number generated.
2. Photographer gets arrested, interviewed and released on police bail.
3. Photographer makes counter allegation, makes statement, another crime number generated.
4. Statements obtained from all witnesses.

5. Medical evidence obtained (if applicable).

6. Photographic evidence obtained and exhibited.

7. Harry gets arrested, interviewed and released on police bail.

8. Further statements obtained from Harry's companions on the night.

9. Both Harry and photographer are charged with assault.

10. Full files are prepared on both.

11. Both appear at magistrates' court for their initial hearings.

12. CPS asks the officer to carry out other enquiries.

13. CPS decides that it's not worth running and the case is discontinued after expenditure of several thousand pounds.

The whole thing could take six months; the witnesses will all be abroad, photographic evidence will be difficult to seize and the officer dealing with the enquiry will also have about 10 to 20 other similarly trivial but relatively complex enquiries running at the same time. If police were called to the scene, then the uniformed officer who first attended will be given the responsibility of completing the enquiry and possibly bringing the pair to court.

Mind you, I am no longer infuriated by the complexity and long-windedness of these trivial 'pub-fight' enquiries. Nowadays when people thank me for taking their statement I say, 'That's fine, it's easier than catching burglars.'

ETERNAL OPTIMISTS

I LIE AWAKE at night worrying that we might get found out. I feel like a hamster in a wheel, running really fast for no apparent reason, waiting for somebody to discover that my job could be done equally well on a part-time basis.

Thankfully, though, given our national pro-bureaucrat disposition, it's not going to happen any day soon.

For example: over the next two or three days I have been allocated about eight hours of overtime in order that some cases can be filed. Currently, I have 15 investigations on the go. Of those, only three will ever contain sufficient evidence to charge. I have about five in which the complainant does not wish to prosecute, but I could still get an administrative detection, so I need to interview the offender. For the rest, it's really just a matter of getting round to the various witnesses who probably didn't see anything and looking at some CCTV. There are also some vehicle enquiries to be done to find out who owns a car that was seen to make off from a shoplifting. Nobody will be arrested and brought to justice as a result of my efforts, but certain crimes will be filed in a dusty drawer labelled 'Detected' as opposed to the drawer below labelled 'Undetected'.

While we don't actually have targets for detections or arrests, the number of both is measured and so it always helps to have at least a couple a week. Ideally, you want easy detections with one offender who will admit the offence without too much investigation.

The cases I am dealing with fall into one of three categories: the depressingly trivial, the no-hopers and the decent jobs.

The depressingly trivial include a harsh word exchanged between former partners, a slap administered to an errant boyfriend and the theft of a few pounds by one sibling from another. If I can persuade the miscreants in some of these cases to admit their offences I will be able to say that I have 'detected' these criminal offences and they will go some way to balance for the thousands of robberies and domestic burglaries that go 'undetected' every year. Yes, it's administrative detections again.

Some complainants actually want the police to prosecute and, while these cases are no less trivial, at least I'll get an arrest out of them: the ongoing Kelly and Sharon nonsense springs to mind.

The no-hopers include an internet fraud where a greedy and naïve man sent a cheque to a Spanish-based property company in the expectation of receiving thousands of pounds in return; the theft, from a factory, of some scrap metal (it looks like scrap and is probably in about a hundred different yards by now, so I don't think we're likely to trace it) and the use of a cloned credit card to purchase petrol across London (I'll send it off to the Met, but by the time they get round to it, the CCTV tapes which may show an offender using the cloned credit card will have long since been changed).

Thankfully, so many people have lost all faith in the police that they no longer bother to telephone us to report incidents, leaving the obsessives and the eternal optimists who make up the bulk of my work.

There are though, a small number of cases in which there is some evidence against an offender and the victim is sane. These are known in my nick as 'decent jobs'. I've got one fraud with good CCTV of an offender with distinctive tattoos and I've got one locker theft where the offender left his fingerprints. Tracing the offenders and building cases against them will be a little tricky, but both cases are 100% worthwhile and will be rewarding if I get a result.

NIGHTS

NIGHTS PROVIDE A BRIEF respite from the treacly bureaucracy that envelops much of what the police force does. As most of the law-abiding classes go to sleep, we develop tactics and targets for catching criminals who work late at night. One of us might take out a plain car or put on a jacket and jeans and walk around likely areas; we might work in pairs and target the neighbourhood of a prolific offender. All too briefly, we feel in control of our own streets: we are actually walking along pavements and checking factory premises, looking into back gardens and speaking to people. For a short while, certain roads in the town have policemen standing at their corners.

Mick only has a few years left and, for reasons I can't understand, still works shifts with us instead of getting himself some sort of cushy desk job.

Last night, we parked the car and got out on foot in an industrial estate that's been targeted a lot lately. We were hoping to land on someone up to no good. As we walked, we chatted. Mick told me that, for many years after he started, it was like this all the time. 'If you had a theft CID would have it off you, simple as that,' he said. 'You didn't have all this "detections" rubbish. If someone didn't want us to do anything, you didn't get a crime number. You didn't deal with common assault, you just used to tell them to speak to a solicitor.'

'Bet you still had the paperwork though.'

'Did we hell. If the Inspector ever found you inside the police station, you'd better have a good reason. We used to leave the station straight after parade, and if you needed a statement form or something like that, one of the cars would bring it to you.'

We got back to the car empty-handed and repeated the procedure around some garages that have recently been broken into. Again, we drew a blank – who knows, maybe we'd been seen by the ne'er-do-wells? – but I had that rare feeling, that I was doing the job I was being paid to do. It's almost a shame that the occupants of the nearby flats weren't awake to see us.

CJS NOW

A FEW MOMENTS OF calm in the canteen at lunchtime today, and I fancied a laugh so I turned, once again, to a back issue of *CJS Now*, the free and desperately-worthy Home Office publication in the very worst traditions of the new Stalinism of political correctness.

The front cover had a picture of Hamid Samiy – a bureaucrat whose specific title is 'Race for Justice Project Manager.'

Inside, Hamid, who works in Hampshire, says: 'Southampton and Portsmouth have lots of refugees and asylum seekers who have been through many difficulties. They are often aged 18 to 25 and have little knowledge of customs or law in this country. They can end up committing offences like driving without insurance or an MOT simply because they don't know it's required. So I put together a book to welcome them… We're going to monitor its impact on crime reduction.'

Not too closely, though, Hamid; you might end up agreeing with me that most asylum seekers who break the law know the law perfectly well, certainly after their first brush with authority, but find it too much trouble to obey it.

In another article, I note that that Local Authorities in East Kent are undoing my vital work in deterring people from calling the police by setting up a multi-language phone line to encourage more victims and witnesses to come forward. According to *CJS Now*, 'In 2002/03, 547 racially-aggravated offences were reported by police in Kent… although this is probably only the tip of the iceberg.' In the public sector, 'Tip of the Iceberg' means 'More funding required now.' Phone lines like this are 'vitally important'. Well, they are to a few people, such as:

- Jyotsna Leney, head of crime reduction for Shepway District Council and chair of the RIRL steering group.
- The rest of the steering group.
- Shafi Khan, Ashford Asian Society's development manager.
- Carol Chastney, unit leader for the CPS in Canterbury, who is assessing the project.
- Mick Cronin, police community liaison officer for South East Kent, who helped launch the RIRL (does that make him a policeman or not?).

Shafi Khan says, 'Ashford's rapid growth could create issues in the future unless we act now.'

CJS Now also examines a government action plan aimed at reducing re-offending. It says it will do this, 'through greater strategic direction and joined-up working'. Meaning: 'by having more people in charge and more forms to monitor things.'

Apparently, the plan contains 'over sixty action points… covering all the key rehabilitation areas, such as housing, health, education, employment and substance misuse.'

But no punishment, it would appear.

Finally, join me in celebrating the birth of the 'Stop and Search Action Team' in an office at the Home Office. The team's work will involve 'spending several days in each force and holding meetings and gathering evidence from community groups, discussing their experiences of stop and search.'

In the UK's Criminal Justice System, this is what passes for 'action'.

SUPPORT STAFF

AS A UNIFORMED police constable with special responsibility for dealing with the rubbish that nobody else wants to deal with, I'm pretty sure of my own position: at the bottom of the pile.

Being certain of this, however, does not stop me being irritated by communications from back office staff asking for clarification and further action when neither the injured party nor the courts require it. In short, I do not like being employed in the expansion of petty bureaucratic empires.

This week I discovered a petty new way of responding to petty enquiries. I received the following email about a neighbour dispute I'd attended which (depending on how you read the log) may or may not have involved a crime being committed:

'PC Copperfield, re: 12 Church Road, there does not appear to be a crime number associated with this incident. According to the log, you attended. I feel this needs clarification. Please telephone me as soon as possible to discuss. Regards Joan (g4 subdivision support admin ops. crime review, allocation).'

I responded thus: 'Dear Joan, I agree, it requires discussion. Please check my schedule and feel free to contact me at any time. Regards PC 9999'

Let her come to me. It's a small victory, but it put a smile on my face.

ENEMIES OF THE STATE

THE STATE DOES AN excellent job of keeping an eye on us via CCTV systems, the coming ID cards (or are they not coming, this week?) and, increasingly, by collecting, cataloguing and storing our DNA.

As a servant of the State it worries me and, if it worries me, it really ought to worry you.

We've done a bit of Sir Robert Peel. Let's look a little deeper.

Sir Robert Peel introduced the regular foot patrol and a uniform which was designed to be dull so it did not dominate or stand out too much. Middle and upper-class people were excluded from the force, because it was felt that they would not be able to deal with the man in the street. Most importantly, though, the constable swore an oath to the law – not to the State.

Today, much has changed: the constable is as much a servant of the Home Secretary as he is of the law, the dark blue coat has been replaced by the bright yellow jacket and the car has seen us abandon the streets. Finally, what do you think about this:

1. The police will take your fingerprints and your DNA if you are arrested for an offence (and keep them on file, even if you're not charged).

2. In some forces, over a third of all 'solved' crime never results in so much as a caution for the offender.

3. If you are arrested for, but not convicted of, shoplifting, it is pretty much standard practice for the police in many forces to search your house whether or not any stolen property is still outstanding.

Back in the 19th century, the fallout from the French revolutionary wars, the Peterloo Massacre and the Corn Laws made 19th Century England a place of enormous political upheaval. The Chartist movement led the way but the introduction of the police (in 1856, all counties in England were required to establish a police force and appoint a chief constable) came to be viewed by many of all social classes as a move towards tyranny.

In 1869, Walter Bagehot wrote: 'I know people... who consider them an infringement of freedom.'

The Birmingham town clerk wrote to the home secretary in 1839: 'I find amongst [council members] a strong feeling of indignation at the [creation of the police] as insulting and despotic, insulting to themselves personally as to members of the Town Council, and despotic as tending to that system of centralisation which every good Englishman must utterly abhor and abjure.'

I think the people of the 19th Century knew what was coming.

YOUR PERSONAL POLICEMAN

NEIGHBOURHOOD BEAT MANAGERS in Devon and Cornwall now have to have their pictures put up on the official police website. Some people printed these photos out and turned them into 'wanted' posters and put them up around Plymouth.

The Police Federation wanted to take legal action to stop it because some of the officers involved complained that they were subjected to more abuse than usual since the photographs appeared but I thought that was evidence of a sense of humour failure. In fact, I laughed out loud when I read about it. You have to admit these toe rags can be quite funny, sometimes.

My photograph has never appeared in our local paper and I intend to make sure it never does. This is in contrast to senior officers, who seem to think that being photographed gurning gormlessly by the local newspaper creates a feeling of safety and security in the local populace. In fact, I see my boss more often in the *Newtown Gazette* than I do in the flesh, which, now I come to think of it, is no bad thing.

Naming individual officers creates problems for the officers. The last thing I want is for someone to contact me to ask how a case is progressing because, the chances are, the answer is going to be, 'Well, not very well, to be honest. There are no other lines of enquiry, I've managed to get it all filed away and I have no intention of ever thinking about it again.'

People seem to think that if they spoke to you about an incident six months ago you will know exactly what they are talking about when they ring up to complain that their new ex-partner is harassing them. It's as though you have then become their personal police officer.

I became someone's personal police officer once. I was assigned to deal with some cars that were parked improperly in the street. I arrived at about 15:00hrs and dished out ten parking tickets. I've never dished out that many before or since, so I thought I had done a pretty good job. I was on nights the following shift and was working away in the office when, at about 04:00hrs, the phone rang and this man said, 'Hello, is that PC Copperfield?'

'Yes. How can I help?'

'I'm Geoffrey Richards. Did you attend my road yesterday and give some tickets out?'

'Yes I did.'

'How many?'

'Ten.'

'That's not very many.'

I was momentarily speechless, but soon regained my composure.

'Well, I'll see if I can give out some more next time I'm round there, sir.'

I thought that would be the end of it, but for about a week afterwards Geoff would leave messages on my voicemail asking me if I had actually given out some more tickets like I'd promised. It's amazing how some people get completely obsessed about things; imagine ringing the police about parked cars at 4am.

Most people are reasonable enough to put their own problems into some sort of context. However, those sort of people never call the police and they are more than made up for by the self-important, the hopeless optimists and the mad.

Ordinary people, who wait their turn and don't really like to bother us, always get the worst service.

TEACHING THE ELEPHANT TO TAP DANCE

WHAT IS A GOVERNMENT FOR? Maintaining law and order and protecting our borders, facilitating international commerce and relations, seeing some sort of fair play between the weak and the strong... I wouldn't quibble with any of that. But the question is: do we want a government poking its noses into every single area of our lives? More to the point, do we want a government taking our money off us to fund its nose-poking? Even more to the point, do we want it wasting billions of our pounds in the process?

Our government wastes so much of our money, which it collects as tax, that it might as well be burned in open pits outside local revenue offices.

To my mind, an ideal Government would be smaller than we have today. Government is almost always either corrupt, wasteful or incompetent and sometimes all three. When faced with a new government initiative, ask yourself: will this reform mean smaller government? If so, it is a good thing.

In the police force, in the absence of any need to actually reduce crime and disorder, we waste your taxes on proving how busy we are. This week, for example, I have been asked to take time out from dealing with family feuds and neighbour disputes in order to give tickets to drivers using mobile phones. It's probably part of a Home Office initiative (something like National Don't Use Your Phone Whilst Driving Week).

I stopped a chap who wasn't exceeding the speed limit, wasn't driving erratically and seemed to be concentrating on the road. He was, however, on his phone at the time.

'Look, officer,' he said. 'I wasn't exceeding the speed limit, I wasn't driving erratically and I was concentrating on the road. What do you lot do when your police radios start up?'

'Hmm,' I said. 'I can see your point, sir. Here's your ticket. Have a nice day.'

I could see his point, too. But what am I supposed to do about it? You lot voted for this government, and the succession of ever more Orwellian governments we've had for the last 50 years or so.

I was told to ask other officers how many tickets they have given out and collate these results and write them down and fax them to somebody, who will in turn collate the results and tell someone else who will then use the success of the operation to justify their promotion. I predict that this particular scheme will be like all the others: a success, but could have been better if we had 'more resources'.

SCHEMING KIDS

MOST OF THE 'young people' I meet are feckless, irresponsible children with no ambition and even less common sense.

When I was young, life seemed to follow a kind of path: school, followed by work, or by a choice between polytechnic or university, and then work.

For the last month I have been trying to get hold of three 'young people' who 'attend' the local 'college' (in reality, a sort of halfway house between compulsory attendance at school and a life of petty crime.)

You'd think it would be easy to find them, wouldn't you? But whenever I try to get in touch with the 'students' they are never at the college. I was back there today, talking to a Mrs Caldwell, their tutor.

'Any sign of Darren, Carl and Connor today?' I asked, cheerily. 'Only last week you said if I called back today…'

'No, I'm afraid they're not here today,' said Mrs Caldwell. 'They should be but… er… they're not.'

'Do you know why?' I asked, eyebrows slightly raised.

'No,' she said.

I am assured that the qualifications they will receive are 'modern and relevant' – that is, not worth the paper they're written on. For the genuinely unemployable, there are innumerable schemes or projects that demand attendance a few hours a week. The aim of such schemes appears to be, from what I've read, to 'empower' young people and 'give them back their self-esteem'. In my experience, the one thing the (non)attendees do not lack is 'self-esteem'. Most young criminals have a terrifically high opinion of themselves and I, for one, would like to see them taken down a peg or two. Not so the courts, though, who insist on sending offenders to 'Enhanced Thinking Courses' and arrest referral schemes, which are really only ways of delaying the inevitable.

Honest toil seems to have gone out of fashion, replaced by navel-gazing and self-absorption; yet with thousands of vacancies for unskilled, physically able youngsters, there has never been a better time to get back some old-fashioned self-respect in the form of a pay packet.

PROPER CRACKERS

I MEET QUITE a lot of mad people in my job. As you know, I'm supposed to say they have 'mental health issues', but it's not as if they're going to be offended when they can barely hear me above the rustling of the newspaper they're trying to eat.

There are a few golden rules given to officers when dealing with the mentally ill. I've forgotten most of them, but two I can recall are: turn your radio down so that they don't think they're hearing voices in their head, and do not simply agree with the insane person's own delusions for the sake of a quiet life.

I'm not sure I give my unqualified support to the second of those rules. In my experience, by the time the police are called to deal with a lunatic who thinks he is being hunted by the Russian mafia, it's already too late. Simply saying, 'Come now, sir, I don't really think you're being tracked by a bounty hunter from Moscow,' isn't going to work. For the sake of everyone present, sometimes you might just as well say, 'I know, we heard you might be at risk, that's why we think you'll be better off with us.'

Mind you, once you've got them in the car, I'd advise listening and giving non-committal answers. It can send them totally up the wall if you agree too much.

The legislation surrounding the insane is, predictably, quite complex, but really the only thing a patrol officer needs to know is that mad people can be arrested under Section 136 of the Mental Health Act and taken to a place of safety. They have to be outside at the time (you can't just go into someone's house and arrest them on suspicion of being mad) and they have to be a danger to themselves or other people; so, for instance, you can arrest someone who's about to jump off a bridge.

Last night's case was quite upsetting for all concerned. We arrived in response to a call from Bill's daughter. I never really understood why we were there, as opposed to an ambulance (another case of, 'If it's not on fire, call the police.')

She had been driven to distraction by her father's complete obsession that people were attempting to break into his house and rape her and her mum. This mania had completely taken him over, to the extent that he had nailed boards across all the windows and forbidden his wife and daughter from coming downstairs.

We watched him running round the house, clutching a broomstick, and saying, 'I bet you think I'm mad don't you? Well let me tell you that there are people out there right now, thinking about coming in the second you leave.'

The rest of the family were clearly at a loss as to what to do next, so we coaxed him outside to check his carpentry from a different angle and locked him up when he wasn't really looking.

Once inside the car, he calmed down a bit and told us about all the other things that had been bothering him.

'They've tried to kill me before,' he said, 'but I got out just in time.'

'Really?'

'Yes, you know them, though, I've seen you with them in Tesco.'

'Well, I can't say I have seen them myself, Bill.'

'Have they ever tried to kill you?'

'No, I must have been lucky.'

'I love the sea, I like the water.'

'Oh yes, so do I.'

'But they tried to drown me once, could you teach me to swim?'

'Well, yes, I could. Perhaps in a few days when you feel better?'

I'm not trying to make light of this, though some of the conversations you have with these people are very funny, in a sad way. Imagine thinking your family is at terrible risk, and no-one believing you? Just because they weren't it didn't mean Bill's agonies and his fear were any more bearable.

His daughter had driven down to the police station and I spoke to her as we waited for a doctor to arrive.

'He'll be alright once he's taken his medication,' she said. 'He just gets like this from time to time, and then he's back to normal. Just my dad, like he always was.'

'I'm sorry you had to call us out,' I said.

'Don't be,' she said. 'We're very grateful.'

NEWS FROM THE FRONT

I HAVE BEEN on the front line this week. If you were out painting Newtown red as part of your pre-Christmas celebrations, you may have even seen me. I was the one wandering about in a reflective jacket and big hat or cruising around in the car with the flashing lights on top. Maybe, like a lot of the people I encountered, you were too drunk to notice or care.

I was on the streets, at night, to fight the war against binge drinking.

Arguably, binge drinking isn't actually a problem – it's just adults drinking as much alcohol as they want to. If it began and ended there – essentially, with a good night out followed by a thumping hangover – this would probably be my point of view. Stupid, not good for you, but your call. But, of course, they can't resist a little side order of argy bargy to go with their alcopops, can they? That's the real problem with binge drinking.

The more cynical amongst you may well take the view that drinking too much and then misbehaving is merely the result of a woeful lack of self-control and a bad upbringing. As we've discussed, the government disagrees: it thinks binge drinking is a disease affecting young people for which there is no known cure other than research and 'more resources'. It believes it is caused by a complex variety of factors and that it's the job of the police and other emergency services to deal with the problem.

My weapons in the war on binge drinking include a briefcase laden with about twenty different forms and a collection of withering comments.

One call was to Newtown's premier nightspot, not known for its outstanding selection of beers and wines (you do get to drink out of plastic pint glasses that glow in the dark though).

On arrival, I immediately diagnosed Tyler as suffering from 'binge drinking'. The symptoms were obvious: a torn shirt, blood issuing from a wound and an inability to shut up. He was surprisingly lucid and clued-up. 'The CCTV will clearly show I was punched first, officer,' was the first thing he said.

'It's dark,' I replied. 'The CCTV will show nothing. I am going to arrest you and the courts will sort it out later.'

Later, I met a 20-year-old bottle-blonde named Nadine. Unfortunately for her, the top she was wearing had shrunk in the wash but at least it gave Newtown's other revellers the chance to see plenty of her.

The root cause of Nadine's problems may well have been similar to Tyler's. Pissed and unable to control herself, she had got into a fight with her ex-boyfriend and his current partner and stood (or swayed) accused of assault.

Swearing and clutching a Bacardi Breezer, she lunged at the other girl as I watched. Her eyes widened in surprise when I arrested her.

'I've got three kids, and I've got a babysitter! You can't arrest me!'

'Ah,' I said. 'Sorry, you're right. We can't go arresting people who've employed babysitters.'

She started to walk away, looking daggers at the other girl.

'Oi!' I said. 'Where are you going?'

'But you said you couldn't arrest me,' she said.

'I was joking. I can and I am. Get in the car.'

It's like shooting fish in a barrel.

At this time of year, there are always people out on the street who think I love talking to them and that they are really funny.

I give them an inch and 30 seconds (I wind the car window down an inch, and give them 30 seconds to convince me they're worth talking to. They usually aren't.)

Others think it's OK to run down the street carrying a traffic cone and that I should not get cross with them when they argue with me.

On Saturday night I had a discussion with a drunk female who wished to pursue a complaint against her boyfriend.

'I want him done, for lying to me,' she said. 'He's been seeing his ex.'

'Hmm,' I said with as much sympathy as I could muster. 'Yes, I can understand your frustration, but while he may have behaved in an immoral way he hasn't actually done anything illegal. For example, theft is illegal and may well be immoral too; adultery is immoral, but isn't illegal.'

'Yerrwhat?'

Normally, I warm to this subject: how do we as a society define crime? Is crime immoral, or is the criminal simply taking a different path? Is morality merely a majority view or are there moral absolutes?

However, I was tired, she was not receptive to new ideas and her kebab was getting cold.

Her inch and 30 seconds had expired, so I was off.

QUICK, THE POLICE ARE COMING

WHEN YOU RING the police and ask them to come round to your house because your life has suddenly taken a turn for the worse, here are some things that you can do to ensure the officer attending feels at home and is able to deal with your complaint normally:

1. Turn the heating up to uncomfortable levels.
2. Take the washing out of the machine and place it on the tops of the radiators, creating that slum/primary rainforest atmosphere.
3. Give your children drinks that are rich in additives, thereby making them dangerously hyperactive.

4. Turn the volume on the television up. Make sure it's not a documentary.

5. Take all the dishes and cutlery and distribute them throughout the house. Smear some ketchup on them, too.

6. Take the children's toys out and throw them down the stairs. Lob a few into the garden.

7. Get the dog really excited.

8. Invite a few relatives round. Tell them you called the police two hours ago and they have only just turned up. Invite them to inform the officers how disgusting this tardiness is.

9. Arrange for friends to ring you on your mobile dozens of times for the duration of the officer's visit.

10. Hide all your books and replace them with videotapes and DVDs.

CHRISTMAS CHEER

CHRISTMAS BRINGS VERY little change in the parade of unfortunates who cross my path, though they are probably a little less tolerant than usual because they know they have an absolute right to a happy, joyful Christmas.

They believe they should be able to enjoy the festivities and not have to put up with the pathetic acts of harassment from their neighbours and ex-partners that constitute entertainment in the underclass. A big telly and some violent video games are all that is required to keep the younger members of the group happy. Alcohol and sex will keep the over-15s out of trouble (though they'll also get them into it, of course).

The Christmas period is surprisingly uneventful and the only reason we leave the station is to evict men who have been unfortunate enough to have fallen foul of their partners.

This is always a depressing experience. Still, they'll have sorted themselves out by the morning and will have learned a valuable lesson: never call the police.

I spent an hour with a man, his wife and her mother. The females wanted him to leave.

'No, we've had enough of him. He's got to go,' said Granny, who struck me as a rancorous old witch. She took me aside and started telling me lurid tales of how the husband kept 'forcing' his wife to do 'things'.

It's a shame he couldn't force her to do a bit of tidying up, I thought.

The most surprising thing was how reasonable the chap was, even though he was being kicked out of his own home. Not only did he understand force policy on domestic incidents, he actually saw the benefits of it.

'Tell you what lads,' he said. 'At least I'll have a bit of peace though, eh?'

Much more fun is the Christmas party gone wrong.

Christmas brings together people who, out of choice, wouldn't spend an evening together outside the office in a million years: workers and their bosses. Large quantities of chilled chardonnay or cheap lager – depending on the generosity of the company in question – are consumed to help people get through the evening.

Blows are frequently traded between both parties and a year's worth of injustices are brought to a head before they are arrested and delivered to the police station.

My favourite part is when the sergeant asks the prisoner what his occupation is. The short delay allows me to say, 'Well, it's in the balance at the moment, Sarge. He's been arrested for assaulting his manager.'

MORE CHRISTMAS CHEER

WELL, SOME OF YOU didn't have a good Christmas, did you?

Those of you who woke up on Christmas Day in the cells at Newtown police station, I bet you weren't too happy. You couldn't wait to say yes to the £80 ticket for disorder, so you could get home and not bother with a court appearance. Those of you who were wanted on fail-to-appear-at-court warrants and were picked up by the police on Christmas Eve and had to wait in the cells until the next available court, you weren't happy were you? No, I know you weren't, because I heard you banging on the cell door and yelling. It was quite upsetting for me, until I left and got home to a full dinner prepared by Mrs C.

Christmas at the Copperfield house was a subdued affair, as it is for most families where one spouse is working. I started early with some paperwork and went to a couple of burglaries. But I spent most of the shift playing Monopoly and Trivial Pursuit. It was British policing at its best, and for once I don't think you can blame us. Food was provided by the officers of the shift: sausage rolls, mince pies and tea and coffee.

Generally it was quiet on Christmas Day, punctuated with those strange, aborted calls: like the kind where a drunken female called in to say she had been beaten up but was fine and didn't want the police to visit, thank you.

Obviously, we still have to turn up, so Kevin and I took off our paper party hats and set off.

Her name was Helen, and she was surprised to see us.

'It's Christmas Day,' she said. 'I told the officer on the phone I didn't want to see you, so why are you here?'

'Because you told us you'd been assaulted,' I replied, rather stating the obvious.

'Yes, but it's Christmas Day. Can't you sort it out afterwards?'

'Not really,' I said, getting out the trowel and spreading it on good and thick. 'We're the police, you see. One of the three emergency services? And you're reporting a crime?'

She blinked at me. 'But I'm busy at the moment.'

'I know the feeling,' I said. 'I've got hotels on Mayfair and Park Lane and by the time I get back someone will have switched them for houses. But the thing is, we've got forms to complete. It'll only take a minute or two.'

After some persuasion we managed to force our way in and complete the relevant documentation, before returning to our in-station board games. She didn't call back, so we were in the clear. Aside from the odd complainant, the other things missing during the Christmas period have been email and voice messages. There's a simple explanation for the lack of email; it's that those who get paid to come up with barmy ideas are on holiday and are unable to 'support' us. Perhaps this year they will all go on strike, leaving us free to get on with policing. On the voice-mail front, it would appear that the persistent complainers have been knocked off their stride by Christmas, but I predict a renewed assault in the New Year.

'Hello, PC Copperfield? This is Mr Willis, please can you give me a ring about my case. I want to know if it has gone to court yet.'

Who is Mr Willis? What case? Has he left a telephone number? No. He'll probably ring back. Who knows, he may even ring when I'm actually at work.

As I say, I managed to get home on time and enjoyed a delicious goose, cooked by Mrs C. We opened our presents and had an early night. By Boxing Day evening, the Christmas spirit had entirely left Newtown and we were dealing with confused old people and angry young people. One young man had completely lost it and locked himself in his bedroom. We attended in response to the parents who said he was smashing the place up. I had been to the address before, and to be honest I couldn't see which part of the house he had smashed up since the last time. After a brief discussion and the completion of a Family Incident form, we were off.

By the miracle of modern bureaucracy (and the manna of the administrative detection) I managed to file three solved crimes without leaving the police station. I had all the raw material (statement stating they didn't want to make a complaint, interview with offender admitting the offence), so I just stapled the relevant documentation together and wrote a brief report on each one about how there was sufficient evidence to file the crime as detected. Each one was signed by me, then the sergeant, then an auditor. Each one will be trumpeted as evidence of improving standards of investigation within Newtown police.

Some things will not change in the New Year.

A MILLION INFLATABLE HOMERS

TWELFTH NIGHT IS the time the Christmas decorations come down and Britain's power stations breathe a sigh of relief.

From early October every year, routine mobile patrol amongst the Newtown council estates is brightened up by illuminations that the inhabitants put up on the outside walls of their houses, and the roofs, and in the gardens and in the windows. On a practical level, the decorations make my job easier because they illuminate my way from the gate to the front door of a property and I can see the discarded electrical items and dog mess before I actually step on them. On an aesthetic level, however, the lights make even the most open-minded police constable feel vaguely queasy.

I make no apology for saying that my own decorations – a simple line of white lights and a wreath upon the door – mark me out as hopelessly out of touch and middle class.

For the most part, Newtown's residents' decorations are a reflection of the meaning of Christmas (an orgy of greed), but there is the occasional electrical reference to something altogether more spiritual: a star glimpsed on the tree inside the property, or an angel clinging to a satellite dish. From Father Christmas riding his sleigh up the side of a house, to a trio of orange, glowing, inflatable snowmen swaying in the breeze, I think I have seen them all.

It must all be incredibly expensive – especially when you consider that inside the property the lights are on and the vast plasma screen/DVD combo has not been turned off since the season's bumper TV guide arrived.

Driving around, attempting to decide which set of decorations is the most tasteless, is a game that the whole shift can enjoy.

'Steve, I've got Homer Simpson, dressed as Santa Claus, climbing down the side of 55 Church Street. He's about 8 foot tall and partially deflated.'

'Roger, Dave. I'm in Valley Road, I've got Bart in a Christmas train and three snowmen plus four, no, make that five Santas and a herd of blue reindeer on the roof of number 16.'

Arriving at a suitably decorated house to investigate a crime last night, my colleague Carl provided the initial critique.

'Jesus Christ, Dave. Look at those snowmen; they look like the living dead.'

'I know,' I said. 'Check out the Father Christmas; I think the dog has chewed his leg off. And those purple and pink lights around the shed door look foul. Ah, good evening Mrs Kellaway! We were just admiring your decorations. Now, I gather you've been having some problems with your ex-husband.'

I. D. ISSUES

WHEN INVESTIGATING ANY CRIME, it is obviously important to establish that the person you have under arrest is the person who committed the crime. Establishing what is known as 'continuity of identification evidence' is vital before any case goes to court.

Several weeks ago now, Barney, our finest CCTV operator, caught an assault on camera, called it in over the radio and managed to follow the offender, on camera, until I caught up with him and carried out the arrest.

All dead exciting, especially as I had to break into a trot between the McDonalds on the High Street and the actual place of arrest outside the snooker club. The description passed over the radio was, 'White male, white shirt, blue jeans with blonde hair… just gone past the McDonalds, yes… that patrol near the snooker club… you're right next to him now… yes that's him, just to your left.'

A good pinch you might say, especially as the CCTV footage is in a class of its own: the pre-fight argument, the punch caught squarely on camera and finally the short pursuit which ended with me putting the cuffs on. Complete continuity from the crime to the arrest.

Sadly, it's all gone a bit downhill from there: the offender went No Comment on interview and the CPS told us to run an identity parade.

Identity parades are run on DVD; they're called VIPER, which stands for Video Identification… something… something.

Anyway, you have to 'invite' the offender to attend – he does not have to, it is entirely optional – at a suitable time both for him and for you. If he doesn't want to attend, your options are limited and you probably won't be able to run the ID parade and will have to proceed without one.

In this case, the offender agreed.

Next, I had to arrange a time for the injured party to attend. By the time I managed to get all this organised, several weeks had gone by and even I couldn't tell who the offender was when he answered his bail at the police station, so it was no surprise to me when neither the witness, nor the victim, could pick my man out.

Fortunately, Barney's CCTV evidence meant we could charge, even though the VIPER was negative.

You'd think ID parades were only set up for really serious offences, but these days VIPER is run for the most insignificant matters. More often than not, in the cases I deal with, it's just used as one more obstacle to prosecution. I suspect that defence solicitors know how unlikely it is that offenders get picked out of a VIPER and that's why they are all in favour of them.

The CPS won't run a case unless it's watertight, and why should they care if patrol officers spend whole mornings on the telephone trying to organise a VIPER?

By the way, naturally we have a whole department dedicated to running VIPER, but the responsibility of ensuring they are arranged and the people turn up falls to… the officer who made the arrest.

THE PRECAUTIONARY PRINCIPLE

THE WIDESPREAD USE of CCTV in British town centres is not without its problems.

The operators directed me to 'a situation' in the town centre on Friday night. I'd barely opened the door of my car before I heard Kelly Broxholme shouting, 'I want 'im done! I want 'im f*ckin' done for harassment. He won't leave me alone.'

Here we go again, I thought as, once more, the wobbling bulk of Ms. Broxholme began to feature prominently in my workload. 'Who's harassing you this time, Kelly?' I asked.

'Him in the blue top, over there,' she said, pointing in the vague direction of a man standing with some friends.

I walked over to the harasser, trying to convey my sincere concern while, at the same time, wondering what to get Mrs C for her birthday in a couple of weeks' time. I took some details from the alleged offender, Nigel.

Nigel denied harassing anyone, including Kelly. 'I dunno what she's on about,' he said. 'Give me one of them lie detectors, mate.'

I really couldn't have cared less. There was no evidence and I let Nigel go, warning him to leave Kelly alone.

'I *was* leaving her alone,' he said. 'She's f*cking *mad*!'

'Well, that's as may be,' I replied. 'But... er... leave her alone more.'

'Is that all you're going to do?' said Kelly, when I walked back over to her.

'What do you suggest?'

'I want 'im done.'

I sighed. To create a crime for Kelly's alleged 'harassment' would set up a trail of bureaucracy which might ultimately result in the arrest, appearance in court and (probable) acquittal of Nigel. I'd much rather just ignore them and carry on with my patrol and see if I can catch some real criminals, or at least deter them.

If it hadn't been for the CCTV cameras I wouldn't be in this situation now.

If we really want to use this system properly, I think we need to be a bit more serious about it. I've written to the government suggesting two key measures (I've not heard back, yet, it must be in the post). The first is to fix loudspeakers to the CCTV cameras so that the police can broadcast messages to individuals.

'Hey, you! Yes, you in the England football top. Pick up that kebab wrapper and don't even think about punching that man in the white shirt.'

It could also be used to broadcast messages to society as a whole.

'Newtown Police would like to remind you that it is an offence to beat your wife. Thank you.'

The CCTV system could be extended to all residential areas and the loudspeaker system could be set up in all new homes.

The second measure would be for the government to introduce the compulsory wearing of 'thudguards' (I suggest rubber helmets, like the ones skateboarders wear) at all times, by all age groups, to reduce injury in the event of becoming embroiled in a fight. What do you think?

Update: While the government has yet to adopt my 'thudguard' idea, it has taken up my suggestion in respect of CCTV loudspeakers. It was a joke, you dummies!

PEARL

MY RADIO SPOKE to me the other day: 'Can you attend 43 Rose Crescent and speak to a Pearl Sorensen? She is reporting having been raped, and she is prepared to speak to a male officer. Can you please attend as a priority?'

Several things ran through my mind. These were:

1. That's the third time this month Pearl's been raped. I wonder if she would benefit from some crime prevention advice.
2. Possible suspects: master criminals capable of carrying out heinous criminal acts without leaving the merest trace of forensic evidence.
3. Rape is one of the few crimes deemed sufficiently serious for CID to investigate, which means that, beyond preserving the scene, my involvement will be limited.
4. Why hasn't my leave been approved yet? I put the form in a week ago.
5. What colour shall I paint the bathroom?

Pearl Sorensen is, as you may have worked out, completely mad. Her allegations of rape run a wide gamut: if it was her GP last week, it's probably a taxi driver today. But, as I say, allegations of rape are taken seriously, until there is evidence to the contrary, and my prompt attendance will help ensure that this is all properly investigated.

I recall this example to illustrate the point that uniformed officers attend a conveyor belt of incidents which, after the end of the shift will probably be forgotten.

Some will be remembered: the stripper who came to the police station to report the theft of her purse will linger in the memory for much longer than the sudden death of a 55-year-old female who had been ill for some time. The sudden death of a woman with children and a loving husband is clearly a tragedy for the family. But I never knew her when she was alive and now she's dead my only responsibility is to complete a form and ensure that there are no suspicious circumstances surrounding her death.

I can recall attending more serious incidents, but for completely the wrong reasons:

Scene preservation at a murder (it was cold and nobody brought me any tea),

A terrorist incident (it was a really hot day and kids kept running under the police tape),

A fatal road accident (had planned to go to the cinema that evening and was really fed up because I had to cancel my plans).

So if I can't even recall the victim of a murder or the circumstances surrounding a fatal road accident, what are the chances of me taking to heart the problems of a volatile relationship in the slums? Slim.

That's not to say the officer doesn't listen to what is being said or profess, at the time, some concern at the situation, but just because you are going through a major crisis in your life it doesn't mean that I am. Being professional doesn't mean I have to empathise with every person I meet: I just need to conduct a good investigation and give some decent advice.

R&SO

I'VE JUST RE-READ the above entry, and I'm worried I might be giving the impression I don't care about Pearl Sorensen. I do, I just don't think I can really help her.

We've had a fair few rapes reported lately. The recent warm weather has brought a large number of rape victims in contact with Newtown police, as well as a slightly smaller number of rapists. The victims usually seem to come forward shortly before I'm about to go off duty on nights, leaving little time for the process of 'evidence gathering'.

As I've said, rape is deemed sufficiently serious to warrant the attention of the professionals over at CID, which means I can hand the job over to them after an hour or two. That's good news, because rape's a very tricky offence, for lots of reasons.

Firstly, it's obviously very serious.

Secondly, it's often extremely hard to prove.

Thirdly, there's a huge political element to the offence. 'Women's groups' (some of them perfectly sensible, others made up of frothing lunatics, none of them speaking for all women) claim that it's a far more common offence than the conviction rates suggest, and politicians are often talking about 'making it easier to secure convictions' in the face of this injustice. All this has created a very polarised, feverish backdrop to the issue.

I'm sure those women's groups, frothing or not, are right about some guilty men going free. After all, burglary, assault and theft (to name but three other offences) are also much more common than the conviction rates. But there isn't a mass outcry suggesting that, for instance, the committers of GBH should have the courtroom odds stacked further against them, as far as I know.

The problem with rape, really, is that it usually comes down to her word against his.

You can prove they've had sex fairly easily. What is very hard to prove is that she didn't say Yes to it. If she has injuries consistent with being violently attacked, or if the rape happened in a public park while she was out jogging, or if it was filmed (it has happened, astonishingly), then you may be onto a winner (and believe me, police officers love to lock up real rapists).

But most of the time when we get a rape reported, the suspect is usually known to the alleged victim and the offence has happened at his flat, or hers, or in one of their cars. He's swiftly arrested, of course, and then begins the process of seizing his clothing and putting it into separate evidence bags. From that, and from medical examinations of the woman and her clothing, we can establish that they have had intercourse.

In her statement, the woman will say that she knows the man, they met at a local pub, she agreed to go back to his flat and then he raped her.

In his statement, the man will say that he knows the woman, they met at a local pub, she agreed to go back to his flat and then they had sex.

How are the courts supposed to pick the bones out of that? Would you send someone to prison for eight years with that level of evidence?

It's his word against hers, and I cannot, for the life of me, see how you will ever get around this fundamental fact without inserting some new injustice into the system. It may be as simple as asking this question: do we want guilty rapists going free, or do we want innocent men locking up?

Generally, our legal system comes down on the side of the innocent, and people tend to agree with this. 'Better for 10 guilty men to go free,' people say, 'than one innocent man be punished.'

In rape, for some reason, the political discourse is slowly being skewed the other way.

I've no idea what percentage of allegations of rape are unprovable. In my experience, however, it's 'a lot'.

Sometimes there's no evidence of penetration, let alone any debate about consent. Sometimes there's no evidence of an offender, no evidence linking the named offender to the crime scene or no evidence that consent was not given. In short, there's no evidence of a crime, other than a very vague statement. These, you're never going to prove unless they change the law to place the burden of proof on the defendant.

To add to that, a surprising number of rapes are literally made up. There are many reasons why women make up allegations. Sometimes they are drunk or mentally ill. Other times they've had sexual experiences with men other than their current boyfriend, perhaps while drunk, and then regret it. (A number of these women report themselves raped and expect us not to do anything about it; they just want to have a piece of paper to show their boyfriend to allay his suspicions. As soon as they see how seriously we're taking their complaint, they start to have doubts, but by then it's too late; there's a crime number and the wheels of justice have started creaking.) Because we do take this offence seriously, as I say. Most people would probably be reassured by the sight of four bleary-eyed, uniformed officers furiously scribbling at the same big desk, booking in property, writing statements or organising a specially-trained officer to deal with the victim. Others will be preserving the crime scene, looking at CCTV systems and trying to locate an offender. In the morning, CID arrive to take on the investigation and follow up all the relevant lines of enquiry. The crime scene will be reopened to the public after SOCO have finished and the doctor will have done a medical on the victim. The victim will have been assigned a liaison from the police and another from victim support.

Dayshift officers arriving always ask the same question. 'Is it a good one?'

By this, they mean, 'Is it a genuine one?'

Responses from the nightshift generally range from a shake of the head to a shrug of the shoulders to the answer, 'Well, something's gone on.'

Outside the station, well away from supervision, the nightshift will tell the whole story and articulate their doubts in the strongest possible terms. 'Load of rubbish Dave. It'll be no-crimed by dinner time.' Or, 'She's been out, had a good time and doesn't want her boyfriend to find out. It's going nowhere.' (These remarks, by the way, are made by female officers just as frequently as by male officers.)

Whatever, we put any personal feelings we have aside.

It's hard even to write about this subject without appearing hopelessly out of touch, or anti-women, or a closet rapist (don't forget, some of the frothers believe all men are rapists).

All I can do is repeat the following points:

1. We believe rape is serious and we treat it accordingly.
2. In many cases, it is not possible to secure convictions as the evidence is simply not there. Where it is there, we will work tirelessly to bang the man up.
3. Not all complainants are telling the truth when they claim they've been raped.
4. Sometimes, the man is telling the truth when he denies raping the woman.
5. Some innocent men are currently being convicted under the current system (inevitably).
6. The law to make it easier to secure convictions will result in more innocent men being convicted.
7. As political pressure grows on prosecutors, so more (and weaker) cases are being brought before the courts. When these prosecutions fail, the police are called into question rather than the politicians.

PS. I chose the title R&SO (Rape & Sexual Offences) because when the offender is brought into custody, we write the offence, name and cell number on a board. In the case of R&SO, to preserve some dignity for the offender, we don't write the word 'Rape', but the letter 'R' instead.

STOP SEARCHING

OF ALL THE DUTIES I perform, one of the most confrontational and controversial is the stop and search.

As a would-be libertarian, I can quite see why: in a free society, one should be able to go about one's business without hindrance from the State. The last thing you want is a uniformed government official asking you to turn out your pockets when you've done nothing wrong. On the other hand, if you've had your wallet stolen by one of a group of three young men, you might think it reasonable that a policeman should be able to search each of them in order to recover it.

Throughout the 1960s and 1970s, the rising burglary and street crime rates led police to stop and search people, using Section 4 of the 1824 Vagrancy Act (the 'sus law', so-called because you could Stop Under Suspicion). The theory was that if you stopped someone, you might find him equipped with the tools of his trade and stop him before he got to use them.

Black men began to suspect that the police were abusing their power by using the sus law to harass them. I've no idea if this is true: I imagine there were some racist coppers who enjoyed pushing black people around, and I imagine some of those black people were criminals. Either way, it all turned into a cause célèbre: in 1981 the Metropolitan police began a stop and search operation called 'Swamp 81' and this culminated in the Brixton riots.

In the resulting Scarman Enquiry later that year, police use of stop and search powers came to be seen as one of the causes of the riots in particular and poor community relations in general. Scarman concluded that the riots were not pre-planned and were an expression of anger by the community. The spark was a stop and search carried out by two police officers. An angry crowd gathered and the officers continued with the search despite their agitation.

Interestingly, during the enquiry, Scarman asked one of the officers involved: 'If you are getting unfriendly reactions from the crowd… are you serving the cause of public peace better by continuing or not continuing?'

The officer replied: 'I think I would be failing in my public duty if I was ever intimidated by a crowd from exercising my authority.'

This exchange shows how much Scarman knew about being a policeman and how insulated he was from real life. It also speaks volumes about the high calibre of the vast majority of Met officers around at the time.

Hostility from ethnic minorities, the Scarman Report (published in November 1981) and the Philips Commission (which reported in January 1981) all combined to form PACE, which provided a clarification of (but not an extension to) the police powers of stop and search. Under PACE, 'reasonable suspicion' is not by itself enough reason to stop and search someone, nor is the subject's belonging to a particular social group (like burglars). Suspicion now has to have some objective basis, and violations of PACE by police officers, particularly in relation to stop and search, are punishable at a disciplinary and even criminal level.

Most stop searches are OK, some aren't. One of my worst, some years ago, could have turned very bad, thanks to a combination of a gobby and aggressive subject and my lack of a legal basis, under PACE, for the search.

I rolled up in the car and spotted a likely lad called Mohammed walking along the pavement. I knew he was a very minor drug dealer so I got out to speak to him with the intention of searching him. Normally, chaps like Mo come over all Ali G and stand there with their hands on their hips and a scornful expression on their faces. But the cheeky so-and-so just carried on walking. 'You can't stop me,' he kept saying, over his shoulder. 'F*ck off.'

Well, that was incorrect as a statement of the law and it was also a silly thing to say to a policeman; we're only human, and we like a challenge the same as anyone else. He'd almost certainly already ditched any drugs (assuming he was carrying any in the first place) when he first saw me but you just can't back down and let them decide when you're going to search them.

So I persisted. 'Hang on,' I said, walking after him. 'I want a word with you.'

I caught up with him just as he was passing the council offices and took hold of his shoulder. He pulled away and started screaming 'police harassment' at the top of his voice.

He clearly had no interest in complying peacefully and I'm sure a lot of you liberal readers are nodding sagely and thinking, *Quite right too, it's a disgrace, this sort of thing*.

Obviously, my response is, 'What if he's got three pounds of crack, a lump hammer and an old lady's pension book on him, and *that's* why he won't agree to a search? What if he's broken into Polly Toynbee's second home (if she's got one) and stolen her first edition of Proudhon's *What is Property: An Inquiry into the Principle of Right and Government*?'

He started swinging his arms and spitting at me, so at that point I had to cuff him. We started rolling around on the ground, Mohammed yelling about racism and harassment, me pointing out, between grunts, that we only really harass criminals. 'I don't do this with everyone I meet, you know,' I said.

By now the fight had gone past the council offices and we were scrapping just underneath a new block of apartments. All the neighbours were looking out of their windows, thinking it was Rodney King all over again going off right under their noses. I imagine a few were hurriedly searching for their video cameras.

I managed to call for back-up – not easy when you're wrestling with an angry youth – and it must have sounded like Mohammed was giving me a real shoeing, because the two other cars turned up really quickly and the drama was over almost as quickly as it had begun.

We sat him on a wall, and I started all over again. After a quick search, I found the world's smallest joint and we let him go with a telling off. Fortunately, he didn't make a complaint. If he had, I might have been in trouble.

Nowadays, I try to imagine that every person I stop and search is a prominent civil rights lawyer; this is no easy task when the subject of the search is a known burglar who clearly knows nothing about the law despite spending so much time on the wrong side of it.

MY EX

IN THE SLUMS, the 'ex' lingers in the background of most domestic crimes like a bad smell. When I go to a house and the informant begins, 'It's about my ex…' you know it's time to dig in for a long session, with a story going back several years.

Even young people have an ex: fat mothers introduce fat female juveniles, aged 14 and dressed like prostitutes, with the words, 'She's having trouble with her ex.'

Tony and Angela are determined to get each other into prison one way or another and, apparently, I'm the man to do it. Ever since Angela started her affair with Ian (we're all now on first name terms), this has gone from fairly inconvenient to really irritating. It all flared up again last week, when I was called to a town centre nightclub where Ian was making a complaint that Tony had punched him. For some reason, perhaps a fit of charity, I arrested Tony and assumed Ian was innocent.

Tony was eventually charged and because Ian was a victim of crime I tried to telephone him to let him know of my success in cracking another case. I couldn't find him but, aware of the domestic situation then pertaining, I telephoned Angela and left the following message.

'Hello, Mrs Giles, this is PC Copperfield from Newtown police station. This message is to let you know that we have charged your ex-husband, Tony, with assaulting your current partner, Ian. If you have any questions please feel free to contact me.'

If only it had all ended there.

Unfortunately, Tony wasn't going to let Ian and Angela get away with this. 'They won't get away with this, officer,' he told me.

He told me he'd been assaulted by Ian. So I gave Tony a crime number of his own and commenced a separate investigation, this time with the roles of victim and offender reversed.

Ian was arrested and charged with assaulting Tony.

Ian couldn't believe this. 'I can't believe this, officer,' he told me.

Tony then remembered that he had received some threatening phone calls from Ian and insisted that this was against the law. 'It's against the law, officer,' he told me.

So I gave him another crime number, this time for harassment.

Angela, who naturally wants Tony in jail so she and Ian can enjoy a life together, doesn't like the way things have been developing. She likes to imply that I am somehow favouring Tony, and even slyly calls my integrity into question with tart voicemail messages. 'Hello, PC Copperfield, this is Ms Jackson,' she'll say, rather pointedly. 'I'm ringing to tell you that Tony has been up to his old tricks again and hanging around outside the house in his car. Do you think you could actually do something to him this time?'

Lately, I've been trying to think of ways to help Tony, Ian and Angela 'move on' from what has been a difficult time for all of them. I know Ian works nights, so I tend to telephone him with regular updates at around 10am. Angela works nearby in an open plan office, so I occasionally drop by to update her in full view of her colleagues. It's all about the personal touch.

The truth is, as in so many domestic situations amongst the underclass, nobody really wants to 'move on' because living in your own soap opera is just too much fun. I occasionally drop hints when any of the parties comes round to the police station and says, 'I tried to ring you yesterday, but you weren't in.'

'I'm sorry,' I say. 'I must have been out trying to catch some criminals.' Then we all laugh, as if the very idea is ridiculous.

Angela was in yesterday. 'I'm really sorry to be taking up so much of your time, Dave,' she said.

'No, no, Angela,' I replied. 'Your current partner has been a victim of crime, this must be investigated and your ex-partner put before the courts. And vice versa, of course. Besides, the overtime will come in handy.'

Exactly what Angela and Tony's children make of all this is open to question, since I haven't met them, but, as Angela said to me as she left, 'At the end of the day it's about justice, innit.'

Quite so, Mrs Giles.

NOSTALGIA

THE THING ABOUT crime and the political Left is that the Left knows things have always been this bad, it's just that, in the old days, child abuse and domestic violence were never reported, and there was nothing much to steal.

The political Right knows that, years ago, people had respect for each other and you could leave your door unlocked.

Both sides then use crime statistics to prove their respective points, both of which probably contain a grain of truth (though I tend towards the right wing view).

Very few ordinary policemen write about life on the beat, but one who did, albeit many years ago, was Harry Daley. Harry joined the Metropolitan Police in 1925 and subsequently wrote a book called *This Small Cloud*. His account is of a remarkably crime-free London (unlike that of today), so please feel free to dismiss his writing as the ramblings of a dedicated fascist working in support of an outdated class structure. Daley never sensed the unpopularity of the police in the whole of his 25 years service.

'How many times have I seen a crowd, staring in attitudes of anxiety... look up with relief at my approach?' he writes. 'Hundreds of times. In the poorer districts of London, people in trouble run to the police station continually, as people ran to the vicarage in Victorian villages. At Wandsworth police station, where I finished my service, a truthful sign could have been displayed over the door, as over the portal of a fairy-tale castle: No person came here for help and went away uncomforted.'

He talks about problems with corruption and what we would now call police brutality early in his service. 'But in my third or fourth year of service, general bribery in the uniform branch was ruthlessly stamped out. At about the same time, violence died a natural death as the standard of recruits improved and better types were promoted. After having a rough time in the street, some policemen naturally were often inclined to have a poke back. But it had to be quick, for soon the impartial station officer and gaoler would be present and beating up would not be tolerated.' He wasn't blind, of course, to the difficulties in bending a truculent yob to the will of the law. 'Order your grandmother to bed as an experiment; if she refuses to go, try to make her against her will. You will be surprised at the violent appearance of the scene, especially if granny is artful enough to trip you up at the top of the stairs. (But) violent policemen were a minority, even amongst the old-timers... Collectively, we could often intimidate the remaining bullies [amongst his police colleagues] to curb their natural aggression.'

And this from James McClure, writing at the same time, but in Liverpool: 'At Rose Hill, they'd call in and ask the man on duty to phone somebody for them… if it was an official they were phoning, they felt the bobby would do it better. They'd pay the tuppence or whatever, and he'd give them a receipt for it. There was a constant stream of late-night callers to look at the station clock to set their alarms. There was another constant stream of late night callers for gas shillings, and certain Bridewell sergeants would keep a special bag of them… First Aid was another thing; kids falling down and cutting their knees, dog bites… They would come in to settle arguments – abstract things that had nothing to do with the police: who won the cup the year before the war? They used the police station as their general information centre.'

I love the idea of ordering your granny to bed early as a form of riot training. And I wonder what Harry and James would make of things now?

BUSY, BUSY, BUSY

I CAUGHT UP WITH a few enquiries of my own today. I drove round to see someone and… he was actually in!

What's more, there was someone else at the house who could act as an appropriate adult (that's appropriate in the legal, rather than moral or traditional, sense).

I took the statement, which was about an incident of criminal damage that occurred well over two months ago, and then I was off to the next enquiry.

This time, it was a theft and a child needed arresting. The last time I met Kyle, I charged him with smashing up a bus shelter. Since then, things had not really improved and I had seen the boy out regularly on the estate at all hours. As soon as I entered the house, I sensed trouble ahead. Kyle's mother was smoking. She clearly had Lorna's 'nerves'.

'KYLE,' she yelled. 'F*CKING COME DOWN HERE NOW!'

'WHAAAAAAAT?' yelled Kyle. Perhaps he's hard of hearing.

When he finally arrived, baseball-becapped and wearing a nylon tracksuit, he stood near the gas fire. I wonder if I'll be able to put him out if he goes up? I thought, but then he moved away from the flame and trudged into the kitchen for a can of Coke.

He returned, glugging, and plonked himself down on the grubby sofa and fixed his eyes on the vast, cinema screen TV along one wall.

'Hello Kyle,' I said. 'I need to talk to you about some items that were stolen from JD Sports in town.'

'Whatever,' he said, eyes not moving from the gaily coloured flickering images of MTV. Well, it makes a change from 'It wasn't me', I suppose.

I outlined the details of this petty crime, skipping lightly over the fact that he'd have to be arrested before I could speak to him.

I turned to his mum. 'And the thing is, I really need to speak to Kyle at the police station and, because of his age, he needs an adult to come with him. I've come to arrange a time when he can come in with you.'

His mum lit another fag. 'Can't you just talk to him here?' she said.

'No, Mrs Ball,' I said. 'It has to be at the station. The boy's on CCTV and the shop are saying it's two Fred Perry polo shirts.'

'Will he get arrested? 'Cos I ain't spending hours down the nick like last time.'

'No, it'll just be a quick interview.' Anything to get the little swine down to the police station.

'Mum, I ain't getting arrested.'

I pacified mum and left them thinking that Kyle won't get arrested. (I've always loved surprises.) We agreed on a date next week.

Further enquiries in the afternoon over the telephone were less successful, as people were out or didn't answer their mobile phones. I finally raised one of them, a chap called Spencer (it's amazing how so many of these chavs use surnames as first names). He was beaten up a couple of weeks ago but, although he made a complaint promptly enough, he has been proving elusive when it comes to making a statement.

'Hello, mate,' he said. 'Tuesday's no good, I can't do Wednesday, Thursday's out…' I held the phone away from my ear. What are we? Some sort of public service?

A recurring theme when I attempt to make appointments with the poor is how busy they are. That's not to say that they are busy in the way that you or I would understand the word. My customers always say, 'I've got a lot going on my life right now.'

What do they mean by that? Decorating? Probably not. Cleaning up the garden? Unlikely. Searching for a job? I don't think so.

JUST FOLLOWING ORDERS

HAVING DEALT WITH a few difficult coves recently, I thought I would explain how I decide whether or not to arrest people.

The simple answer is: I don't.

If your neighbour says that you assaulted him, and that that's how he got the 1cm cut to the face, you'll be arrested. Even if there were no other witnesses and you and your neighbour have always got on well, you will still be arrested.

It's not a question of whether I believe the allegation. I may even think it's utter rubbish. But if there are, objectively, 'reasonable grounds to suspect' (which, in reality, means 'the slightest suspicion'), you're coming with me.

OK, I might ring you and ask you to come down to the police station, so that the whole thing can be done at a mutually convenient time, but one way or another you will be going to the police station and you will be interviewed on tape. After the interview, you will be fingerprinted, photographed and your DNA will be taken. I know, it's not fair because you haven't done anything. In fact, for the record, I think it is the Police State in action and it should be changed, but there we are.

The whole thing will take a couple of hours and then you'll be free to go. You'll probably be burning with embarrassment, anger and a new and lingering distrust, even hatred, of the police, but that's by the by.

Discretion is slowly being taken away from officers.

We are allowed to decide whether or not to take action in the following examples:

Speeding
Bad driving
Other motoring offences (not if you fail the roadside breath test)
If you are found with a penknife over the regulation length
Drunk and disorderly
Swearing and other abusive behaviour in the street

But we are not allowed to use common sense in cases where an individual makes a complaint against another person.

They usually involve assaults, so I suppose it's only right that the police investigate, and investigate robustly, to the fullest extent of their powers. If you're a victim then that, surely, is the least you can expect.

A few tips to bear in mind.

1. There's no such thing as common sense when it comes to the police.
2. I can arrest you even if I'm on my own and I'm not wearing my hat. It's amazing how many people think we have to be in pairs and wearing headgear.
3. However stupid I may look, I probably know the law better than you do, but don't let that stop you from complaining. When you complain, make it original; don't just put 'wrongful arrest', because that's boring. And put it in writing so I can photocopy the letter and put it away in my file. Then I can get it out whenever I need a laugh.
4. Do not agree to turn up for interview, then fail to materialise. Nothing annoys me more than this – I'll come round your house at 07:30hrs on a Sunday morning, or I'll find out what day you're going on holiday and come round then instead.

SWAN CATCHING

YEARS AGO, POLICE officers went on swan-catching courses. God knows why, but they did.

They were run by the RSPCA and involved a day out by a large body of water. You would goad a swan into attacking you and it would rush at you, wings outstretched. As the 'catching officer', you would stand your ground until the last minute and then dodge out of the way. As you did this, you had to tread lightly upon its wingtip, causing it to lose balance and fall to the floor. You then simply gathered the swan up, holding it both by the body and supporting its neck. Advanced catchers could then catch another swan, without letting go of the first. Swans are surprisingly light, apparently.

Swans (and geese) terrify me: it's something to do with those enormous webbed feet and all that hissing and the way how, when alarmed, they stand about six feet high and flap their wings aggressively. Fortunately, the course was abandoned many years before I joined. I can see why: what's the point of catching one when you can just shoo it away or call the RSPCA?

Some courses are like that: even after you pass them, you still have a nagging doubt at the back of your mind.

I got that feeling the other day, when I passed a 'Stinger' course. A Stinger is a thing with spikes that you fling across a road in the path of a vehicle. The vehicle's tyres are punctured and it grinds to a halt. The occupants decamp, attempt to leg it but are hampered by their poor levels of fitness and are captured by the police (in theory). To practice using the Stinger, we all went up to a nearby racetrack and took it in turns to throw it out in front of the 'suspect' car and quickly pull it back before the pursuing 'police' vehicle ran over it (our stinger had rubber spikes).

'This is a laugh, eh, Dave?' said my colleague, Andy. 'It's dead easy, as well. Can't see why we've not been using these things for years.'

It was, I have to admit, great fun and it was certainly easy, compared (I imagine) with swan catching.

The thing is, a lot has got to go right before you can use the Stinger and, while I'm certain it would be extremely satisfying to use it successfully, I suspect it will be some time before I am in the right place at the right time.

SEARCHING QUESTIONS

I'VE TALKED ABOUT stop-search before, but this week it threw up another good example of that old favourite of mine, the law of unintended consequences.

As we know, black and Asian people complain that they are disproportionately stopped and searched by police officers (and it's true, statistically, they are). I suspect that one of the things they hate most about it is the formal and officious way most of these searches are carried out but, regrettably, that's made inevitable by the general furore over the issue, got up by doubtless well-meaning pressure groups, community leaders and politicians.

Let me explain.

If you stop and search someone, you are supposed to tell them a number of things before you start:

G – Grounds for the search
O – Object/purpose of the search
W – Warrant card (to be produced if in plain clothes)
I – Identity of the officer
S – Station to which attached
E – Entitlement to a copy of the search record
L – Legal power used
Y – (Tell them) 'You are detained for the purposes of the search.'

While I'm not sure it's any improvement on 'Keep your hands where I can see 'em!', it does handily spell out 'Go wisely' so it's easy to remember.

Anyway, the other day I got pulled up by a new starter for not going through the full script; he wasn't being critical, he just wanted to know why I hadn't bothered with the full gubbins. Thinking about it, he was right: it's no good showing new police officers the wrong way to go about things, because they'll only get themselves into trouble and I'll be to blame.

The subject was a well-known white (that's important) Newtown drug dealer. He had been searched so many times before that he had a pocket full of search records and a resigned expression when I pulled him over. G, O, I, S, E, L, and Y were all known to both of us and I was in uniform so W was covered, too.

So my opening gambit was, 'Hello, Ron, got any drugs on you?'

'No, not today.'

'Fair enough, you know the score.'

He got out of the car and emptied his pockets.

'How's the missus and kids these days, Ron? Your eldest must be doing her GSCEs soon?'

And it continued in this vein for a minute or two – but for the fact that my hands were in his pockets, a casual passer-by might have assumed we were old friends. Eventually, I established he was, indeed, drug free and he was on his way with a sly grin and a cheery wave. It was all quite civilised, even chummy.

Even if we'd found something, the search itself would not have been invalidated; it would take a good defence solicitor to exclude such evidence, because we don't have the exclusionary rule in UK law. But here's the important bit: it might have opened the door to a complaint. After all, I'd not followed the letter of the law.

What has this got to do with ethnicity?

Well, for individual officers, stop-search means risking a complaint every time they stop and search a non-white person, because non-white people are predisposed to feel they're being unfairly targeted (they're not by me, I can assure you, but they still think they are). Consequently, non-whites – even ones very well known to us – don't get the friendly, low-key, 'Hello, Ron, how's the wife and kids?' approach. Instead, they get, 'You have been seen acting suspiciously by CCTV near some cars. I am searching for evidence that you are going equipped. I am PC1234 Copperfield. I am based at Newtown police station. You are entitled to a record of the search. This search is conducted under section 1 of PACE 1984. You are detained for the purposes of the search.'

Plus, I've also called for assistance because I don't want to be accused of any misconduct and witnesses are handy in this regard.

The end result is that Ron the white drugs dealer gets totally different treatment from Steve the black car thief, which is not what people intended.

WORRYING STUFF

TWO THINGS HAVE been troubling me lately: Quality council housing and investigating internet fraud.

Mrs C has been on about redecorating the downstairs of Copperfield Towers so I have, of late, been taking a keen interest in the kitchen/diners of the slums and, let me tell you, it's been an education. The local housing association has almost completed a refurbishment and rebuilding project and people have just started to move into the new houses. Not for the underclass the pokey kitchen and cramped living room, separated by a cold hallway lit by a single unshaded bulb. No, no, no. They watch television in one half of an enormous living room and leave the second half to a pile of laundry about the height of a child. The kitchens are also huge, with room for a washer, drier and a dishwasher. Work surfaces (in reality, surfaces upon which fast-food is eaten) and cupboards match and the whole thing looks like a winner in the Ideal Home exhibition. I've even taking to running my road accident tape measure along a few walls to get a few ideas for my own house, using the ruse that I need to get the exact measurements to put in the statement.

'Why are you measuring up my house? You're not going to contact the council are you?'

'No, not at all. I just think that it's important that your statement is correct. If we're going to find these burglars, we need all the detail we can get. See how it reads now: I entered my hallway, which is 3m x 2.5m with a dado rail around it at a height of 1m. The front door is uPvc and I have painted the walls with Dulux Harvest Gold.'

'I can't see how it helps, all that stuff.'

'Oh yes, it really does. You see, it's all evidence.'

Yes, yes, I know lots of people live in poverty and don't have enough to eat, let alone matching appliances, but it just goes to show the kind of work these people have to put into a new place before it begins to resemble the kind of slum we are all familiar with.

Although I've enjoyed my visits to these places, I have mainly been stuck (even more than usual) in the office attempting to investigate internet crime. Mainly, we're talking fraud.

I bet you thought/hoped this sort of thing was handled by a crack squad of geeks with all the latest hi-tech tools, liaising with the FBI and Interpol. Well, at the moment, it's just me. I start each investigation knowing that it will be unsolved, but, in order to satisfy the crime auditors, I have to show I have made all the relevant enquiries. This means faxing eBay with all the details of the crime, so they can tell me the culprits are based in Holland, and faxing the relevant bank with details of the cloned credit card along with the form from the injured party giving me access to his account. I then telephone the bank to chase up the enquiry (this takes a number of attempts and a long time on hold) before they tell me that the transactions occurred in Thailand.

In most forces, crimes are allocated to officers on a first-come, first-served basis, so the first person to meet the injured party gets to investigate the crime. While this is fair and reasonable most of the time, it means that every officer is dealing with one or two internet/ bank frauds, each of which takes a good couple of hours to sort out on the phone and even more time in writing up the crime to satisfy the auditors. Furthermore, with each officer working shifts, it can be weeks before any meaningful work is carried out on the crimes anyway. We do have a 'Hi-tech Crime Department' (you'll recall that they make me laugh when they ask me to 'fax the details through'; I always want to reply, 'Tell you what, I'll write them on a piece of vellum using a quill and send it over by pigeon.'). They 'deal with internet crime' in the same way the domestic violence unit 'deals with domestic violence'; that is, they tell me to let them know if I need any help or advice and, in the meantime, good luck.

Internet crime is a rapidly-growing problem which requires unique investigative skills. Precisely which investigative skills am I exercising when I am sitting in an office, armed with CS, a baton and a stab vest, on the phone to an internet auction company and at the same time responding to a dispatcher who wants me to attend a violent domestic on the other side of town?

BLACK COMEDY AND CANTEEN CULTURE

EVEN IF YOU DON'T know much about how the police work, you'll probably know about our 'canteen culture'. Due to the fact that we're all sexist and racist, we cannot be trusted to adopt the liberal orthodoxy, and our conversations are often covertly monitored by professional standards departments in order to weed out the counter-revolutionaries amongst our ranks: people, perhaps, who insist on using words like 'brain storm' (which apparently offends the mentally ill) instead of 'cloud burst', or those who do not know the word of the week for people who are not white.

The culture in any group is defined by its more experienced members and problems can emerge if those in charge fail to exercise leadership. In the police, this has led to quite serious incidents, where junior officers have been pressured into withholding evidence or lying (although, these days, that's more difficult, with CCTV and advances in forensic evidence. Generally, as I've said before, police corruption is a figment of most people's imagination. It is simply not worth it.)

There is, though, a dominant culture amongst most officers who work outside police stations (as opposed to those who stay indoors and operate computers) and it's defined as much by people and situations that officers deal with on the streets as by key individuals within the shift. For example, if a sergeant has a particular enthusiasm – commercial burglaries, say – then the rest of the shift get enthused, too, and spend their time racing around industrial estates catching burglars. On the other hand, if you have a sergeant who insists on every report being War and Peace, then most of the shift is going to be indoors writing.

I've always fitted in to most of the groups I've worked with, mainly because I tend to keep my ideas to myself (no, seriously) and avoid making a fuss when I'm asked to do something. More importantly, though, I actually like the people I work with and the culture within the shifts. Most junior officers are conservative, only adopting radical liberal views when they reach senior positions, and have a healthy distrust of authority. This leads to cynicism and many opportunities for japes.

Japes abound in the police, from typed complaints about officers from the Pakistani embassy, to completed fictional files created in the officer's name about which he will know nothing but about which he will receive numerous queries. Best of all, though, police officers get to laugh about all the things you aren't really supposed to. I can't go into details for obvious reasons, but I'm sure all officers have made, heard and laughed at inappropriate jokes about some of the most serious crimes in the statute books. It's almost impossible to complete an enquiry involving dogs without someone shouting up on the radio, 'Any leads?'

You have to be on your guard after having an accident in a police car because half the people who ring you up to inform you of impending legal action are fellow officers trying to disguise their voices. Confess some weakness in a forthcoming court case in which you're giving evidence and people will wind you up about it for weeks.

It's difficult to remain politically correct when you're dealing with crimes rather than hand-wringing about them. It's all very well guarding a murder scene, but where's the fun if you can't steal all the chocolate bars out of the packed lunches? A call to attend a serious stabbing feels like you've got away scot free, especially if you were originally on your way to a domestic incident that's so trivial nobody has attended for the last week.

STOLEN PROPERTY

ONE OF THE BENEFITS of having a vast bureaucracy instead of a police service is that many more crimes are 'detected' than would otherwise be the case. The system of 'crime audit' that exists in many forces ensures that all crime is correctly counted and administrated to the extent that the very administration of crime becomes significantly more important than reducing it, or even 'solving' it, in the traditional sense.

However, most of us still get a bigger kick out of the traditional side of the job.

I spent today dealing with podgy Josh Rogers. It was a simple enough case. 'I've just seen podgy Josh Rogers ride off on my bike,' said a small youth.

Always happy to help, we belt round to podgy Josh's house and speak to Mrs. Rogers, Josh's mum.

'Mrs Rogers, does Josh own a bike?'

'No... er... yes. He's... er... just been given one.'

'Can I come in?'

'Yes... Josh! F*CKIN' COME 'ERE.'

A fat youth with piggy eyes appears. I address myself to him. 'Josh, I'm going to give you one chance to help yourself here. Are you ready?'

'Yes. But I didn't nick that bike.'

'What bike, Josh?' and the rest, as they say, is history.

There's nothing quite like finding stolen property: you obtain a description from the complainant, you search a house and... there it is! I've had the same feeling when recovering blood-soaked clothing or other critical evidence. You solemnly put the evidence into a bag, ask the subject to sign the relevant sections of the search form and inform him of what's going to happen next, all the time thinking, Gotcha! It's a marvellous feeling: I really have to try not to laugh out loud.

I suppose it is a reflection of the inefficacy of modern policing that recovering even small amounts of stolen property can generate so huge a feeling of warmth and self-congratulation. Despite all the advances in police bureaucracy, it's still fun to catch thieves, even stupid ones like podgy Josh Rogers.

Oh, and speaking of reducing police bureaucracy, I have noticed a twin-track approach to the problem:

1. By making the letters on any given form smaller and increasing the number of boxes to complete, you can maintain the same number of forms while gathering much more 'vital information'.

2. By combining several forms into one, you can actually reduce the number of forms while maintaining the same level of bureaucracy.

LIGHTS, CAMERA, ACTION

'VIOLENT DOMESTIC IN PROGRESS, screams can be heard. 14b Edwards Road,' said the voice on my radio.

I recognised the address: it was Maxine and her heroin-addled ex. Their details were imprinted on my mind and also on a piece of paper, detailing the worst, most troublesome relationships in Newtown, which nestles permanently in my briefcase for ease of future reference.

An immediate response was required. I was already halfway through my meal, so the call would be answered within the required time and I could still finish my last sandwich and tasty morsel of cake.

I rolled down to the car and, with blue lights and sirens on, off I went. En-route, I triggered a 'safety camera'. Fortunately, I'm in the clear: 'Speed camera triggered on Church Road, control.'

When the ticket comes through, I will simply attach a copy of the computer printout of the incident, a photocopy of my pocketbook, a detailed explanation of what went on, another completed form and send it all back (twice, the first lot having got lost in the system) and the ticket will be waived.

I don't drive all that fast, or very well, and I have no natural talent when it comes to being behind the wheel, unlike PC Mark Milton. Milton achieved his 15 minutes of infamy when he was charged after driving at 84mph in a 30mph zone and 159mph on the M54 to 'familiarise' himself with his new car.

This outraged the public and the media, and I can't say I blame them, really. We spend our professional lives dishing out millions of speeding tickets to otherwise fairly innocent members of the public and then, when they report actual crimes to us we send them letters saying 'You've been a victim of a fairly minor and, to us, insignificant crime, fancy some counselling?'

We can't be surprised if the public get angry and we lose their support.

As it happened, Maxine's ex, Paul, had gone by the time I got there. They'd just had yet another argument. I was able to deal with the documentation in double quick time, without having to ask for details of all of Maxine's children. I wasn't able to say if the mess inside the flat constituted 'signs of a struggle' or merely 'failure to tidy up'. Probably a bit of both. I'm sure I'll be back next week.

COPPERFIELD'S GUIDE TO PROTESTERS

I LIKE PROTESTERS, within reason. At least they're getting off their backsides and protesting about things, rather than just harrumphing and changing TV channels.

A while back, it was the G8 and celebrity scruff, activist and former Boomtown Rat 'Sir' Bob Geldof calling for a million soap-dodgers to descend upon Edinburgh and bring an end to world poverty; a year or two before that they were rampaging through London smashing up branches of McDonalds and giving Winston Churchill a grass Mohican. As far as I know, they didn't really bother with Moscow this year. I'm sure that was down to travel costs or not being able to get time off work. Nothing to do with the average Muscovite policeman's likely response (robust and old-fashioned) to gobby students/hippies/ anarchists prancing about shouting the odds.

Personally, the prancing gobbiness doesn't bother me. It's a free country and if you want to make a fool of yourself in public, that's up to you. No, it's the rampaging I'm not so keen on. It's no longer enough to wear a rubber wristband and wave a few placards; now you have to cause problems for thousands of genuinely innocent bobbies.

The Edinburgh G8 was a case in point. Thousands of English coppers were shipped north to link arms and protect the windows of local branches of Starbucks just so Sir Bob and a load of middle-class crusties could develop a warm glow of smug self-satisfaction and get themselves on the telly in the process. I tore myself away from the domestic miseries of Newtown for half an hour to check out some of the protest organisers' websites. They made fascinating reading. 'Dissent – A Network of Resistance Against the G8' was one I particularly enjoyed. 'We are asking that all local groups consider renting mini-buses for the period of the convergence,' they wrote, that phrase 'period of the convergence' neatly indicating that self-important jargon has even found its way into the world of the nose-ringed anarchist. 'Renting a mini-bus is actually a cheap way for a group of people to get up to Scotland, and will help with travel to and from the convergence space which will be remote.'

I emailed to say that there would probably be a few police carriers going up half-full from England and that there might be some spaces on board. Similarly, the odd carrier might be oversubscribed and if there was any space left in one of their minibuses, perhaps they could let their local force know? We could all resume hostilities on the other side of the border, I said. They didn't respond, which I found a bit odd: after all, they must have been car-sharing environmentalists.

They also had a handy guide for dealing with the police. Its advice included: 'Note as well that the police will bluff on the law so if you challenge them directly to state the law they are hassling you under they will back down. Police will seize on any perceived doubt or weakness, so show them that you are confident in facing them down even if you are nervous on the inside.' The guide adds, 'It helps to remember that you are struggling for justice, while they are seeking to protect corrupt governments and destructive corporations.'

I'd never thought of it like that before. I thought I was in it for the overtime.

Anyway, here's Copperfield's guide for dealing with protesters, wherever you may find them:

1. Identify your protester using the following police-style mnemonic:
   B – Balding
   O – Oxfam clothes
   G – Getting on a bit
   S – Sandals
   A – Acting like a tw*t
   P – Pony tail
   BOGSAP. It has a certain ring, doesn't it?

2. Remember, they may look confident, but they're really nervous on the inside. If you're not sure, just bluff on the law.

3. Take the little bars of soap and bottles of shampoo from your hotel and throw them at the protesters. They love the irony.

4. Use the phrase 'I'm only following orders' as often as possible. This will have the effect of calming the protesters, like a beekeeper approaching a hive with his smoke generator (that's what I call an analogy).

5. If anyone asks, say you're from the Met and all you know is that you're there to protect Global Capitalism/Big Business/War-mongering Corporations.

6. Remember, they are struggling for justice while you are on time-and-a-half for 16 hours a day. Many of you will be on rest day rate; many of *them* are on the dole. You are being put up in hotels while they will be sleeping in their own filth. Take heart, and think about your next payslip!

The worst thing about protesters, actually, is the war stories. I didn't make it to the G8 but I know there were a few confrontations from which the police always walked away clear winners. Those of us left behind had to put up with tales of derring-do for weeks afterwards. 'Well, when I was in Scotland I did such-and-such…' 'You should have seen me with those three blokes…' 'I put on two stone eating shortbread and deep fried Mars bars…'

I believe it was quite hard work, so I have to say (through gritted teeth) that they probably earned their overtime. But stop going on about it, for goodness' sake.

By the way, the current trend for charity wristbands is going the way I predicted it would. I recently filled out a crime report where the modus operandi ran as follows: 'Offender pinned IP to the ground and removed his charity wristband. Offender then made good his escape.'

Further, as recent press reports revealed, my suspicion that all the wristbands were being made in sweatshops where the workers are free to earn as much as 50p per week turned out to be true, too. Still, if you must wear a wristband, wear one that's worthwhile. You could support our soldiers with a camouflage one, for instance. I'm thinking of starting a police one, with ACAB printed on it. The money will go behind the bar at the King's Head for the next Christmas party.

I SAY! DESIST I TELL YOU!

I WAS READING OUR trade magazine *Police Review* in the nick this morning. It has just finished a debate on whether or not ordinary patrol officers should carry Taser. For those of you who don't know, Taser is a stun gun that fires a couple of electrodes attached to wires. The electrodes stick to your clothing, you get an electric shock and you fall to the ground. The debate is irrelevant because ACPO has already decided to issue Taser to AFOs (Authorised Firearms Officers) only; the rest of us will have to make-do with a stick, a tin of CS and a nice line in biting sarcasm.

The *Police Review*/NOP poll showed that 80% of officers wanted the Taser, which means 20% must have thought, 'No thanks, I'd rather risk seriously injuring myself and my colleagues by having to wrestle a subject to the ground.'

Who are these nutjobs?

The Home Office is opposed to Taser. It says, 'The policy in this country has long been that the police should generally not be armed and that gives a character to our policing that we should not readily give up. Safe as it is, there is no doubt that Taser is an aggressive response and the government believes that it should only be used in strictly controlled conditions.'

I agree in principle. After all, Peel's dictum was that physical force should only be used 'to the extent necessary to secure observance of the law or to restore order only when the exercise of persuasion, advice and warning is found to be insufficient'. The thing is, 'persuasion, advice and warning' cut very little ice in Newtown at 02:30hrs on a Saturday. I'd like to take that Home Office spokeswoman on a tour of Newtown at closing time and see if we come across any 'strictly controlled conditions' suitable for Taser deployment.

'No, no, PC Copperfield! Using Taser is too aggressive in this situation. Allow that 6ft tall, heavily-built, drunken male to come closer still before threatening to beat him with your baton. If the worst happens and you get injured, at least you'll leave the character of our policing intact.'

A representative of the 20% opposed to Taser wrote in a letter to *Police Review*: 'The clamour for Taser appears to be symptomatic of a worrying trend for some officers to avoid confrontation when their own safety is at risk.'

Unsurprisingly, the Inspector who wrote this worked at an incident handling centre in Surrey, where the main risk of a 'confrontation' probably occurs in the queue for the canteen.

Personally, I'm not all that bothered about Taser. My priorities are a reliable photocopier and enough staples to last the shift. I'd also like a chair in custody, for when I have to wait an hour to book in a prisoner.

Incidentally, while perusing *Police Review*, my eye was drawn to a full page interview with PC Emma Chapman: used to be a man, is now a woman. Emma says s/he has had no problems in his/her job, but that doesn't stop him/her adding: 'The service does need some more encouragement to actively recruit from transgender communities.'

Clever boy/girl Emma, I see an air-conditioned office and a job title with the words Transgender Liaison Support Initiative Group Outreach Police Worker rearranged into some sort of order.

Later, I drove up to Weatherby to speak to Paul, Maxine's ex. I was there about an hour listening to him going on about his plans to get a solicitor and get custody of the kids. He told me he was off the gear, but it didn't look like it to me and I suspect he only wants the kids so he can sell them for more heroin. Paul hadn't actually committed any offence (unless you count being a pain in neck to Maxine and ruining his kids' future) but I thought he would benefit from a word from me asking him to stay away.

'She's always ringing me up, though.'

This is probably true, but I continued. 'Well, find another girlfriend and stay away.'

'But I just want to see the kids, officer.'

'Come off it Paul, you don't want to see the kids, you just want Maxine's money.'

We carried on for a while but it soon became apparent that for as long as Maxine was prepared to give Paul money, he would keep turning up at her house and I would end up racing across Newtown in response to Maxine's calls.

REAL COPPERS

I DON'T MIND PEOPLE knowing what I do for a living, though it can get a bit boring at parties.

I can't beat my fellow police blogger Brian (of the now-defunct Brian's Brief Encounters). Here's his list of automatic responses to the questions you always get asked.

Yes, I enjoy my job.

No, I'm not on duty now.

Yes, I have seen some gruesome sights. Let me think. Perhaps you'd like to hear about the two-week-old hanging, complete with maggots, as you tuck into that prawn vol-au-vent? Maybe that sushi will taste nicer if I relate the tale of the car crash decapitation from the other week?

No, I have nothing to do with speed cameras.

No, I don't have a Lodge friend who is in charge of speed cameras.

No, I don't know why your five-year-old burglary hasn't been solved yet.

No, nor where your last-but-one car is.

No, I don't watch it.

No, I don't know Tony Stamp, or Reg Hollis.

Yes, I do have my own handcuffs.

No, I leave them at work.

No, I don't plan to drive myself home.

No, after seven glasses of Chilean Rioja, I think you should consider a taxi.

Yes, even though we've had a big meal.

No, to the best of my knowledge, none of them moonlight as strip-o-grams.

No, I don't think they'll change their minds for your mate's 40th.

Andy, a colleague of mine, prefers not to say what he does. He says that he is a clerk who works for the courts system. This has more than a little truth to it, given that these days we're so busy writing that we don't have time to get out on the streets and deter crime. The obvious solution to this, of course, is to make full-sized cardboard cut-outs of real police officers and put them in areas where there is a crime problem. This lunatic scheme has proven so popular that local newspapers from Cornwall to Durham are picturing the real officer, face to face with his own cardboard cut out. How funny is that? No, really, is that funny? A more useful (and easier to answer) question might be, 'How effective is that?' especially after the shoplifter realises It's not a real policeman, but a cardboard cut-out instead.

The next stage is surely to provide the two dimensional, law-enforcement mannequins with voice boxes so they could say things like, 'Evenin' all', 'Warm night' and that old favourite, 'Move along, nothing to see here.'

So, cardboard coppers maintain a presence on the street while the real officers can get on with the business of writing reports.

CANINE CRIME

MOST VICTIMS DON'T like going to court. Some will, but lots make statements saying they don't want to prosecute and others make statements saying they do wish to prosecute, only to withdraw the statement at a later date.

Nevertheless, the crime they initially reported to the police remains on the books and the offender is interviewed with the aim of getting a clear-up as per the administrative detection scam I've already outlined. This is an entirely bureaucratic, time-consuming operation; the only advantages of it are that it keeps lots of people in work and makes our crime figures look better.

The latest news about the rise in violent crime and the shocking clear-up rates got me thinking: how can the police make a difference?

I've thought about it for a while, mainly while massaging my wrist in between form-filling, and I have come up with the following solution: We should create, through bureaucratic smoke and mirrors, a rise in Canine Crime. Think about it. Currently, dog-bites are classified as either 'Dog out of control in a public place' or 'Nuisance, animal'. The first step in PC Copperfield's Operation Fido would be to re-classify such incidents as 'Violence against the person' (which, technically, they are). A crime of violence thus created, the next step is to 'detect' the crime.

I take a statement from the victim and then I speak to the dog. 'Of course,' I say, 'you may well have to be put down.'

The dog stares up at me with big brown eyes and a tongue falling half way out of its mouth.

'OK,' I say. 'Look. I'll take a statement, you admit to it and we'll leave it at that. It's just for my figures.'

So, I interview the dog (because the interview has to be PACE compliant, there is an appropriate adult present in the form of the owner). I put it to him, step by step, he nods and barks a bit and fetches the odd stick and, at the end, he signs using his paw. Add the victim statement to the admission and I have a detection. Looking at the bigger picture, the vast majority of canine crime could be solved, increasing the police detection rate for violent crime.

The consequent blame for the rise in canine crime could be laid at the doors of the RSPCA and would not be down to the police.

INVESTIGATING PETTY CRIME

JUST IN CASE you're missing the point of all this – sorry, but I deal with a lot of people who do, both in and out of the police – let's talk about James. He's a nice lad who hasn't been expelled and goes to a real school. His mum helps him deliver the Newtown Advertiser when she gets back from work. The house is a 'tea house' meaning, whenever I've gone in the past, I've always had a cup of tea there. What's more James is a good witness: quiet and not too emotional, he even wears a watch, so he knows what time his bike was nicked.

Without his bike, James' paper delivery empire will crumble – even with the assistance of his mum, it would be impossible to accomplish in less than two hours.

No force was used in the theft, just a simple, 'Oi, fatso, get off the bike.'

He only had to wait a couple of hours before I was able to see him and take a statement from him. The good news was that James knew the three lads – Ryan, Conor and Duayne – who had taken his bike, so it was simply a matter of getting them to court. All three live on the estate, so I had no problem picking them up. None of them go to school on a regular basis and all of them have limited criminal records.

I already knew what they would say. 'Yes, I was there, but I didn't do it. No, I don't know where the bike is.'

Furthermore, I knew what their mothers would say: 'I've asked him if he's done it and he said he didn't, so you've got to believe him.' Here's a breakdown of the steps that were taken to investigate the matter.

1. Statement from James: 1 hour.
2. Crime report: 15 minutes,
3. Arrest, wait for solicitor, interview, photograph, fingerprint and DNA then bail offender Ryan: 2 hours.
4. Section 18 search for bike of Ryan's house (and waiting for authorisation): 1 hour.
5. Arrest, wait for solicitor, interview, photograph, fingerprint and DNA then bail offender Conor: 2 hours.
6. Section 18 search for bike of Conor's house and waiting for authorisation): 1 hour.
7. Arrest, wait for solicitor, interview, photograph, fingerprint and DNA then bail offender Duayne: 2 hours.
8. Section 18 search for bike of Duayne's house and waiting for authorisation): 1 hour.

9. Further witness statement from witness Kara (including travelling and other arrangements): 1 hour.

10. Further witness statement from witness Josie (including travelling and other arrangements): 1 hour.

11. Prepare report for CPS to obtain CPS advice (x2 because they always lose the first one): 1 hour.

12. Prepare charges and then charge Ryan, Conor and Duayne: 1 hour.

13. Prepare court file for not-guilty plea and subsequent trial of Ryan, Conor and Duayne: 3.5 hours.

14. Complete further tasks as directed by prosecutor/police liaison team (total): 2 hours.

15. In-house progress reports as required by the police: 1 hour.

TOTAL TIME: Just over 20 hours, or two-and-a-half shifts, which means a lot of time not dealing with any more calls for service by anyone else in Newtown.

I'm not sure if knowing that the police really go to all this trouble and take half a week to investigate a petty theft is reassuring, or frightening. Although I was actually out of the police station for six hours, all I did was drive to someone's house, take a statement, then drive back to the police station, so I wasn't 'patrolling' in the traditional sense of the word. The 20 hours was spread over about two months and I had to try to fit it in with about ten other similar crimes as well as responding to other calls for service.

I never got to find the stolen bike, but the three offenders were found guilty, given a community punishment and referred to the Youth Offending Team (whatever that is).

I only mention this now, because I've only just got the result in from our Court Liaison Unit. The actual incident occurred six months ago.

PC David Copperfield

KEEPING UP WITH
THE JONESES

THE JONES/TRUELOVE FAMILY are our biggest customers –
literally, and metaphorically. They live in a large, three-bedroom house
on the Long Road estate: Maureen Truelove (fat and loud), Kevin
Jones (her partner, fat and aggressive) and her offspring, Courtney
(14, fat and uncooperative) and Wayne (16, skinny and slothful). In
an estate with more than its fair share of unpleasant families, these
are the worst of the lot. They have turned their garden into a waste
tip, their house is in an advanced state of disrepair and their electrical
products are top-notch. In short, they are a family from hell.

I've had a pleasant break from them for a number of months,
though three weeks ago I was contacted by a tearful Maureen telling
me she wanted her neighbour arrested for slander ('Civil matter
Maureen. Speak to a solicitor.')

I've had to call on them this week though.

'Hello,' I said, with a cheery smile. 'I've come to see Wayne.'

'F*cking hell,' said Maureen. 'What's he F*CKING done this
time?'

'Well,' I said. 'We think he's probably stolen a top from JD in town.'

'WAYNE,' shouted Maureen. 'GET F*CKIN' 'ERE.' Wayne got
halfway down the stairs and shouted down to us. 'I AIN'T F*CKIN'
DONE NUFFINK.'

'WELL WHY ARE THE F*CKIN POLICE HERE THEN?' asked
Maureen. A reasonable enquiry, I thought.

We carried on for some time in the same vein, with all parties
alternatively shouting at me, then at each other, before Wayne agreed
to come with me to the police station.

That was just one meeting with them.

The police are consistently involved with them for a number of
other reasons including:

– Kevin and Maureen are always drunk and beating each other
up
– They hate their neighbours and are always being 'harassed'
by them

238

– They hate their neighbours and are always 'harassing' them
– Wayne is a persistent shoplifter and delinquent
– Courtney likes to throw her not inconsiderable weight around the estate

I'd like to work for a private company managing the Jones/ Truelove Account. I could do them a price list, discounted, naturally, as they would be 'Gold Card' holders. We'd give them a direct line, 24 hours a day, to any one of a small team of staff dedicated to solving their problems. The price list would be something like this:

Double-crewed emergency response vehicle: £200 (£350 after 22:00hrs and at weekends), thereafter £100 per half-hour.
Normal visit by a member of staff: £75 call-out, thereafter £50 per hour
Statement taking (at company HQ), witnesses: £30 (any size).
Statement taking, Injured Party: £50 (any size)
Non-crimes, advice etc: £60 per hour
Harassment investigations: £500 per neighbour arrested (charging neighbours with harassment, a further £150)
All other investigations: £300 per arrest (charging with criminal offences, a further £150)
Referral to other agencies: £50 per letter
Arresting Jones/Truelove family juveniles at home: £200
Arresting Jones/Truelove family adults by appointment at company HQ: £150
All interviews: £20 per five minutes
Custody space: £70 per hour
Solicitors: free on legal aid

The obvious question is, Who would pay the bills?
I would set up a separate company called Copperfield Holdings and take on all the work related to the Jones/Truelove family (and a few other big 'service user families') to make the whole thing pay. I would do most of the work myself, retaining the power of arrest etc., and charge it back to the police.

The more I think about it, the more I think it's the way forward.

P.S. To work out how much it actually costs at the moment, and how inefficient the police really are, double everything in the price list.

AMERICAN RIFLEMAN ARRIVES!

AFTER READING THROUGH page after page of politically correct news from trade journals like *Police Review* and Newtown Constabulary's own freesheet, I felt a tremendous sense of relief when my copy of *American Rifleman* dropped though the letterbox at the end of its long journey from the land of the free and heavily-armed.

This is the magazine you get when you join the National Rifle Association (NRA); it contains gun news, gun features, pictures of guns, stories about guns, advertisements for guns and opinions about guns.

This edition has a feature on Florida's 'Castle Doctrine', by one Chris W. Cox.

In the UK, you are only able to use 'reasonable force' to deter aggression (as we saw earlier, with 'hot' burglaries).

That's all fine and dandy, but it presupposes two things: firstly, that you can work out, in the blink of an eye, exactly what 'reasonable force' is in the circumstances in which you find yourself (and believe me, an army of detectives and CPS lawyers will spend weeks and maybe months trying to prove you got it wrong afterwards) and, secondly, that you're able to use that force to protect yourself.

Take the case of Muglin Southerman, a kitchen fitter from Manchester.

Mr Southerman was standing in a pizza takeaway when a gang of youths walked in. One of them asked him for a light, and when he didn't provide them with one, they dragged him out of the shop and attacked him like savages. Witnesses said he was hit with an iron bar and his head was kicked 'as if it was a football'. Mr Southerman, a father of three, died.

At what point would he have had an accurate appreciation of the amount of force required to save his life? Probably not when they first started jostling him in the takeaway. Maybe not when they dragged him outside, when he was still thinking They'll leave me alone in a minute. Perhaps when he was lying on the floor with someone being David Beckham with his face? But by then it was probably too late.

Let's say he had immediately realised the danger he was in; what chance would he have had against a gang of yobs? (And even assuming he punched the first yob to the ground and the others ran off, would the courts, not knowing what was otherwise to happen, have accepted this was reasonable?)

I think this case perfectly illustrates why the doctrine of reasonable force is a flawed one: it's fine for barristers who spend their well-remunerated lives buried in abstract legal texts, and it's great for High Court judges, who seldom use pizza takeaways in Manchester. But in the real world, it's a nonsense.

What has all this got to do with *American Rifleman* and Castle Doctrine?

Well, most people remember the Tony Martin case. I've already mentioned hot burglaries and the Monckton murder. Most of the debate about reasonable force surrounds what happens when you discover an uninvited guest rifling through your drawers at home. The attitude of the British police tends to be: 'Yes, you can use reasonable force. But we'd rather you stayed upstairs out of the way and let them get on with it. And if you do get involved, we'll arrest you.'

Castle Doctrine (based, quaintly, on the old but very out-of-date saying, that an Englishman's home is his castle), says three things about this:

1. It establishes, in law, the presumption that a person who forcibly enters your home or occupied vehicle is a criminal who is there to cause death or great bodily harm; therefore, you may use any manner of force, including deadly force, against that criminal.

2. It removes the 'duty to retreat' if you are attacked in any place in which you have a right to be. You no longer have to turn your back on a criminal and try to run when attacked, as our courts like you to. Instead, you may stand your ground and

fight back, meeting force with force, including deadly force, if you reasonably believe it is necessary to prevent death or great bodily harm to yourself or others.

3. It provides that persons using force authorized by law shall not be prosecuted for using such force. It also prohibits criminals and their families from suing victims for injuring or killing the criminals who have attacked them.

In short, it gives rights back to law-abiding people and forces judges and prosecutors who are prone to coddling criminals instead to focus on protecting victims.

At the moment, it's only the law in Florida, but the NRA is hoping it will spread across the US. It won't come over here any time soon, though. Wayne LaPierre, NRA Executive Vice President, has this to say about the UK: 'Never forget that the Brady (an anti-gun pressure group) idea of Utopia is Great Britain, where the disarmed populace is subject to prosecution for any form of self defence, and where armed criminals control not only urban neighbourhoods but the rural countryside.'

Guns are another controversial subject. I know not everyone agrees with me that law abiding people should be able to arm themselves if they so desire.

To that, I'd say two things.

1. Criminals arm themselves with impunity.

2. Muglin Southerman *might* be alive today if he'd pulled out a pistol and told the gang to leave him alone (I know the counter-argument, that they'd all have been armed, too; but they *were*, just not with guns, and they *might* have thought twice about starting on him if there was a chance he'd have been armed too).

LaPierre for PM, anyone?

A GAME OF SOCA

I LIKE THE SOUND OF SOCA (The Serious and Organised Crime Agency). If its logo is anything to go by – a roaring big cat, astride the globe, pouncing on an unseen enemy – it should be a ripping success.

As it happens I've got a couple of jobs that I'm writing up especially for SOCA, in the expectation that they'll take them on. These are:

– A case of bullying at St John's School, in which the female IP has been sent abusive text messages from different pupils in different form years (ORGANISED). Mother is very upset and may well have to withdraw her child unless the bullying stops (SERIOUS).

– The theft of a credit card and its subsequent use to the value of £2,000 (SERIOUS) in various locations around the country and the internet (ORGANISED).

I bet they bat them back to me, probably with some helpful emailed suggestions. Tell you what, why don't I try and join? SOCA is just the kind of thing that ambitious police officers love: surveillance, drugs, plain clothes, nice cars and serious villains. Unfortunately, it's just the kind of thing that most victims of crime will never see the point of; all they want are a few more coppers on the streets, as opposed to in the office.

I read recently that 60% of muggings are not reported because the police aren't interested.

The Home Secretary responded by saying, 'Clearly, we need to ensure that the service is equipped to deal with future challenges. This is why we have established a Serious Organised Crime Agency.'

I predict that, while SOCA may, from time to time, put large amounts of guns and drugs on the table, it will have no interest in or effect on muggings.

One of the senior people in SOCA is going to be Lt Gen Sir Cedric Delves. Gen Delves is a highly impressive character: he fought in the Falklands with the SAS, where he remained undetected behind enemy lines for 10 days in an observation post overlooking Port Stanley.

Ten days? I know of officers who have remained undetected for years behind desks inside police stations.

DETAINED PERSON'S RIGHTS

I LOCKED UP a Kurdish Iraqi man at the weekend.

'How long am I going to be in here, you bastards?' he shouted, from the comfort of his en-suite cell.

'I bet you wouldn't talk like that in Abu Ghraib,' I remarked cheerfully, as I carefully counted out his change into a plastic bag before sealing it and recording the amount: £3.67.

A short time later, his local girlfriend telephoned to ask for his keys.

'Have you got Faruk?' she said, in the unmistakeably hoarse tones of the fishwife. ''Cos if you have, that's f*ckin' great, that is, thanks a lot, 'cos I'm locked out of the flat. He's got the f*ckin' keys.'

You might think this would be an ideal time to bring in the Data Protection Act. 'Sorry,' I wanted to say. 'But I'm not allowed to confirm that we've locked up your boyfriend.'

Instead, I had to get a patrol to drive round and deliver the keys to this awful woman.

I sometimes wonder why we don't just dispense with the illusion of being police officers and devote ourselves full-time to being social workers for the people we come into contact with. I'm forever being dispatched to fetch medication, interpreters, friends, relatives or appropriate adults for people who've been arrested for various offences. The theory is that just because we've arrested them that doesn't mean they're guilty, and therefore we should inconvenience them as little as possible. If we had nothing else to do, and were on top of crime, and they were generally innocent, fair enough. As it is, we've loads to do, we're not on top of crime and they're generally guilty, so tough (we ought to say).

What's more, I seem to spend more time worrying about people I've arrested than the victims. OK, sometimes there isn't much to choose between the two, but it annoys me when Superintendents, doctors and defence solicitors keep asking me how much longer I'm going to be; not to mention the custody sergeant who (for entirely understandable reasons) wants them out of there as soon as possible.

Earlier in the week, I had to accompany a burglar to the local hospital because an injury he had sustained in the course of one of his crimes had become infected (poetic justice indeed).

I had to sit next to him in the waiting room for an hour or so and eventually I had to answer the call of nature. I removed one end of the handcuffs and attached them to the immovable waiting room chair before going to the toilet. Afterwards, I collected a few things from the car, so I was gone a little while. On my return he said he felt humiliated, like an animal.

People of Newtown, I do what I can.

I DON'T KNOW MUCH, BUT I KNOW WHAT I LIKE

I ONLY PURCHASE the *Newtown Gazette* to find out about the latest changes at the top of Newtown Police. On more than one occasion, I've telephoned my Inspector only to be told, 'No Dave, I was your Inspector last week.'

Things change so fast in the police. They even introduce new forms while you're in the middle of an investigation, so that when you try and file it you find out that you need a particular check-sheet or other that you didn't need only a week or so earlier. The public often seem to know more about crime fighting than I do.

'What sort of car is that?' someone asked me yesterday, as I was putting some cones in the boot.

'Er... hang on I'll have a look.' I pulled the hatchback down and looked at the badge. 'It's a Ford of some kind.'

'I bet it's tuned though, eh?'

'Well, it's just a car really, with some buttons for the blue lights.'

Another person asked me about informants. 'Do you have a snout?' he said.

'Not really... should I? I mean, do I need one?'

'You know, an informant like.'

'Oh, God, no. People tell me too much as it is. The less I know, the less I have to tell people.'

I was relating this 'snout' story to Mrs C last night and she said, 'You do have some laughs in your job, though, don't you?'

'Oh yes,' I said. And I do, all the time. There's loads of good things about it. It's just that there's loads of bad things, too.

So, for no particular reason and in no particular order, here are my top ten and worst ten things I like/dislike about work at the moment:

Top Ten

1. Drunks who commit offences when I'm looking.
2. Catching burglars on or near the scene of the crime, preferably after a short foot chase.
3. Aggressive old people.
4. People who get into massive brawls and then refuse to provide details and, despite sustaining injuries, don't want any further police action taken.
5. People who make complaints about me when I'm expecting them to.
6. People who say, 'I'm sorry to have wasted your time officer' and really mean it.
7. Handing serious crimes on to CID.
8. Having CID say to me, 'We'll have that one off you, Dave.'
9. Finding stuff on searches.
10. Walking around.

Worst Ten

1. Being accosted by drunks who wish to report that someone has slapped them and they want them 'done'.
2. Drunk drivers who pretend not to be able to blow into the tube.
3. Suspects who admit the offence on interview then go bandit in court.
4. Waiting in custody.
5. Suspects who don't turn up on police bail.
6. Counter-allegations of petty offences.
7. Administrative personnel who clearly regard administration as more important than police work.
8. Suspects who live off the force area.

9. Parents who insist their child could not have done anything wrong because they know their kids.
10. Driving everywhere.

DETECTING

DETECTIVES INVESTIGATE MOST of the crime that you read about in national newspapers or see on television. If it's a really serious crime like a murder, a relatively senior officer will head the investigation and appear on the news asking for witnesses to come forward and reassuring the rest of us that the killer will be caught (take this with a pinch of salt if you live in Nottinghamshire). An unfortunate by-product of all this publicity is that lots of people I meet are under the impression that their particular case will also be dealt with by detectives.

In statistical terms, detectives investigate a tiny minority of crimes reported by the public. That's not to say they don't do very much, it's just that the investigations they carry out are much more detailed and thorough than those carried out by their uniformed colleagues. Even so, most investigations are time consuming, frustrating and boring.

I met a disgruntled Newtown young offender called Lewis the other day.

'I had five mates round at the weekend, yeah?' he said. 'Just a party, like. Anyway, this morning I noticed me money had gone.'

Inwardly wincing, on behalf of his neighbours, at the thought of Lewis and five of his mates having a weekend house party, I feigned interest. 'Oh yes,' I said. 'How much has gone missing, and where from?'

Two hundred pounds, and from his cash box. It was a delicious irony; Lewis is a well-known thief. But I could tell from his indignation that the irony had eluded him.

'It had to be one of them bastards,' he said. 'No-one else come in all weekend and I've got the only key to the house, yeah?'

'Oh dear,' I said. 'With friends like those, who needs enemies?'

'Yerwot?'

'Never mind. Let's see what we can do.'

I knew, right from the off, that this was going nowhere. I'll have to get the cash box fingerprinted some time in the next week or so, but it will yield nothing. Lewis's five now-ex-friends will have to be interviewed but they live miles away in Weatherby, which is in a different force area to ours. I'll have to get officers from Weatherby to speak to them (PACE compliant) and ask them if they took the money. All five will deny any involvement, Lewis will not get his £200 back and the case will be filed as undetected.

The following day, another member of the public reported being assaulted by three people who then got into a taxi and drove off. The number of the taxi was taken and possible identities for the trio provided. Each of these will have to be arrested and their accounts taken; each will provide alibis that will have to be investigated; each will deny being there and an identity parade will have to be done for each person. This will take months, literally.

Once again, the result of the enquiry is already in no doubt: the victim will be unable to identify the offenders because he was drunk at the time, there will be no CCTV evidence and CPS will not run the case.

That's two simple cases reported to the same officer over two days which will result in hours and hours of enquiries spread over several weeks and, in each case, the officer knew within a few minutes of speaking to the injured party that there would never be enough evidence.

It is cases like these that form the bedrock of a detection rate. Sometimes there will be sufficient evidence to charge someone, sometimes there won't. Beyond a certain point, the law of diminishing returns begins to bite: if we spend more time investigating crime, we might be able to push up the detection rate a point or two, but at what cost? The officers who could be out on patrol are stuck in the police station arranging futile appointments with witnesses months after the event. If they aren't doing that, then they are putting together files for the CPS which they already know will never run in a month of Sundays.

I have between 10 and 20 of these crimes on the go at any one time, each requiring a varying number of arrests and/or statements. The crimes aren't particularly serious and about half the victims have already forgotten about them.

I can't remember the last time I did anything worthwhile.

ANTI-TERROR EMAILS

TERRORISM HAS ARRIVED in Newtown. It has made about as much impact as the recent arrival of 'culture' to Britain's shores: lots of people have a vague idea what it is, but everybody is doing their best to see it never gets a foothold here.

The townspeople are assisting the police by reporting a large number of suspicious packages in shopping centres, near chip shops and in car parks.

Needless to say the suggested police response to such threats is contained in a number of emails, all of which I delete immediately without opening. Which means if I ever do come across a terrorist and actually deal with him, I'll be lying if I give an interview in which I use the phrase 'The training just took over, really.' It will have been pure luck.

Anyway, yesterday someone dialled 999 to report a suspicious bag in the shopping centre.

On arrival, I found one corner of the shopping centre had been cordoned off by the private security people.

'We haven't done the full evacuation yet,' said one of them. 'We thought we'd wait for you to have a look at it first.'

So they're worried enough that it's a bomb to call us, but not enough to get everyone out. Ever get the feeling that you're being used and abused?

'Well,' I said. 'I'm sure it's nothing to worry about. What does it look like?' Like I'm an expert on what bombs look like. I mean, I've seen a few in films. They usually have red digital counters which helpfully show you how long you've got before they go off. Now, if I can just find the counter…

'I suppose it looks like a bag of shopping, really,' replied the security guard/bomb expert, a bit dubiously.

'I suppose it could actually be a bag of shopping, then?' I said.

'We don't know what it is,' he replied, slightly defensively. 'That's why we called the experts.'

'Oh,' I said, looking round in relief. 'There are experts here? Why didn't you say?'

'No,' he said. 'I mean, that's why we called you.'

'Right,' I said. 'Let's have a look then.'

He walked me tentatively over to what looked like a carrier bag full of rubbish in one corner, next to WH Smiths. Then the training just took over. I bent down and picked it up. It was a carrier bag of rubbish. 'It's a carrier bag of rubbish, I think,' I said. 'I could get it analysed, but I'm fairly confident.'

'Can't be too careful, I suppose,' said the security guard.

'That's right,' I said. 'You've done the right thing. You never know, after all. Call us any time.'

I walked back out of the shopping centre and slung the bag into a bin near the police car.

I should add at this point that it's rare that a sensible member of the public points out a suspicious package: it always seems to be Newtown's lunatic fringe that feels most at risk from Islamic fundamentalism. Suspicious packages don't require much in the way of investigation (at least, by me) so I don't mind dealing with them.

Of course, even now this is being pored over gleefully by Al-Qaeda members in their caves. 'Look, Osama, the British police do not even read their emails. Let us strike now, while the infidel is sleeping.'

SNATCH

THE POLICING STRATEGY of intensive foot patrol has long since been ditched and we've been told that zero-tolerance is too confrontational. Our policing strategy is called 'intelligence-led policing'. This means we make up for a lack of front line officers by trying to predict when and where crime will occur, in the hope that we can actually prevent it by being in the right place at the right time. Policing by crystal ball might work better. I'm not a fan.

A handbag snatch in Newtown town centre summed up the failings of intelligence-led policing last week.

It happened mid-morning, so the dayshift was operating at full strength: six officers. Only two were actually mobile at the time, the other four were dealing with emails and paperwork that had accumulated over their rest days. The police station itself was a hive of activity and, by coincidence, I had just been into the intelligence office to answer a query they had about a stop-search I had done a month or so previously. Their office was up to full strength, with (from memory) seven people at their desks, all typing fast.

Our filing and archive staff were also hard at work, pushing trolleys laden with paper files from one room to another.

The victim had just been to the chemist to get her prescription and was about to get on the bus to go home when a young man wearing a hooded top cycled past her and snatched her handbag. It happened more or less in the town centre, but so quickly that there were very few witnesses. A helpful member of the public called the police, bringing into action a well-oiled and expensive machine.

The first to respond was the town centre CCTV operator. She scanned the area with the cameras, but the location of the offence was such that the thief would have been well out of range within only a minute or two.

The only other mobile unit and I made an area search, after obtaining a description of the offender over the radio, but we only got to hear about it about fifteen minutes after the event so it was like trying to find a needle in a haystack, when the needle's on a bike and left the haystack a quarter of an hour ago, riding like Lance Armstrong.

My role in all this, as the officer attending, was to investigate the crime and provide some help to the victim, Freda. She was quite calm, although a little tearful when we finally managed to get through to her husband to let him know what had happened. Together we cancelled all the cards we could think of and then I set about getting a statement from her.

'You know,' she said. 'I don't think I would recognise him again. I'm ever so sorry.'

'I really don't think you've got anything to be sorry about Mrs Miller,' I said. Another case of a real victim apologising to us while time-wasters bother us incessantly.

'I just want the photos back, you see,' she said. 'I didn't have hardly any money with me, just the photos of my son and his wife who are in Australia.'

'Well, I'll get you home as soon as we've done this, then I'll have a good look round and see if I can find the bag.'

'Oh, thanks for trying. What should I do about my bus pass?'

'I think you'll just have to contact the council so that they can get you another one.' Her gratitude was touching, although I really didn't know where to begin looking for the bag.

This is not a common crime in Newtown, to be honest. Snatching a lady's handbag takes some nerve and you have to be fairly ruthless or desperate to try it. In this case, the offender had clearly weighed up the risks and decided he would never be caught.

Newtown police, like every other police force in the country, are caught between detecting crime once it has happened, and preventing crime from happening in the first place.

When you look at the resources (in financial terms) that were on duty at the time of the offence, they were undeniably impressive: experienced police officers and detectives, intelligence analysts, an expensive CCTV system, new police cars, a top-notch administrative system for cataloguing and recording crime accurately, highly skilled forensic experts, managers with experience in running large organisations and a large police station only a few hundred metres away.

But let's look at what Newtown police was actually able to offer Mrs Miller as she waited for the bus: two officers and a CCTV system. Because of the large number of incidents requiring attention, both those officers were in cars and en-route to calls outside the town centre. The CCTV system was working, but pointing in another direction and in any case never caught the actual crime, which when you think about it, isn't at all surprising.

A uniformed officer walking the street exerts a powerful influence: you should try it (obviously, you'll have to join the police first; if you do it without joining it's an offence. Strip-o-grams are a grey area). Innocent people exhale as you pass, relaxing the tight grip they have on their handbags or their children, drivers fasten their seatbelts, people smile and say hello, cyclists move off the pavement, youths stop shouting and skateboarding and move along. Criminals take avoiding action, but too late to avoid a conversation with me: 'Not on the rob today are we, Kyle?'

It doesn't take much to drive them away, but like vultures they come back all too soon. It might have taken just a glimpse of an officer's hat in the distance to deter the thief from stealing Mrs Miller's handbag, but the chances of one appearing any time soon are about the same as us finding the person who stole her handbag.

By the way, the bag was found and the pictures were still in it. The look of happiness on her face when I took it round to her... well, it makes it all worthwhile.

PENALTY POINTS

PENALTY POINTS, the totting up procedure, variable speed limits, illegal window tints, tyre tread depths... these are all things which I know nothing about. I was definitely there when they taught it, and I even passed an exam in the subject, but after leaving training school I got interested in catching crooks. Still, hats off to anyone who knows their traffic law: the public need to be protected from defective vehicles.

I can tell if someone is disqualified from driving, because the computer says so, and I can tell if you're drunk because there's a light that comes on on the machine that tells me to arrest you. If it's dark and your car has a couple of bright(ish) lights at the front and a couple of red or orange ones at the back then you're safe. I can just about, when pressed, sound like a traffic officer.

'Are you pregnant, sir?'

'No.'

'Then can you tell me why you're not wearing a seat-belt?'

Given my ignorance of current traffic law, it will come as no surprise to you that most of the questions I get asked are about cars. There's an old saying in the job that goes, 'If you don't know, ask.'

But on the other hand, if you're on your own and the other person clearly doesn't know any more than you, why not just guess?

Most of the answers to traffic questions take the form of numbers: legal width of a tyre, maximum height of a letter on a licence plate, number of flashes per minute on an indicator. Consequently, most of my answers take the form of random numbers, thus:

'Officer, I was wondering what the minimum tread depth was on a tyre.'

'Well, I think it's five.'

'Hello officer, could you tell me what the speed limit is if I'm towing my caravan?'

'Yes sir, it's 48.'

'Thank you, and on a dual carriageway?'

'Why, then it rises to 62.'

'Officer, what's the loudest my horn can be?'

'132.'

'And in decibels?'

'94.'

My ignorance of the modern police car meant that I once was unable to turn off the blue lights.

'No, after you. No, I'm not in a hurry. What these? No, there's no problem, I just can't seem to turn them off.'

PEARL AGAIN

PEARL SORENSEN has gone. It couldn't really last. She fulfilled the main criteria of a customer of Newtown Police in that she:

1. Had 'mental health issues'.
2. Was a neighbour from hell.
3. Persistently complained about her neighbours.

Lots of our slum-dwellers fulfil at least one of the criteria above, but Pearl covered all the bases. She consumed so much in the way of police resources, that almost every officer on the shift had a crime which involved her as an injured party, key witness or offender. I can recall on one occasion SOCO dusting for fingerprints when the aluminium powder from their previous visit was still on the window.

My most recent visit was due to her rape allegation, which was in due course followed up by detectives. Their investigation was first-rate (no surprises there) but those involved unfortunately became Pearl's dearest friends and she subjected them to numerous letters of thanks and 'hot tips' about other crimes in the area, all of which were entirely fictional.

As luck would have it, and because the sergeant thought I had a rapport with Pearl on account of my previous visits, I was sent to her flat to talk to her. As she opened the door, the smell of cat excrement was so strong, it almost knocked me over. Pearl is about 4ft tall and in her 40s, very fat and generally dressed in a t-shirt from the Niagara

Falls. I'm not really a betting man, but I'd put my house on the fact that Pearl has never been to the Niagara Falls and doesn't even know what they are. She has an 'under bite' such that her jaw sticks out and makes her look permanently miserable.

'What's been going on then, Pearl?' I said.

She showed me her diaries, which I pretended to read. I've tried before. They are gibberish.

'Weeeell, I ain't sayin' I know exactly,' she said, 'but I've got my suspicions.'

This would have been a good time to leave, but I carried on the investigation.

'What makes you suspicious, Pearl?'

'Screamin',' she said, narrowing her eyes. 'Screamin' all the time. That little babby is always screamin'. I fink it's being abused. They said I should report it to the police.'

'Who said you should?' I asked, curious to know who, apart from the police, were feeding Pearl's delusions.

'It was on the telly last night.'

And that was about the size of it: Pearl heard a crying baby and thought it was child abuse. The fact that she had also watched a programme on television about it the previous evening meant she felt it was her duty to give us a ring.

Modern crime recording standards are quite complex but, in essence, if you report a crime to the police, we record a crime. This works for 90% of the population who are both sane and work for a living, but when it comes to the remaining 10% the system breaks down. Such was the story with Pearl, who regularly reported the theft of items of underwear from her flat (which was locked and showed no signs of forced entry) and being raped by the milk/post man.

Pearl is classed, in the jargon of our times, as 'vulnerable' and so requires an appropriate adult and video interview whenever she makes an appearance at the police station. This is naturally arranged and various enquiries undertaken over a period of weeks at the end of which the matter is filed.

I used to undertake enquiries and call out SOCO because to collude with Pearl in her bizarre imaginings was easier than convincing our own crime registrars that a crime had not in fact occurred. The words 'daft old bat' don't look good on any crime report. Trust me, I've tried.

So, what did it for Pearl? In the end the Newtown Slum Housing Association (or Noosh, as our social workers call it) decided that she had to go for the greater good of the other tenants, so she packed her things and moved over the force boundary.

I remained sympathetic to Pearl to the end as clearly she should have been in a home being properly cared for, rather than been cast out into 'the community' (as the Church Road Estate is called). But I suspect that by treating all of her fictitious allegations seriously, as per the crime recording standards, we were merely adding fuel to the fire.

BEYOND THE LIMITS

I HAD A WELCOME BREAK from the tedium of Newtown yesterday. I drove to the countryside to conduct farm-to-farm enquiries. I must have spent half an hour longer than I needed to at each location, drinking coffee with the morning sunshine flooding into the kitchen. No televisions had to be turned off, the houses were pleasantly warm, not uncomfortably so, and I was greeted by men who were not wearing tracksuits and women without tattoos. I had taken a risk in not telephoning ahead, but in the end it made no difference: only one person had to be summoned back to the farmhouse by his wife, all the others were taking advantage of recent wet weather by tending to their gardens.

Most were anxious not to detain me, fondly imagining that I had better things to do, but almost all reported similar experiences of having small but valuable items of equipment stolen by gypsies. Unfortunately for them they were not reporting a fashionable racist or domestic crime, which means that I'll probably not get back to these people any time within the next few years.

Derbyshire Police have been working on a project to reduce prejudice against gypsies. It's called 'Moving Forward', although calling it 'Move Somewhere Else' would have been more appropriate if you'd have asked these farmers. The aim of the project is, '… to develop ways in which policing performance can be improved by engaging more with the community. The project has used a community partnership throughout seeking out experienced trainers from the

Gypsy and Traveller communities and has itself modelled initiatives for community engagement as well as making recommendations for ongoing development.' Sounds like the kind of thing that has senior people nodding sagely, without actually understanding what it means.

Other issues I discussed with the farmers included fox hunting, which I was quizzed about at some length, and firearms laws, the intricacies of which they knew more about than me.

Vast tracts of rural England are not policed, so having a policeman in the house was a novel experience for all of the people I met. The only other times they had seen a police officer was during the hunt or when they had their guns inspected.

I'm not sure whether farmers are the last hope of this country, in the same way that Winston Smith regarded the proletariat as the only thing that could stop Big Brother in George Orwell's 1984, or whether farmers are the last inhabitants of a country which has already disappeared.

Anxious not to go back to Newtown's adult cry babies too soon, I took my lunch indoors at a country pub.

Upon my return to the Church Road Estate I was at last able to continue with the proper tasks of the modern police officer and took a long statement from a 12-year-old girl about nuisance text messages she was receiving on her mobile phone from an ex-boyfriend. Ex! At 12! I'm getting too old for this.

MORE NONSENSE

I DEALT WITH TWO drunks for the price of one today: both had been locked up on a Monday night for being drunk and disorderly, so I was sent to write out tickets for both of them.

When I got into custody, I found 'Honest' Pete Wright sitting on one of the chairs near the desk.

The last time I saw him, he didn't look all that well: he confessed to being back on the gear (as if there was some time in his recent history when he was off it), but said he was hopeful of getting on a detox course.

He looked absolutely dreadful. His face was like a skull covered in skin, with false, slightly dull, eyes. Pete was never going to be used for the next Colgate campaign, but now his teeth were completely rotten; the ones that weren't yellow were black. He'd been locked up around five hours earlier by the night shift, who had been called to a burglary in progress at some sheltered housing just off the Church Road Estate. Pete was arrested running down the road as the first patrol drove up. The purse was found a few feet from where he was arrested. Apparently, he'd been into an old lady's house and swiped the purse off the table. As luck would have it, the old dear's daughter was visiting at the time and called us and we had some lads nearby.

I volunteered to fingerprint him and after completing the paperwork, I took him through into the documentation room.

'You've moved up from shoplifting I see, Pete,' I said.

'Yeah,' he said. 'You just get a bit desperate after a while.'

'What happened to going back into catering?'

'Dunno.' He shrugged his shoulders.

'You're in a right f*cking state now. Have you looked in the mirror lately?'

'Well, I'm not that bothered now am I?' he said. 'I'm going to prison anyway.'

'Good job too, from the look of you. Oh, and I never did find out who burgled your flat.'

'Yeah well, never mind. I bet it was them kids.' Keeping up the pretence to the end, that's Pete.

I went back to the office to get all the drunk and disorderly statements together and after sorting that out, I went to the canteen for my meal break. The latest copy of *CJS Now* was lying around. I read this:

'District Judge Philips reminds us that we should not refer to drug users as "clean". The opposite is dirty and drug users are human beings and entitled to their dignity. The suggestion that they are dirty does not help.'

I thought about Pete Smith, and his filthy teeth and BO, and how I'd seen him dissolving in front of my eyes over the last year or so. I thought about how this well-meaning nonsense actually ruins peoples' lives. I thought about the old lady whose purse had been taken. I wondered who on earth thinks *CJS Now* is a part of this picture.

BEST JOB EVER?

IN THE IDLE moments between switching biros or reaching for the stapler as we manned our desks in the police station yesterday, we fell to discussing 'the best job ever'.

By general consent, Steve's suggestion – the Heathrow robbery in 2004 – was top of the heap. It doesn't really get any better than arresting six men on the plot of a £40 million gold bullion robbery at an international airport. Following a surveillance operation, more than 100 officers, some of them armed, were waiting for the robbers who held up airport staff with knives, guns and 'cudgels'.

'The only thing I don't get,' said Sandra, 'is where the hell do you find 100 policemen?'

I dug out an old diary.

'Well, it was a Monday,' I said. 'They'd have had a lot of officers on duty to deal with the weekend prisoners.'

That's the Met, mind you. We do things differently in our force. Had the same robbery have occurred in Newtown on a Saturday night at peak holiday time, it would have been down to Bill and myself to make the arrests and interview the prisoners.

'Could you please attend the Heathrow depot, we have received intelligence that an armed raid is planned. The situation has been risk-assessed. Ensure that you are wearing your stab-proof vests, keep an escape route open at all times and if you feel threatened, withdraw.'

On second thoughts, if there was an opportunity to get involved in an interesting operation, a load of officers would turn up at the station to do the exciting bit and Bill and I would be called in afterwards to take statements, book in the property and conduct all the minor CPS enquiries: none of the glory, all of the responsibility.

Still, I did volunteer to be a policeman and I do get paid.

While in Newtown we have a hard enough job keeping tabs on our own small army of villains, I cannot imagine how the Met manage with every crook in the country, and many from abroad, migrating to London.

Sometimes the police get it right, and I think CO19 (the Specialist Firearms Command of the Metropolitan Police) will remember this job for a while.

CLOCKING OFF

THE BEST TIME for our little gang is with about an hour to go on our last night shift. Newtown at this time is a dangerous place: I can hardly keep my eyes open driving the police car, while the town's working men cycle off to begin work at the various little industrial estates around the edge of town.

By about 05:30hrs yesterday, we were all back inside the police station, sitting in the office with cups of tea made by our most recent recruit. The huge police station was completely empty, as was the car park. Bill and I had had an arrest in the early hours and, as the junior partner, I had prepared the prisoner handover package a while ago. I read it through, making sure that the various bits of paper were there and I hadn't missed anything important like the address of a drunken witness or something. Having one in the traps after a bit of a scrap gave us all something to laugh about. CCTV had reported it and Bill ran up behind him taking him to the floor, just like he'll be doing on the rugby field tomorrow. I could clearly be seen kneeling on the offender's head while he struggled to get free. The rest of the shift arrived within seconds and the handcuffs were on.

We reviewed the statements and I read through Bill's. 'It says here that you told him to calm down. When did you do that?'

'As I was running towards him.'

'Didn't do much good,' I pointed out.

'Only because you were kneeling on his head.'

Despite all the problems, being a police officer is one of the best jobs in the world: you get into some entertaining and challenging situations and you get to work with funny and dedicated people. Sitting around the table in the office, drinking tea and going over some of our shift's most entertaining scrapes, I couldn't think of anything else I really want to do.

Sadly though, even our most enthusiastic constables are losing heart.

Despite claims to the contrary, there really is no end in sight to the problem of police bureaucracy: every few months brings another form to be completed, putting yet another procedural hurdle between you and actually getting out on patrol and doing what you joined for.

We like what we do because it's interesting and we get to help people. What's more, we occasionally get to catch bad people and in doing so make the place safer. We understand that a certain amount of what we do will be routine and many of the people we meet will not appreciate the work that we do. For those of us at the front line though, there are fewer and fewer opportunities to do anything worthwhile as we become crime recorders rather than crime fighters and the uniformed constable becomes nothing more than a filing clerk.

At 07:00hrs, we knocked it on the head, leaving the dayshift to pick up where we had left off.

Epilogue

I've had rather a busy time of it since we first published *Wasting Police Time*.

To my astonishment – well, I was only a humble bobby – I found myself in most of the papers (from *The Daily Mail* to *The Guardian*) and on things like Newsnight, Five Live (with both Simon Mayo and Victoria Derbyshire) and lots of other national TV and radio programmes. Nick Cohen of *The Observer* – a strange bedfellow, you might think – chose *Wasting Police Time* (along with Frank Chalk's *It's Your Time You're Wasting*, also published by Monday Books) as one of three 'best political books' of the moment.

They even produced a BBC Panorama special about me. I walked along the street in my pointy hat, drove round in a panda car and gave them the benefit of my views on a range of subjects. This would have been hard if I'd still been undercover but I was able to appear as myself (ie, not as PC David Copperfield) because by that point I was leaving the UK police farce and going to work as a policeman in Canada.

Being in the job, the stuff in these pages wasn't news to me (or any other front line officer), but clearly a lot of it was news to the media (and the general public).

If there is anyone outside the police who ought to know what's really happening to law and order in modern Britain, you might think it would be the Police Minister – who, when the book first came out, was Tony McNulty MP (later found to have been claiming thousands of pounds in second-home expenses on a London house where his parents lived, even though it was only eight miles from his actual home. This was all above board, apparently.). Sadly, if you thought McNulty would be up to speed with policing, you'd be disappointed. Challenged about the contents of this book in the House of Commons, he replied that it was 'more of a fiction than Dickens'.

Unfortunately for the law-abiding taxpayer, it's not a work of fiction (as McNumpty later admitted); if anything, I downplayed much of the lunacy of modern policing.

Not much has changed since this book first came out. If anything, things have got worse – for instance, shoplifters will no longer have to pay their fixed penalty notices as long as they say they're really sorry and they won't do it again, honest. Which is almost unbelievable, really. You can steal stuff from a shop, and *nothing* will happen to you. Why don't we all do it?

Police bureaucracy has 'moved on' a little (though it hasn't 'gone away', or 'reduced', or even 'improved slightly') but most of it hasn't made much difference to the lives of working, front-line bobbies: a new form here to replace an old one there, a new unit created in this office, a couple of over-complex new computer systems installed in that one.

The only really significant change, at my level, is the abandonment of the system of 'administrative detections'. Maybe this came about after we revealed this shady practice to the wider world in the first edition, or maybe it didn't. Either way, it would be wrong to leave that element of the book unchanged so we've, er, changed it. However, there are several references to administrative detections in other areas of the book and, rather than rewrite those, we've left them in; they help to make up the snapshot of what it was like to be a British bobby in late 2006 and, anyway, all that's really happened is we've swapped one set of forms for another. We're still not catching all that many burglars, drug dealers and muggers.

We've also tidied up one or two mistakes while we were at it, and made a few other minor amendments.

Anyway, for those of you who missed it on Panorama, my real name is Stuart Davidson and I worked for Staffordshire Police. Hope you enjoyed the book!

PC David Copperfield, January 2011

Glossary

I thought it might assist non *Bill*-obsessives and general non-police readers if I provided a basic list of some of the many common acronyms, words and phrases that litter a police officer's life.

ABCs – Acceptable Behaviour Contract. Drawn up by a team of well-meaning but deluded 'carers' in response to a young hooligan's anti-social behaviour. See also *ASBO*.

ACAB. A smudgy blue tattoo often seen on the knuckles of criminals. They tell us it stands for 'Always Carry A Bible' but we suspect it stands for 'All Coppers Are Bastards'.

ACPO – Association Of Chief Police Officers. A group of liberal-minded, unelected, desk-bound senior politicians, sorry, police officers, who provide the strategic direction for the Police Service.

Administrative Detections. A now-discontinued but probably soon-to-be-revived method of solving mostly trivial crime without convicting, or even arresting, anyone. As opposed to 'sanctioned detections' which often result in a charge or a formal caution. See also *Ethical Crime Recording*.

Arrest Referral Schemes. After arresting someone, usually a drug addict, we try to make them see the error of their ways by sending (or referring) them to treatment, in the mistaken belief that this will stop them thieving.

ASBO – Anti-Social Behaviour Order. Part of the Crime and Disorder Act 1998. An order from a court prohibiting a person from doing something that is generally considered unpleasant, although not sufficiently serious to warrant prison. Breaching an ASBO can land its subject in jail for up to five years. Which we like. Or would do, if it ever happened.

CID – Criminal Investigation Department. A team of detectives that investigate more serious and complex crimes.

CJS – Criminal Justice System. The expensive machinery for not really dealing with crime, criminals and disorder. Encompasses police, probation, prison, magistrates, lawyers and judges.

Class A Drugs. The most dangerous drugs like heroin and cocaine.

Class B Drugs. Amphetamine (when not prepared for injection) and barbiturates.

Class C Drugs. Cannabis (unless that's back up to Class B now, I forget), steroids and some tranquillisers (like valium)

Community Punishment Orders. Used to be called Community Service. Entails a number of hours of unpaid, menial work in the community. Trouble is, the criminals being 'punished' never turn up for it.

Community Rehabilitation Orders. A sentence for a criminal offence. Involves sitting down with a probation officer and discussing ways of keeping out of trouble, like not stealing, drinking too much or getting into fights.

Court Liaison Unit. An office bound unit that sends communication from police officers to the *CPS* (qv) and vice-versa.

CPS – Crown Prosecution Service. Organisation staffed by borderline incompetent lawyers headed by politically correct maniacs which (in England and Wales) decides whether to prosecute criminals on the evidence provided by the police. NOTE: THE POLICE DO NOT CHARGE PEOPLE. SO IF YOUR ATTACKER/BURGLAR/ CAR THIEF IS NOT CHARGED EVEN WHEN IT'S BLINDINGLY OBVIOUS THAT HE IS GUILTY, DO NOT BLAME US. WE'RE JUST AS PISSED OFF AS YOU ARE WHEN THE CPS REFUSE CHARGE, HONESTLY. Often referred to by police officers as the Criminal Protection Society, or Couldn't Prosecute Satan.

Crime Audit Desk. An office-bound department in every borough or division of every force which ensures that all investigations and incidents (even the most minor) comply with Home Office guidelines ie that various bits of paper are stapled into the correct order, that the correct number of crime numbers are allocated and that crimes are recorded correctly.

D&D – Drunk and Disorderly. A common enough offence committed by being drunk and trying to fight police officers, and losing.

Defence solicitors. Co-conspirators funded by the taxpayer to assist unimaginative criminals in dreaming up alibis, excuses and explanations. Only joking.

Dispatchers. The first line of defence against the timewasters who frequently call the police. They are also responsible for allocating particular officers to incidents over the radio.

Diversity. The ridiculous notion that society does not consist solely of white men. Often the subject of a two or three day course in which police officers are brought face to face with their prejudices.

Enhanced Thinking Courses. A type of therapy undertaken by convicted criminals in which they address their offending behaviour and think about how they will conduct themselves in the future. Perhaps.

ECPO – Enhanced Community Punishment Order. 'Punishment with a purpose'. Yet another government scheme devised to avoid sending criminals to jail.

Ethical Crime Recording. An intensely time-consuming and bureaucratic system of recording even the most petty incident as a crime, even when nobody wants anything done about it. (See also *Administrative Detection*).

Human Rights Act. Now infamous legislation under which individuals (including criminals) are given rights. Often devoid of common sense, the HRA takes precedence over UK law.

IP – Injured Party. Politically correct term for victim.

IPCC – Independent Police Complaints Commission. The organisation responsible for setting standards for the way in which police complaints are dealt with. It also investigates serious incidents where someone has died or been seriously injured as a result of some police activity (eg a death in custody, or a fatal road accident following a police pursuit).

KFC. Deep-fried chicken, featuring Colonel Harland Sanders' secret blend of 11 herbs and spices, which is traditionally provided for criminals who hurl bricks at the police from rooftops.

Lambert and Butler. The serious smoke, for the discerning criminal.

MG (Manual of Guidance) forms. An interminable and highly labour-intensive series of forms devised by bureaucrats at the *CPS* (qv) to accompany a suspect charged with a criminal offence to court.

Misper Enquiries. Enquiries into missing persons – usually kids who have run away from care homes or school to play in the amusement arcades and drink cider in the park.

Nominals. The major criminals in any particular area.

PACE. Police and Criminal Evidence Act 1984. Legislation brought in as a result of police misconduct in the past to ensure that suspects are dealt with fairly by police officers, and have a 95% chance of getting off even when caught red-handed.

PCSOs – Police Community Support Officers. A government idea that ensures a uniformed, cheap alternative to police officers on the street, while allowing police officers themselves to get on with writing reports, filing and stapling.

Police Authority. A group of local worthies that constitute the 'governors' of each regional police force. Together with the Home Office and the Chief Constables they form the tripartite arrangement that runs the police.

Police Federation. The 'trade union' that represents all police officers up to and including the rank of Chief Inspector.

Professional Standards Department. The department within each police force that investigates corruption as well as most complaints made by the public. They couldn't catch me, try as they might!

Restorative Justice. Often seen as an alternative to conventional justice as dispensed by the courts, Restorative Justice seeks to get the offender to apologise to the victim. So that's alright, then. Because they are sorry. No, really they are.

RfR&D – Respect for Race and Diversity. That part of the selection procedure that deals with diversity (qv) and which all prospective police officers must pass.

RIPA – Regulation of Investigatory Powers Act 2000. Provides rules for the police and other bodies on interception of communication data, surveillance and police informants.

RV Point – Rendezvous point. Often established in firearms or other critical incidents as a staging or meeting point some distance from the actual crime scene.

SEARCH (Selection Entrance Assessment for Recruiting Constables Holistically). The selection procedure undergone by all prospective police officers. See also RfR&D.

Section 4 POA. Section 4 of the Public Order Act usually means threatening someone in the street.

Section 5 POA. Section 5 of the Public Order Act is swearing in the street.

SOCO – Scenes of Crime Officers. Called Crime Scene Investigators (CSI) in the US, here in the UK they do the same job but without the palm trees, boob jobs and plotlines.

Stop and Search. Under Section 1 of *PACE* (qv) police officers are allowed to stop and search people they suspect of possessing evidence (usually drugs or stolen property) relating to a criminal offence, even if they swear blind they ain't done nothing.

Street Bail. When a suspect is arrested for a offence he is normally brought immediately to a police station and then released (bailed) after questioning. Street bail, however, is given immediately after arrest (for a minor offence), without bringing a suspect to a police station. It is done in order to save time.

Sus Law – Stop Under Suspicion. Legislation used by the police to stop and search (qv) offenders who appeared to be behaving suspiciously and about to commit a crime. Became very unpopular in the black community and was given as the excuse for rioting in Brixton in 1981. Replaced by *PACE* (qv) and the Criminal Attempts Act.

Tagging. The attachment of a 'tag' around an offender's ankle after (or as an alternative to) a prison sentence. A monitoring company is then able to check on the offender's movements and shrug their shoulders and do nothing when the offender breaches the terms of the tagging.

Taser. A gun that releases a high voltage into an offender causing him to fall to the floor. Very effective and only used by trained firearms officers in the UK.

TICs – Taken into Consideration. Often an offender, when banged to rights for one or two offences, will confess to a string of other offences which will be 'taken into consideration' by the sentencing judiciary, in the expectation that he will not receive a significantly longer prison sentence, but will be able to 'wipe the slate clean'. A fraud on victims, basically.

VIPER – Video Identification Parades by Electronic Recording. A witness watches a series of suspects recorded onto a DVD in an attempt to identify an offender. A 'virtual identity parade'.

VMEs – Visible Minority Ethnics. Very politically correct term for people who are not white. Note: will be out of date by time of publication.

Youth Offending Team. Either a gang of steamers, or a team of people (often referred to a do-gooders) who identify the specific needs and requirements of specific offenders in line with a national model. Jail isn't often given as one of them.

Zero Tolerance. A method of policing famously implemented by Chief William Bratton of the NYPD (qv), in which police arrest people for minor offences in order to improve the quality of life for law-abiding citizens. In the UK however, it is no more than a soundbite.

Also from Monday Books

Perverting The Course Of Justice / Inspector Gadget
(ppbk, £7.99)

A senior serving policeman picks up where PC Copperfield left off and reveals how far the insanity extends – children arrested for stealing sweets from each other while serious criminals go about their business unmolested.

'Exposes the reality of life at the sharp end'
– *The Daily Telegraph*

'No wonder they call us Plods... A frustrated inspector speaks out on the madness of modern policing'
– *The Daily Mail*

'Staggering... exposes the bloated bureaucracy that is crushing Britain' – *The Daily Express*

'You must buy this book... it is a fascinating insight'
– *Kelvin MacKenzie, The Sun*

In April 2010, Inspector Gadget was named one of the country's 'best 40 bloggers' by *The Times*.

From all good bookshops, online from www.mondaybooks.com or via 01455 221752.

Diary Of An On-Call Girl
True Stories From The Front Line / WPC EE Bloggs
(ppbk £7.99)

IF CRIME is the sickness, WPC Ellie Bloggs is the cure... Well, she is when she's not inside the nick, flirting with male officers, buying doughnuts for the sergeant and hacking her way through a jungle of emails, forms and government targets.

Of course, in amongst the tea-making, gossip and boyfriend trouble, real work sometimes intrudes. Luckily, as a woman, she can multi-task... switching effortlessly between gobby drunks, angry chavs and the merely bonkers. WPC Bloggs is a real-life policewoman, who occasionally arrests some very naughty people. *Diary of an On-Call Girl* is her hilarious, despairing dispatch from the front line of modern British lunacy.

WARNING: Contains satire, irony and traces of sarcasm.

"Think Belle de Jour meets The Bill... sarky sarges, missing panda cars and wayward MOPS (members of the public)." - *The Guardian*

"Modern policing is part Orwell, part Kafka ... and part Trisha." – *The Mail on Sunday*

From all good bookshops, online from www.mondaybooks.com or via 01455 221752.

In Foreign Fields / Dan Collins

(ppbk, £7.99)

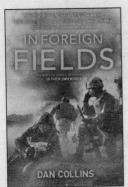

A staggering collection of 25 true-life stories of astonishing battlefield bravery from Iraq and Afghanistan... medal-winning soldiers, Marines and RAF men, who stared death in the face, in their own words.

'Enthralling and awe-inspiring untold stories'
– *The Daily Mail*

'Astonishing feats of bravery illustrated in laconic, first-person prose' – *Independent on Sunday*

'The book everyone's talking about... a gripping account of life on the frontlines of Iraq and Afghanistan'
– *News of the World*

'An outstanding read' – *Soldier Magazine*

From all good bookshops, online from
www.mondaybooks.com or via 01455 221752.

Sick Notes / Dr Tony Copperfield

(ppbk, £8.99)

Welcome to the bizarre world of Tony Copperfield, family doctor. He spends his days fending off anxious mums, elderly sex maniacs and hopeless hypochondriacs (with his eyes peeled for the odd serious symptom). The rest of his time is taken up sparring with colleagues, battling bureaucrats and banging his head against the brick walls of the NHS.

If you've ever wondered what your GP is really thinking - and what's actually going on behind the scenes at your surgery - *SICK NOTES* is for you.

'A wonderful book, funny and insightful in equal measure'
– Dr Phil Hammond (Private Eye's 'MD')

'Copperfield is simply fantastic, unbelievably funny and improbably wise... everything he writes is truer than fact'
– British Medical Journal

'Original, funny and an incredible read' *– The Sun*

Tony Copperfield is a Medical Journalist of the Year, has been shortlisted for UK Columnist of the Year many times and writes regularly for *The Times* and other media.

From all good bookshops, online from www.mondaybooks.com or via 01455 221752.

Second Opinion: A Doctor's Dispatches from the Inner City
Theodore Dalrymple (hdbk, £14.99)

No-one has travelled further into the dark and secret heart of Britain's underclass than the brilliant Theodore Dalrymple. A hospital consultant and prison doctor in the grim inner city, every day he confronts a brutal, tragic netherworld which most of us never see. It's the world of 'Baby P' and Shannon Matthews, where life is cheap and ugly, jealous men beat and strangle their women and 'anyone will do anything for ten bags of brown'. In a series of short and gripping pieces, full of feeling and bleak humour, he exposes the fascinating, hidden horror of our modern slums as never before.

'Dalrymple's dispatches from the frontline have a tone and a quality entirely their own... their rarity makes you sit up and take notice'
– *Marcus Berkmann, The Spectator*

'Dalrymple is a modern master'
– *Stephen Poole, The Guardian*

'The George Orwell of our time... a writer of genius'
– *Denis Dutton*

From all good bookshops, online from
www.mondaybooks.com or via 01455 221752.

Not With A Bang But A Whimper / Theodore Dalrymple
(hbk, £14.99)

In a series of penetrating and beautifully-written essays, Theodore Dalrymple explains his belief that a liberal intelligentsia is destroying Britain. Dalrymple writes for *The Spectator*, *The Times*, *The Daily Telegraph*, *New Statesman*, *The Times Literary Supplement* and the *British Medical Journal*.

'Theodore Dalrymple's clarity of thought, precision of expression and constant, terrible disappointment give his dispatches from the frontline a tone and a quality entirely their own... their rarity makes you sit up and take notice'
- Marcus Berkmann, The Spectator

'Dalrymple is a modern master'
- The Guardian

'Dalrymple is the George Orwell of our times... he is a writer of genius'
- Dennis Dutton

From all good bookshops, online from www.mondaybooks.com or via 01455 221752.

When Science Goes Wrong / Simon LeVay

(ppbk, £7.99)

We live in times of astonishing scientific progress. But for every stunning triumph there are hundreds of cock-ups, damp squibs and disasters. Escaped anthrax spores and nuclear explosions, tiny data errors which send a spacecraft hurtling to oblivion, innocent men jailed on 'infallible' DNA evidence…just some of the fascinating and disturbing tales from the dark side of discovery.

'Spine-tingling, occasionally gruesome accounts of well-meant but disastrous scientific bungling'
– *The Los Angeles Times*

'Entertaining and thought-provoking'
– *Publisher's Weekly*

'The dark – but fascinating – side of science… an absorbing read' – *GeoTimes*

From all good bookshops, online from www.mondaybooks.com or via 01455 221752.

A Paramedic's Diary / Stuart Gray

(ppbk, £7.99)

STUART GRAY is a paramedic dealing with the worst life can throw at him. *A Paramedic's Diary* is his gripping, blow-by-blow account of a year on the streets – 12 rollercoaster months of enormous highs and tragic lows. One day he'll save a young mother's life as she gives birth, the next he might watch a young girl die on the tarmac in front of him after a hit-and-run. A gripping, entertaining and often amusing read by a talented new writer.

As heard on BBC Radio 4's Saturday Live and BBC Radio 5 Live's Donal McIntyre Show and Simon Mayo

In April 2010, Stuart Gray was named one of the country's 'best 40 bloggers' by *The Times*

From all good bookshops, online from www.mondaybooks.com or via 01455 221752.

So That's Why They Call It Great Britain / Steve Pope

(ppbk, £7.99)

From the steam engine to the jet engine to the engine of the world wide web, to vaccination and penicillin, to Viagra, chocolate bars, the flushing loo, the G&T, ibruprofen and the telephone... this is the truly astonishing story of one tiny country and its gifts to the world.

From all good bookshops, online from www.mondaybooks.com or via 01455 221752.